THE WONDER WOMAN CHRONICLES

VOLUME ONE

ALL STORIES WRITTEN BY WILLIAM MOULTON MARSTON. ALL COVERS AND ART BY HARRY G. PETER, UNLESS OTHERWISE NOTED.

ALL-STAR COMICS NO. 8
-DECEMBER 1941-JANARY 1942-
Cover: *Everett E. Hibbard* 3

INTRODUCING WONDER WOMAN 4

SENSATION COMICS NO. 1
-JANUARY 1942-
Cover 13

WONDER WOMAN COMES TO AMERICA* 14

SENSATION COMICS NO. 2
-FEBRUARY 1942-
Cover 27

DR. POISON* 28

SENSATION COMICS NO. 3
-MARCH 1942-
Cover 41

A SPY IN THE OFFICE* 42

SENSATION COMICS NO. 4
-APRIL 1942-
Cover 55

SCHOOL FOR SPIES* 56

SENSATION COMICS NO. 5
-MAY 1942-
Cover 69

WONDER WOMAN VERSUS THE SABOTEURS* 70

SENSATION COMICS NO. 6
-JUNE 1942-
Cover 83

SUMMONS TO PARADISE* . . 84

WONDER WOMAN NO. 1
-SUMMER 1942-
Cover 97

WONDER WOMAN, WHO IS SHE? 98

THE ORIGIN OF WONDER WOMAN* 99

WONDER WOMAN GOES TO THE CIRCUS! . . . 112

WONDER WOMAN VERSUS THE PRISON SPY RING* . . 125

THE GREATEST FEAT OF DARING IN HUMAN HISTORY! 138

SENSATION COMICS NO. 7
-JULY 1942-
Cover 151

THE MILK SWINDLE* 152

SENSATION COMICS NO. 8
-AUGUST 1942-
Cover 165

DEPARTMENT STORE PERFIDY* 166

SENSATION COMICS NO. 9
SEPTEMBER 1942
Cover 179

THE RETURN OF DIANA PRINCE* 180

*These stories were originally untitled and are titled here for reader convenience.

The comics reprinted in this volume were produced in a time when racism played a larger role in society and popular culture, both consciously and unconsciously.

WONDER WOMAN CREATED BY WILLIAM MOULTON MARSTON

Dan DiDio SVP – EXECUTIVE EDITOR ☆ Sheldon Mayer – EDITOR ORIGINAL SERIES
Georg Brewer VP – DESIGN & DC DIRECT CREATIVE ☆ Bob Harras GROUP EDITOR – COLLECTED EDITIONS
Bob Joy EDITOR ☆ Robbin Brosterman DESIGN DIRECTOR – BOOKS

DC COMICS

Paul Levitz PRESIDENT & PUBLISHER ☆ Richard Bruning SVP – CREATIVE DIRECTOR ☆ Patrick Caldon EVP – FINANCE & OPERATIONS
Amy Genkins SVP – BUSINESS & LEGAL AFFAIRS ☆ Jim Lee EDITORIAL DIRECTOR-WILDSTORM
Gregory Noveck SVP – CREATIVE AFFAIRS ☆ Steve Rotterdam SVP – SALES & MARKETING ☆ Cheryl Rubin SVP – BRAND MANAGEMENT

DC Comics, 1700 Broadway, New York, NY 10019
A Warner Bros. Entertainment Company
First Printing.

ISBN: 978-1-4012-2644-2
Printed by World Color Press, Inc., St-Romuald, QC, Canada 2/17/10

Cover art by Rodney Ramos after Harry G. Peter.

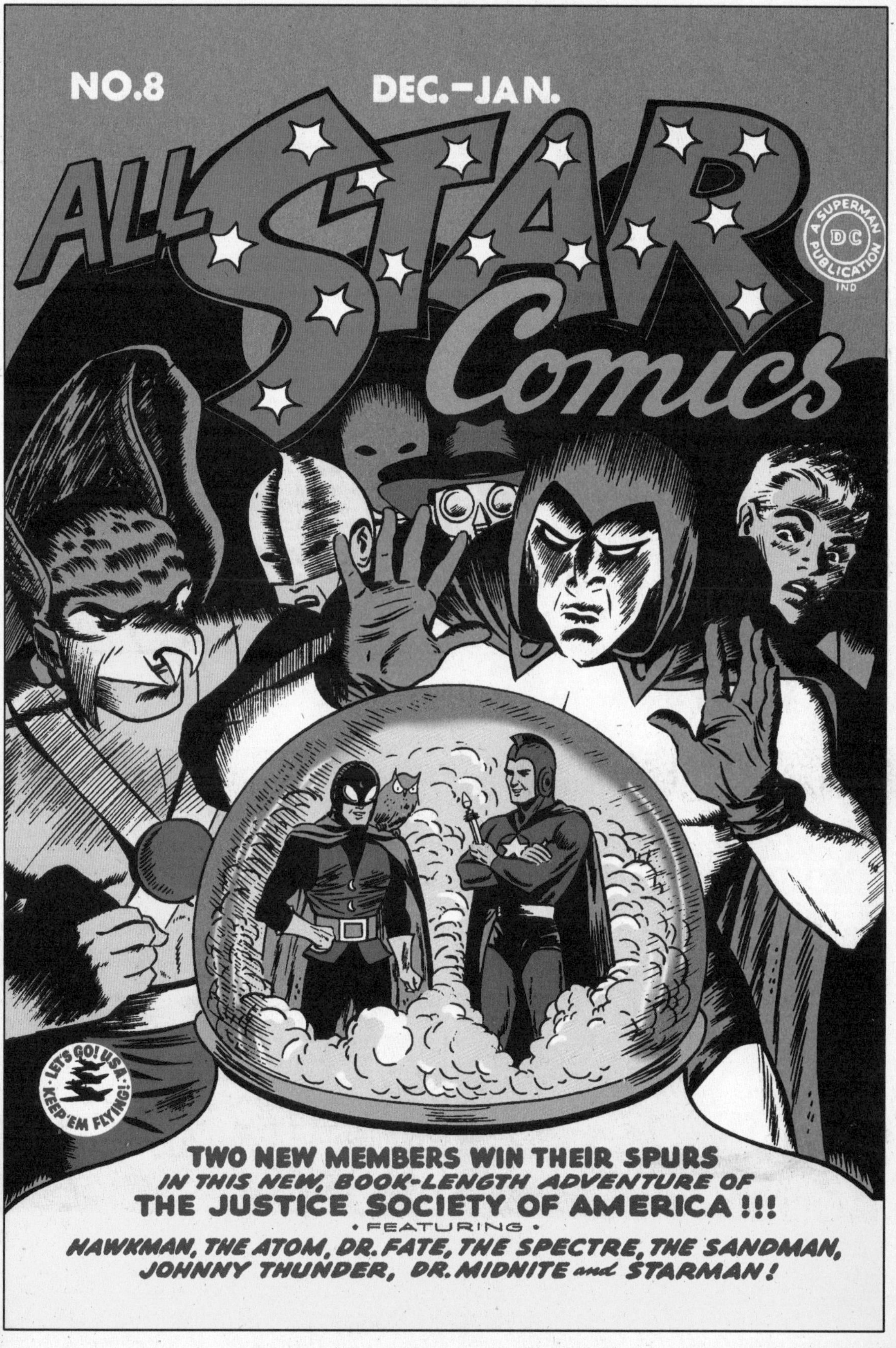
NO.8
DEC.-JAN.
ALL STAR Comics
A SUPERMAN DC PUBLICATION IND
LET'S GO! U.S.A. KEEP 'EM FLYING!
TWO NEW MEMBERS WIN THEIR SPURS
IN THIS NEW, BOOK-LENGTH ADVENTURE OF
THE JUSTICE SOCIETY OF AMERICA !!!
• FEATURING •
HAWKMAN, THE ATOM, DR. FATE, THE SPECTRE, THE SANDMAN,
JOHNNY THUNDER, DR. MIDNITE and STARMAN!

Introducing Wonder Woman

TRADE MARK APPLICATION PENDING

by CHARLES MOULTON

AT LAST, IN A WORLD TORN BY THE HATREDS AND WARS OF MEN, APPEARS A WOMAN TO WHOM THE PROBLEMS AND FEATS OF MEN ARE MERE CHILD'S PLAY— A WOMAN WHOSE IDENTITY IS KNOWN TO NONE, BUT WHOSE SENSATIONAL FEATS ARE OUTSTANDING IN A FAST-MOVING WORLD! WITH A HUNDRED TIMES THE AGILITY AND STRENGTH OF OUR BEST MALE ATHLETES AND STRONGEST WRESTLERS, SHE APPEARS AS THOUGH FROM NOWHERE TO AVENGE AN INJUSTICE OR RIGHT A WRONG! AS LOVELY AS APHRODITE— AS WISE AS ATHENA — WITH THE SPEED OF MERCURY AND THE STRENGTH OF HERCULES —— SHE IS KNOWN ONLY AS WONDER WOMAN, BUT WHO SHE IS, OR WHENCE SHE CAME, NOBODY KNOWS!

TO BEGIN THE STRANGE HISTORY OF "WONDER WOMAN," LET US GO OUT OVER THE SEA AND FOLLOW IN THE WAKE OF A PLANE, ENTIRELY OUT OF GASOLINE! AS WE WATCH, IT FLOUNDERS HELPLESSLY IN THE SKY, AND FINALLY CRASHES ON THE SHORES OF AN UNCHARTED ISLE SET IN THE MIDST OF A VAST EXPANSE OF OCEAN....

BURSTING FROM THE SURROUNDING FOLIAGE, TWO BEAUTIFUL FIGURES RACE TOWARD THE WRECKED PLANE...

LOOK, PRINCESS, A STRANGE PLANE!

WELL, WHAT ARE WE WAITING FOR? COME ON, LET'S SEE IF ANYONE IS HURT!

2

PRINCESS, IT'S—IT'S—

A MAN! A MAN ON PARADISE ISLAND! QUICK! LET'S GET HIM TO THE HOSPITAL.

3

CARRYING THE FULL GROWN MAN AS IF HE WERE A CHILD, THE YOUNG WOMAN STEPS THROUGH THE FOLIAGE AND ENTERS THE STREETS OF A CITY THAT FOR ALL THE WORLD SEEMS TO BE BORN OF ANCIENT GREECE!

A MAN!

HOW DID HE GET HERE?

SOMEONE TELL THE QUEEN THERE'S A MAN ON PARADISE ISLAND!

IS HE ALL RIGHT? WILL HE LIVE?

I DON'T KNOW. HE'S HAD A CONCUSSION. WE WON'T KNOW ANYTHING FOR DAYS. I WONDER WHAT THE QUEEN WILL DO WITH HIM. HE CAN'T BE MOVED.

SUDDENLY, HIPPOLYTE, THE QUEEN, ENTERS THE HOSPITAL ROOM...

MOTHER!

THE QUEEN!

I HEARD THAT THERE WAS A MAN HERE, BUT I COULDN'T BELIEVE IT. WHO IS HE?

HIS PLANE CRASHED ON THE BEACH OF THE ISLAND THIS MORNING. THE PRINCESS AND MALA BROUGHT HIM HERE. I FOUND THESE PAPERS IN HIS POCKET.

"CAPT. STEVEN TREVOR, U.S. ARMY INTELLIGENCE SERVICE." HMM. WE CAN'T LET HIM DIE. SEE THAT HE GETS THE BEST OF ATTENTION. KEEP HIS EYES COVERED SO THAT, IF HE SHOULD AWAKE, HE WILL SEE NOTHING! HAVE HIS PLANE REPAIRED, FOR HE MUST LEAVE AS SOON AS HE IS WELL! KEEP ME INFORMED OF HIS PROGRESS!

IN THE ENSUING DAYS, THE PRINCESS, THE QUEEN'S ONLY DAUGHTER, IS CONSTANTLY AT THE BEDSIDE OF THE UNCONSCIOUS MAN, HELPING — WATCHING —

YOU OUGHT TO GET SOME SLEEP, PRINCESS. YOU HAVE BEEN ON THE JOB NOW FOR FOURTEEN HOURS.

NEVER MIND ME. WE - WE MUST MAKE HIM WELL.

LEAVING THE PRINCESS TO WATCH OVER THE INJURED PILOT, THE DOCTOR SEEKS AUDIENCE WITH THE QUEEN....

WHAT HAS HAPPENED THAT YOU DISTURB ME AT THIS HOUR? IS THE MAN—

NO, HE IS ALIVE. IT IS THE PRINCESS I AM WORRIED ABOUT. I DON'T THINK SHE OUGHT TO BE ALLOWED IN THE HOSPITAL ANYMORE. SHE ACTS RATHER STRANGELY ABOUT THAT MAN.

SO SHE IS IN LOVE! I WAS AFRAID OF THAT! YOU ARE QUITE RIGHT, DOCTOR. I SHALL TAKE STEPS IMMEDIATELY.

THAT WOULD BE WISE. IT'S FOR THE CHILD'S OWN GOOD.

5

AND SO THE PRINCESS, FORBIDDEN THE PLEASURE OF NURSING THE ONLY MAN SHE CAN RECALL EVER HAVING SEEN IN HER LIFE, GOES TO HER MOTHER, HIPPOLYTE, THE QUEEN OF THE AMAZONS!

BUT MOTHER — I DON'T UNDERSTAND— I MUST SEE HIM! I MUST KNOW WHO HE IS, HOW HE GOT HERE! AND WHY HE MUST LEAVE? I—I LOVE HIM!

I WAS AFRAID, DAUGHTER, THAT THE TIME WOULD SOME DAY ARRIVE THAT I WOULD HAVE TO SATISFY YOUR CURIOSITY. COME— I WILL TELL YOU EVERYTHING!

AND THIS IS THE STARTLING STORY UNFOLDED BY HIPPOLYTE, QUEEN OF THE AMAZONS, TO THE PRINCESS, HER DAUGHTER!

In the days of Ancient Greece, many centuries ago, we Amazons were the foremost nation in the world. In Amazonia, women ruled and all was well. Then one day, Hercules, the strongest man in the world, stung by taunts that he couldn't conquer the Amazon women, selected his strongest and fiercest warriors and landed on our shores. I challenged him to personal combat—because I knew that with my MAGIC GIRDLE, given me by Aphrodite, Goddess of Love, I could not lose.

And win I did! But Hercules, by deceit and trickery, managed to secure my MAGIC GIRDLE— and soon we Amazons were taken into slavery. And Aphrodite, angry at me for having succumbed to the wiles of men, would do naught to help us!

Finally our submission to men became unbearable—we could stand it no longer—and I appealed to the Goddess Aphrodite again. This time not in vain, for she relented and with her help, I secured the MAGIC GIRDLE from Hercules.

With the MAGIC GIRDLE in my possession, it didn't take us long to overcome our masters, the MEN—and taking from them their entire fleet, we set sail for another shore, for it was Aphrodite's condition that we leave the manmade world and establish a new world of our own! Aphrodite also decreed that we must always wear these bracelets fashioned by our captors, as a reminder that we must always keep aloof from men.

And so, after sailing the seas many days and many nights, we found Paradise Island and settled here to build a new World! With its fertile soil, its marvelous vegetation—its varied natural resources—here is no want, no illness, no hatreds, no wars, and as long as we remain on Paradise Island and I retain the MAGIC GIRDLE, we have the power of Eternal Life—so long as we do not permit ourselves to be again beguiled by men! We are indeed a race of Wonder Women!

That was the promise of Aphrodite—and we must keep our promise to her if we are to remain here safe and in peace!

That is why this American must go and as soon as possible!

Come, let me show you the Magic Sphere you've heard me talk about. It was given to me by Athena, the Goddess of Wisdom, just after we conquered the Herculeans and set sail for Paradise Island! It is through this Magic Sphere that I have been able to know what has gone on and is going on in the other world, and even, at times, forecast the future!

That is why we Amazons have been able to far surpass the inventions of the so-called man-made civilization! We are not only stronger and wiser than men—but our weapons are better—our flying machines are further advanced! And it is through the knowledge that I have gained from this Magic Sphere that I have taught you, my daughter, all the arts and sciences and languages of modern as well as ancient times!

But let us see where your American captain came from and how he got here. Watch closely—

WHAT THE MAGIC SPHERE REVEALS...

SIR, I'VE COME TO REPORT THAT I HAVE AT LAST UNCOVERED INFORMATION AS TO WHO THE LEADERS OF THE SPY RING ARE. I'D LIKE PERMISSION TO CLOSE IN ON THEM *PERSONALLY!*

BUT THAT'S RIDICULOUS, CAPTAIN. YOU'RE THE MOST VALUABLE MAN IN THE ARMY INTELLIGENCE DEPARTMENT. WE CAN'T RISK LOSING YOU!

THAT MAY BE, SIR. BUT THESE MEN ARE DANGEROUS AND CAPTURING THEM IS A JOB I'D RATHER NOT SHIFT ON ANYONE ELSE'S SHOULDERS. I'D HOPED YOU'D UNDERSTAND, SIR.

HMM. I BELIEVE I DO, SON... I BELIEVE I DO.. GO TO IT, AND THE BEST OF LUCK TO YOU!

THAT NIGHT, STEVE TREVOR DRIVES TO A HIDDEN AIRFIELD NOT FAR FROM AN ARMY AIR BASE...

THOSE RATS HAVE THEIR PLANES HIDDEN HERE. VON STORM SHOULD DRIVE PAST HERE ANY MINUTE. IF I CAN CAPTURE HIM—THEIR LEADER—A CLEAN-UP JOB WILL BE SIMPLE.

MEANWHILE IN ANOTHER CAR, APPROACHING STEVE'S HIDING PLACE...

TONIGHT WE STRIKE. WE SEND OUR PLANES INTO THE STRATOSPHERE WHERE THEY CANNOT BE SEEN, AND BOMB AMERICAN AIR FIELDS AND TRAINING CAMPS. SINCE OUR PLANES WILL NOT BE IDENTIFIED, IT CANNOT BE CONSTRUED AS AN ACT OF WAR—

SUDDENLY, AS THE CAR PASSES STEVE'S HIDING PLACE....

VAS IST?

JUST TAKE IT EASY, BOYS - YOU'VE GOT COMPANY!

IF YOU'LL BE GOOD ENOUGH TO STOP THE CAR AND STEP OUT QUIETLY, THERE WON'T BE ANY TROUBLE, GENTLEMEN—

THE DRIVER SWERVES THE CAR SUDDENLY AND CRASHES INTO A TREE . . . . .

GOOT WORK, FRITZ!

HA, GENTLEMEN! THE QUICK THINKING OF OUR DRIVER HAS NETTED FOR US AN AMERICAN OFFICER.

HE IS NOT HURT, JUST UNCONSCIOUS. HE WILL COME IN HANDY FOR OUR PLANS, NICHT WAR?

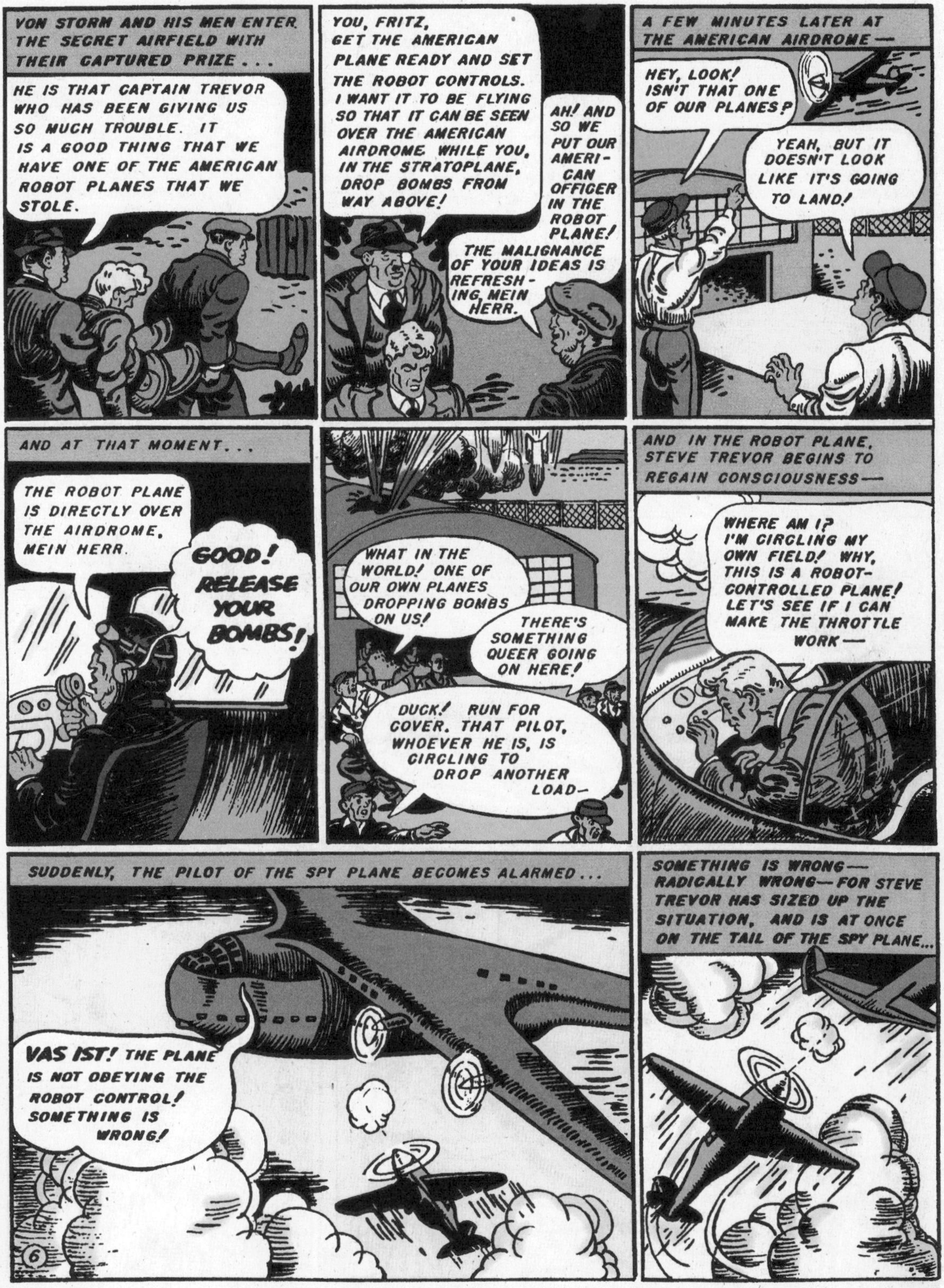
VON STORM AND HIS MEN ENTER THE SECRET AIRFIELD WITH THEIR CAPTURED PRIZE . . .
HE IS THAT CAPTAIN TREVOR WHO HAS BEEN GIVING US SO MUCH TROUBLE. IT IS A GOOD THING THAT WE HAVE ONE OF THE AMERICAN ROBOT PLANES THAT WE STOLE.
YOU, FRITZ, GET THE AMERICAN PLANE READY AND SET THE ROBOT CONTROLS. I WANT IT TO BE FLYING SO THAT IT CAN BE SEEN OVER THE AMERICAN AIRDROME WHILE YOU, IN THE STRATOPLANE, DROP BOMBS FROM WAY ABOVE!
AH! AND SO WE PUT OUR AMERICAN OFFICER IN THE ROBOT PLANE!
THE MALIGNANCE OF YOUR IDEAS IS REFRESHING, MEIN HERR.
A FEW MINUTES LATER AT THE AMERICAN AIRDROME—
HEY, LOOK! ISN'T THAT ONE OF OUR PLANES?
YEAH, BUT IT DOESN'T LOOK LIKE IT'S GOING TO LAND!
AND AT THAT MOMENT...
THE ROBOT PLANE IS DIRECTLY OVER THE AIRDROME, MEIN HERR.
GOOD! RELEASE YOUR BOMBS!
WHAT IN THE WORLD! ONE OF OUR OWN PLANES DROPPING BOMBS ON US!
THERE'S SOMETHING QUEER GOING ON HERE!
DUCK! RUN FOR COVER. THAT PILOT, WHOEVER HE IS, IS CIRCLING TO DROP ANOTHER LOAD—
AND IN THE ROBOT PLANE, STEVE TREVOR BEGINS TO REGAIN CONSCIOUSNESS—
WHERE AM I? I'M CIRCLING MY OWN FIELD! WHY, THIS IS A ROBOT-CONTROLLED PLANE! LET'S SEE IF I CAN MAKE THE THROTTLE WORK—
SUDDENLY, THE PILOT OF THE SPY PLANE BECOMES ALARMED...
VAS IST! THE PLANE IS NOT OBEYING THE ROBOT CONTROL! SOMETHING IS WRONG!
6
SOMETHING IS WRONG— RADICALLY WRONG— FOR STEVE TREVOR HAS SIZED UP THE SITUATION, AND IS AT ONCE ON THE TAIL OF THE SPY PLANE...

FRITZ, THE PILOT OF THE SPY PLANE, IS PANIC-STRICKEN AS HE REALIZES THAT HE HAS A SKILLED OPPONENT ON HIS TAIL... HE RADIOS FOR INSTRUCTIONS...

VON STORM! THE AMERICAN HAS RECOVERED CONSCIOUSNESS. HE IS TURNING THE ROBOT PLANE AGAINST ME. I CAN'T SHOOT HIM DOWN! WHAT SHALL I DO? HELLO VON STORM, DO YOU HEAR ME?

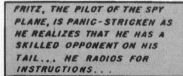

VON STORM IS FURIOUS AT THE WAY HIS PLANS ARE GOING —

YOU FOOL! DON'T LET HIM SHOOT YOU DOWN! THEY MUST NOT FIND OUT THIS PLAN! THEY MUST NOT KNOW YOU DROPPED THOSE BOMBS! GET HIM AWAY FROM HIS FIELD—

THE STRATOPLANE TURNS TAIL AND RUNS — STEVE FOLLOWS...

HE'S TURNED TAIL, THE SKUNK! I'VE GOT TO SHOOT HIM DOWN, BUT HE KEEPS MOVING TOO HIGH FOR ME. I'LL CATCH HIM IF IT'S THE LAST THING I DO!

ALWAYS OUT OF SHOOTING RANGE, THE BLACK PLANE KEEPS STEVE FOLLOWING UNTIL THEY ARE FAR OUT AT SEA

I WONDER HOW LONG HE'S GOING TO KEEP THIS UP! WELL, AS LONG AS THERE IS GAS LEFT IN THIS CRATE, I'M GOING TO STAY WITH HIM—

HOURS PASS AND MANY MILES — HUNDREDS OF MILES — PASS WITH THEM, BUT STEVE KEEPS DOGGEDLY ON THE TRAIL OF THE ENEMY PLANE UNTIL FINALLY HIS GAS BEGINS TO RUN LOW —

RUNNING SHORT OF GAS! LOOKS LIKE HE HAS ME LICKED! WAIT! WHAT'S THAT BELOW? CAN IT BE AN ISLAND? IT SEEMS SURROUNDED BY CLOUD FORMATIONS!

WELL, DAUGHTER, THERE'S THE HISTORY OF YOUR CAPTAIN UP TO THE VERY MOMENT HIS PLANE CRASHED ON PARADISE ISLAND!

BUT MOTHER, HE MUST BE TAKEN BACK TO AMERICA TO FINISH THE JOB HE STARTED!

GETTING HIM BACK WOULD BE A PROBLEM. LEAVE ME ALONE, MY DAUGHTER. I MUST CONSULT WITH APHRODITE AND ATHENA, OUR GODDESSES. I MUST SEEK THEIR ADVICE!

YES, MOTHER.

IT WOULDN'T BE ANY TRICK AT ALL FOR ME TO FLY HIM BACK MYSELF, BUT MOTHER WOULD NEVER HEAR OF IT.

IN THE QUEEN'S SOLITUDE, THE SPIRITS OF APHRODITE AND ATHENA, THE GUIDING GODDESSES OF THE AMAZONS, APPEAR AS THOUGH IN A MIST...

HIPPOLYTE, WE HAVE COME TO GIVE YOU WARNING. DANGER AGAIN THREATENS THE ENTIRE WORLD. THE GODS HAVE DECREED THAT THIS AMERICAN ARMY OFFICER CRASH ON PARADISE ISLAND. YOU MUST DELIVER HIM BACK TO AMERICA —— TO HELP FIGHT THE FORCES OF HATE AND OPPRESSION.

YES, HIPPOLYTE, AMERICAN LIBERTY AND FREEDOM MUST BE PRESERVED! YOU MUST SEND WITH HIM YOUR STRONGEST AND WISEST AMAZON — THE FINEST OF YOUR WONDER WOMEN! — FOR AMERICA, THE LAST CITADEL OF DEMOCRACY, AND OF EQUAL RIGHTS FOR WOMEN, NEEDS YOUR HELP!

YES, APHRODITE, YES, ATHENA. I HEED YOUR CALL. I SHALL FIND THE STRONGEST AND WISEST OF THE AMAZONS. SHE SHALL GO FORTH TO FIGHT FOR LIBERTY AND FREEDOM AND ALL WOMANKIND!

AND SO THE AMAZON QUEEN PREPARES A TOURNAMENT TO DECIDE WHICH IS THE MOST CAPABLE OF HER SUBJECTS...

BUT MOTHER, WHY CAN'T I ENTER INTO THIS TOURNAMENT? SURELY, I HAVE AS MUCH RIGHT —

NO, DAUGHTER! I FORBID YOU TO ENTER THE CONTEST! THE WINNER MUST TAKE THIS MAN BACK TO AMERICA AND NEVER RETURN, AND I COULDN'T BEAR TO HAVE YOU LEAVE ME FOREVER!

THE GREAT DAY ARRIVES! FROM ALL PARTS OF PARADISE ISLAND COME THE AMAZON CONTESTANTS! BUT ONE YOUNG CONTESTANT INSISTS ON WEARING A MASK...

IF YOU ARE ALL READY, LET THE TOURNAMENT BEGIN — AND MAY THE BEST MAIDEN WIN!

THE TESTS BEGIN! FIRST...THE FOOT RACE! A TRAINED DEER SETS THE PACE! AS THE DEER EASILY OUTRUNS THE PACK, SUDDENLY THE SLIM MASKED FIGURE DARTS FORWARD, HER LEGS CHURNING MADLY...

AND NOT ONLY CATCHES UP WITH THE DEER — BUT PASSES IT!

AS THE TESTS OF STRENGTH AND AGILITY GO ON THROUGHOUT THE DAY, MORE AND MORE CONTESTANTS DROP OUT WEARILY, UNTIL NUMBER 7, THE MASKED MAIDEN, AND MALA — NUMBER 12 — KEEP WINNING EVENT AFTER EVENT...UNTIL EACH HAS WON TEN OF THE GRUELLING CONTESTS!

AND NOW A DEADLY HUSH BLANKETS THE AUDIENCE. THE QUEEN HAS RISEN...

BULLETS AND BRACELETS!

BULLETS AND BRACELETS!

BULLETS AND BRACELETS!

BULLETS AND BRACELETS!

CONTESTANTS 7 AND 12. YOU ARE THE ONLY SURVIVORS OF THE TOURNAMENT! NOW YOU MUST GET READY FOR THE 21ST, THE FINAL AND GREATEST TEST OF ALL — BULLETS AND BRACELETS!

8

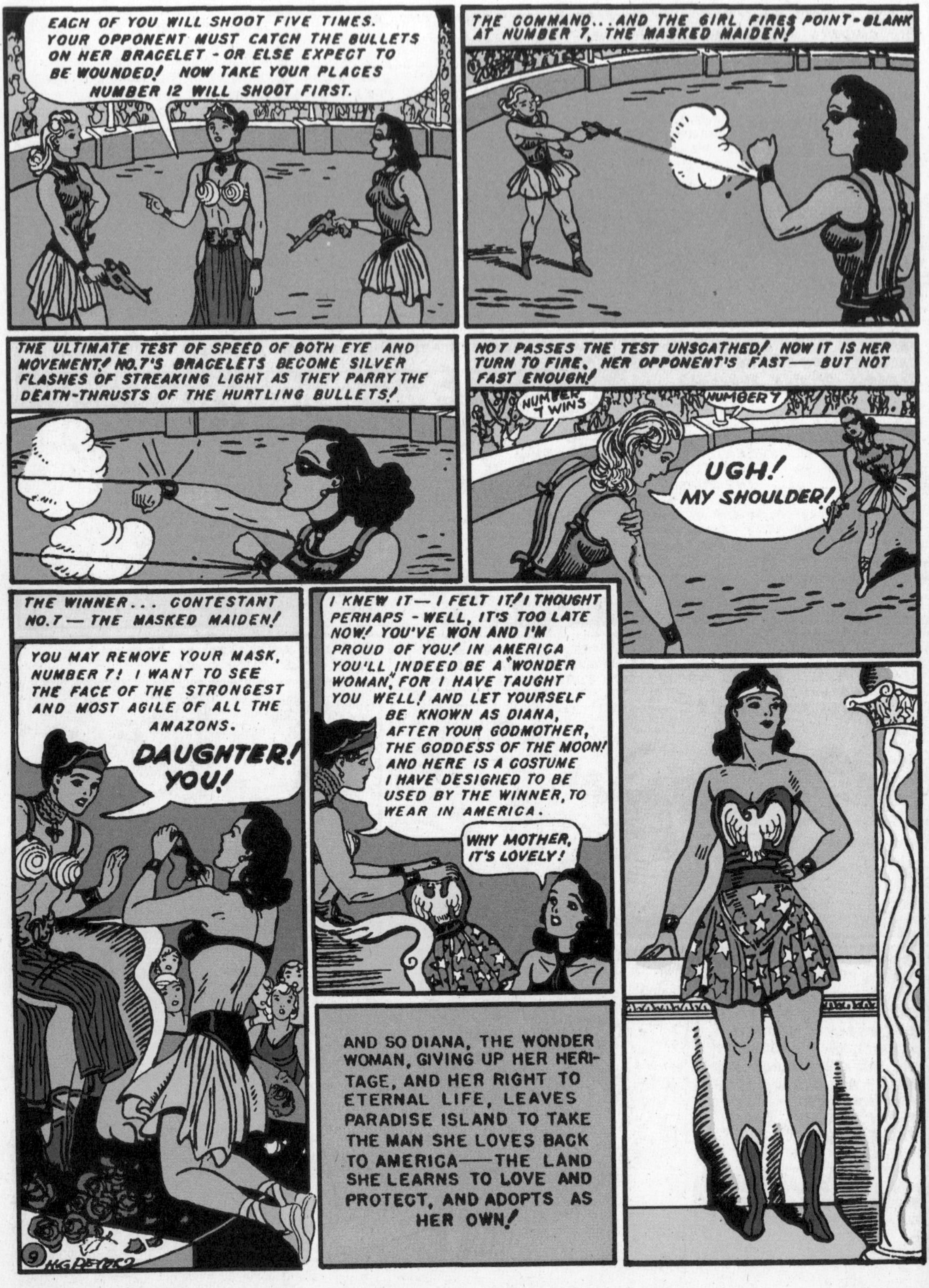
EACH OF YOU WILL SHOOT FIVE TIMES. YOUR OPPONENT MUST CATCH THE BULLETS ON HER BRACELET - OR ELSE EXPECT TO BE WOUNDED! NOW TAKE YOUR PLACES NUMBER 12 WILL SHOOT FIRST.
THE COMMAND...AND THE GIRL FIRES POINT-BLANK AT NUMBER 7, THE MASKED MAIDEN!
THE ULTIMATE TEST OF SPEED OF BOTH EYE AND MOVEMENT! NO.7'S BRACELETS BECOME SILVER FLASHES OF STREAKING LIGHT AS THEY PARRY THE DEATH-THRUSTS OF THE HURTLING BULLETS!
NO 7 PASSES THE TEST UNSCATHED! NOW IT IS HER TURN TO FIRE. HER OPPONENT'S FAST— BUT NOT FAST ENOUGH!
NUMBER 7 WINS
NUMBER 7
UGH! MY SHOULDER!
THE WINNER... CONTESTANT NO.7 — THE MASKED MAIDEN!
YOU MAY REMOVE YOUR MASK, NUMBER 7! I WANT TO SEE THE FACE OF THE STRONGEST AND MOST AGILE OF ALL THE AMAZONS.
DAUGHTER! YOU!
I KNEW IT— I FELT IT! I THOUGHT PERHAPS - WELL, IT'S TOO LATE NOW! YOU'VE WON AND I'M PROUD OF YOU! IN AMERICA YOU'LL INDEED BE A "WONDER WOMAN," FOR I HAVE TAUGHT YOU WELL! AND LET YOURSELF BE KNOWN AS DIANA, AFTER YOUR GODMOTHER, THE GODDESS OF THE MOON! AND HERE IS A COSTUME I HAVE DESIGNED TO BE USED BY THE WINNER, TO WEAR IN AMERICA.
WHY MOTHER, IT'S LOVELY!
AND SO DIANA, THE WONDER WOMAN, GIVING UP HER HERITAGE, AND HER RIGHT TO ETERNAL LIFE, LEAVES PARADISE ISLAND TO TAKE THE MAN SHE LOVES BACK TO AMERICA—THE LAND SHE LEARNS TO LOVE AND PROTECT, AND ADOPTS AS HER OWN!
9

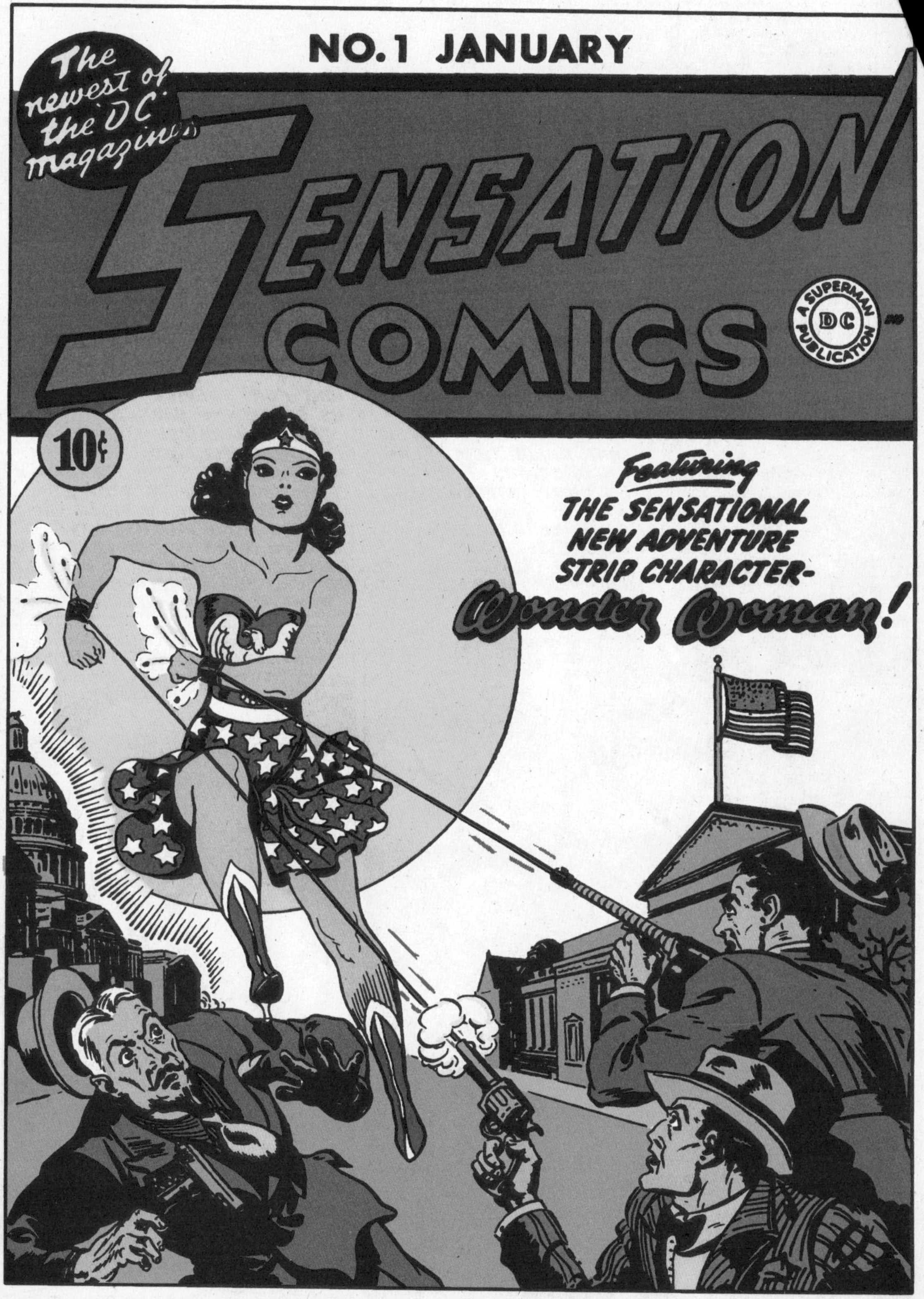
NO.1 JANUARY
The newest of the 'DC' magazines
SENSATION COMICS
A SUPERMAN DC PUBLICATION
10¢
Featuring
THE SENSATIONAL
NEW ADVENTURE
STRIP CHARACTER-
Wonder Woman!

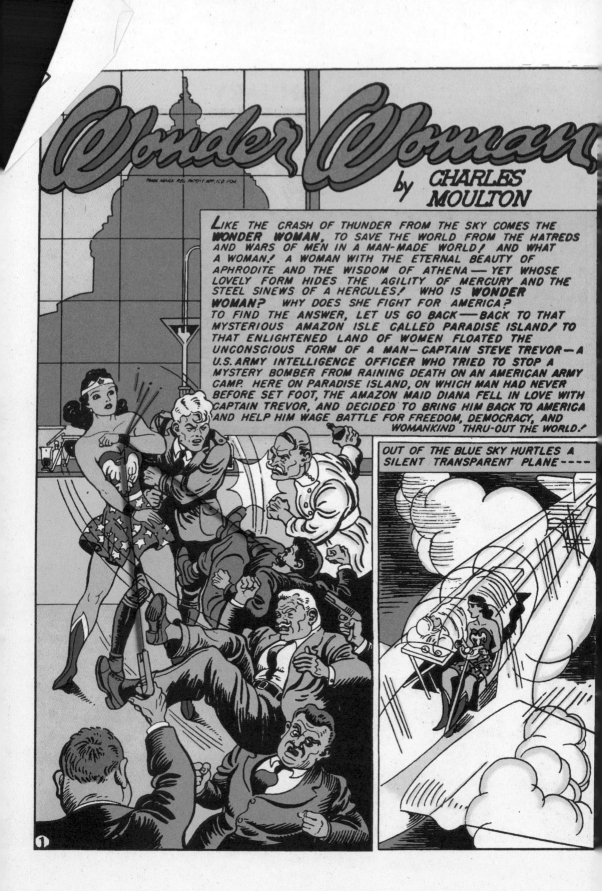

Wonder Woman

by CHARLES MOULTON

LIKE THE CRASH OF THUNDER FROM THE SKY COMES THE **WONDER WOMAN**, TO SAVE THE WORLD FROM THE HATREDS AND WARS OF MEN IN A MAN-MADE WORLD! AND WHAT A WOMAN! A WOMAN WITH THE ETERNAL BEAUTY OF APHRODITE AND THE WISDOM OF ATHENA — YET WHOSE LOVELY FORM HIDES THE AGILITY OF MERCURY AND THE STEEL SINEWS OF A HERCULES! WHO IS **WONDER WOMAN?** WHY DOES SHE FIGHT FOR AMERICA? TO FIND THE ANSWER, LET US GO BACK — BACK TO THAT MYSTERIOUS AMAZON ISLE CALLED PARADISE ISLAND! TO THAT ENLIGHTENED LAND OF WOMEN FLOATED THE UNCONSCIOUS FORM OF A MAN — CAPTAIN STEVE TREVOR — A U.S. ARMY INTELLIGENCE OFFICER WHO TRIED TO STOP A MYSTERY BOMBER FROM RAINING DEATH ON AN AMERICAN ARMY CAMP. HERE ON PARADISE ISLAND, ON WHICH MAN HAD NEVER BEFORE SET FOOT, THE AMAZON MAID DIANA FELL IN LOVE WITH CAPTAIN TREVOR, AND DECIDED TO BRING HIM BACK TO AMERICA AND HELP HIM WAGE BATTLE FOR FREEDOM, DEMOCRACY, AND WOMANKIND THRU-OUT THE WORLD!

OUT OF THE BLUE SKY HURTLES A SILENT TRANSPARENT PLANE----

AND AT THE CONTROLS IS AN AMAZON MAIDEN, NAMED DIANA BY HER MOTHER, QUEEN OF THE AMAZONS, AFTER HER GODMOTHER, GODDESS OF THE MOON!

HE'S STIRRING! PERHAPS I'D BETTER REMOVE HIS BANDAGES!

OH-H-H!

WHERE--? I'M IN HEAVEN! THERE'S AN ANGEL SMILING AT ME--- A BEAUTIFUL ANGEL!

HE'S FAINTED! HE'S STILL VERY WEAK. HE CALLED ME AN ANGEL--- A BEAUTIFUL ANGEL. THAT'S THE FIRST TIME A MAN EVER CALLED ME-- BEAUTIFUL!

ON--- ON SPEEDS THE PLANE UNTIL IT REACHES ITS DESTINATION—WASHINGTON, D.C.!

AT LAST I'M HERE — IN THE CAPITAL OF THE UNITED STATES!

DIANA BRINGS THE TRANSPARENT PLANE DOWN ON AN ABANDONED FIELD ON THE OUTSKIRTS OF WASHINGTON.

THIS DESERTED BARN SHOULD DO NICELY AS A HIDEOUT FOR MY PLANE!

PICKING UP STEVE TREVOR, SHE RACES SWIFTLY TO THE WALTER REED HOSPITAL.

GOOD THING IT IS STILL VERY EARLY IN THE MORNING SO THE STREETS ARE DESERTED.

AND INSIDE---

THIS IS CAPTAIN STEVE TREVOR OF THE ARMY INTELLIGENCE! HE'S HAD A BRAIN CONCUSSION! SEE THAT HE'S TAKEN CARE OF!

WHO—WHAT?

BUT-BUT WAIT! WHO ARE YOU?

I'LL SEND YOU A FULL REPORT SOMETIME! 'BYE!

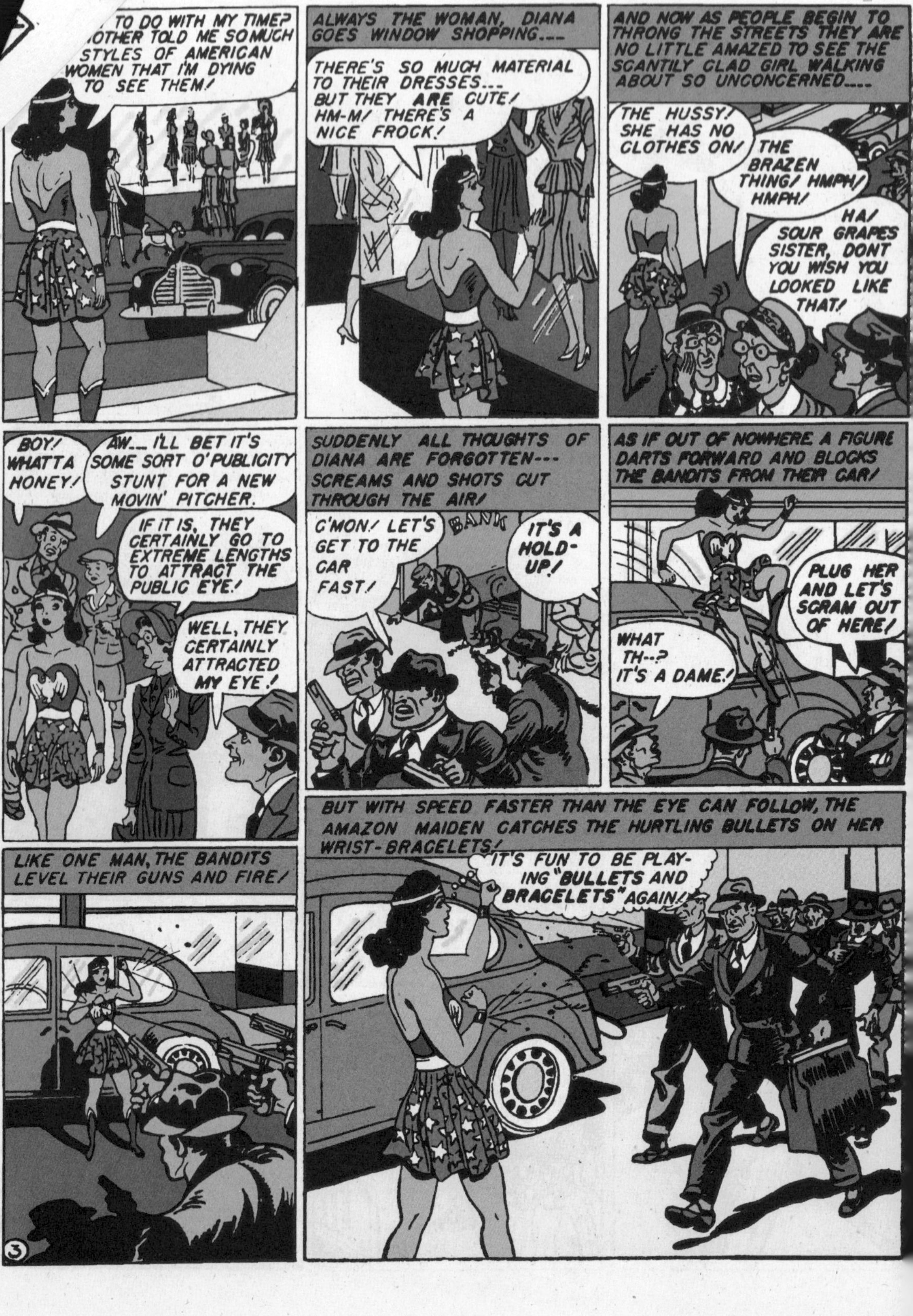
TO DO WITH MY TIME? OTHER TOLD ME SO MUCH STYLES OF AMERICAN WOMEN THAT I'M DYING TO SEE THEM!
ALWAYS THE WOMAN, DIANA GOES WINDOW SHOPPING---
THERE'S SO MUCH MATERIAL TO THEIR DRESSES... BUT THEY ARE CUTE! HM-M! THERE'S A NICE FROCK!
AND NOW AS PEOPLE BEGIN TO THRONG THE STREETS THEY ARE NO LITTLE AMAZED TO SEE THE SCANTILY CLAD GIRL WALKING ABOUT SO UNCONCERNED----
THE HUSSY! SHE HAS NO CLOTHES ON!
THE BRAZEN THING! HMPH! HMPH!
HA! SOUR GRAPES SISTER, DONT YOU WISH YOU LOOKED LIKE THAT!
BOY! WHATTA HONEY!
AW... I'LL BET IT'S SOME SORT O' PUBLICITY STUNT FOR A NEW MOVIN' PITCHER.
IF IT IS, THEY CERTAINLY GO TO EXTREME LENGTHS TO ATTRACT THE PUBLIC EYE!
WELL, THEY CERTAINLY ATTRACTED MY EYE!
SUDDENLY ALL THOUGHTS OF DIANA ARE FORGOTTEN--- SCREAMS AND SHOTS CUT THROUGH THE AIR!
C'MON! LET'S GET TO THE CAR FAST!
BANK
IT'S A HOLD-UP!
AS IF OUT OF NOWHERE A FIGURE DARTS FORWARD AND BLOCKS THE BANDITS FROM THEIR CAR!
PLUG HER AND LET'S SCRAM OUT OF HERE!
WHAT TH--? IT'S A DAME!
LIKE ONE MAN, THE BANDITS LEVEL THEIR GUNS AND FIRE!
3
BUT WITH SPEED FASTER THAN THE EYE CAN FOLLOW, THE AMAZON MAIDEN CATCHES THE HURTLING BULLETS ON HER WRIST-BRACELETS!
IT'S FUN TO BE PLAYING "BULLETS AND BRACELETS" AGAIN!

SHE'S PLAYIN' WITH 'EM! SHE'S PLAYIN' CATCH WITH 'EM!

AND NOW I'M GOING TO PLAY *CATCH* WITH YOU!

DIANA'S HAND CLOSES LIKE A STEEL CLAMP ABOUT THE BANDIT'S WRIST ---

WH-?

CATCH!

WHA - WHAT'S GOIN' ON AROUND HERE?

I DON'T KNOW. I HEARD SOMEONE SAY "IT'S A HOLD-UP." GOOD-BYE!

WAIT! WE WANT TO ASK YOU A FEW QUESTIONS!

SOME OTHER TIME, WHEN I'M ON THE "QUIZ KIDS" PROGRAM!

AS DIANA DARTS AWAY, ONE MAN SLIPS FROM THE EDGE OF THE CROWD ---

DID YOU SEE HER SLAP THOSE BANDITS AROUND?

AND DID YOU SEE HER SLAP THOSE *BULLETS* AROUND? NOW *THAT* WAS SOMETHING!

WONDER WHO SHE IS?

WAIT! SHE'S ...NG FASTER! ...TEP ON THE GAS ...O CATCH UP TO HER!

EVEN AS THE CAR WHIPS FORWARD, DIANA PUTS ON A GREAT BURST OF SPEED.

WHAT TH'—SHE'S GOING FASTER AND THE CAR'S DOING 35 MILES PER!

FASTER SPEEDS THE CAR, AND FASTER SPEEDS THE HUMAN METEOR AHEAD!

HOLY SMOKE! I'VE GOT THE CAR AT 50 MILES PER HOUR—AND I STILL HAVEN'T CAUGHT UP WITH HER!

FASTER---FASTER---FASTER-- FASTER- UNTIL DIANA COVERS GROUND AT A MILE A - MINUTE!

60 MILES AN HOUR-- AND SHE'S STILL AHEAD! I'M GOING TO OPEN UP THIS BUGGY TO THE LIMIT!

FASTER AND STILL FASTER---UNTIL AT 80 MILES PER HOUR, THE CAR DRAWS ALONGSIDE THE MILE-A-MINUTE MAIDEN!

HEY--- WAIT-- I JUST WANT TO TALK TO YOU ABOUT A BUSINESS PROPOSITION!

SAY--WHAT ARE YOU? WHEW! YOU WERE BURNING UP THE ROAD!

WHAT'S THIS--- BUSINESS PROPOSITION-- YOU TALKED ABOUT?

MY NAME IS AL KALE! I BOOK ACTS FOR THEATRES! NOW I DON'T KNOW WHAT YOUR RACKET IS AND I DON'T CARE. ALL I KNOW IS THAT THOSE SPEEDY LEGS OF YOURS, OR THAT "BULLET" TRICK COULD NET US A FORTUNE!

YOU MEAN YOU WANT TO PUT ME ON A STAGE?

EITHER ON THE TRACK OR THE STAGE! RACING—OR THAT "BULLET" TRICK IN THE THEATRES. IT WOULD BRING YOU PLENTY OF MONEY!

YES, I WILL NEED MONEY. AND I DO HAVE TO KILL TIME TILL STEVE RECOVERS CONSCIOUSNESS---

I'LL DO IT! I'LL PUT ON MY "BULLETS AND BRACE-LETS" ACT FOR YOU! BUT THE RACING IS OUT!

THAT'S O.K. WITH ME. WE'LL CLEAN UP WITH THAT "BULLETS" ACT ANYWAY! BOY-OH-BOY-OH-BOY-

AND "CLEAN UP" THEY DO---FOR THE "BULLETS AND BRACELETS" IS A GREAT ATTRACTION AND A SOURCE OF WONDER TO ALL!

THE PAPERS GIVE THE "WONDER WOMAN" PLENTY OF PUBLICITY----

BUT AT LAST, ONE DAY THERE APPEARS AN ITEM THAT ATTRACTS **WONDER WOMAN'S** ATTENTION----

BUT YOU CAN'T QUIT NOW! WE'RE KNOCKIN' 'EM DEAD! WE'RE MAKING MORE MONEY THAN---

MAKING MORE MONEY DOESN'T INTEREST ME ANY MORE! I'M SORRY, BUT I'M THROUGH WITH THE ACT!

I CAN'T HOLD HER. SHE DIDN'T SIGN ANY CONTRACT. WHEN I THINK OF ALL THE DOUGH WE COULD--- **DOUGH** ---SAY---I GOT HER DOUGH THAT SHE TOLD ME TO HOLD FOR HER! HMMM---

KALE---GONE---AND WITH ALL MY EARNINGS! I----THERE HE IS-GETTING INTO HIS CAR!

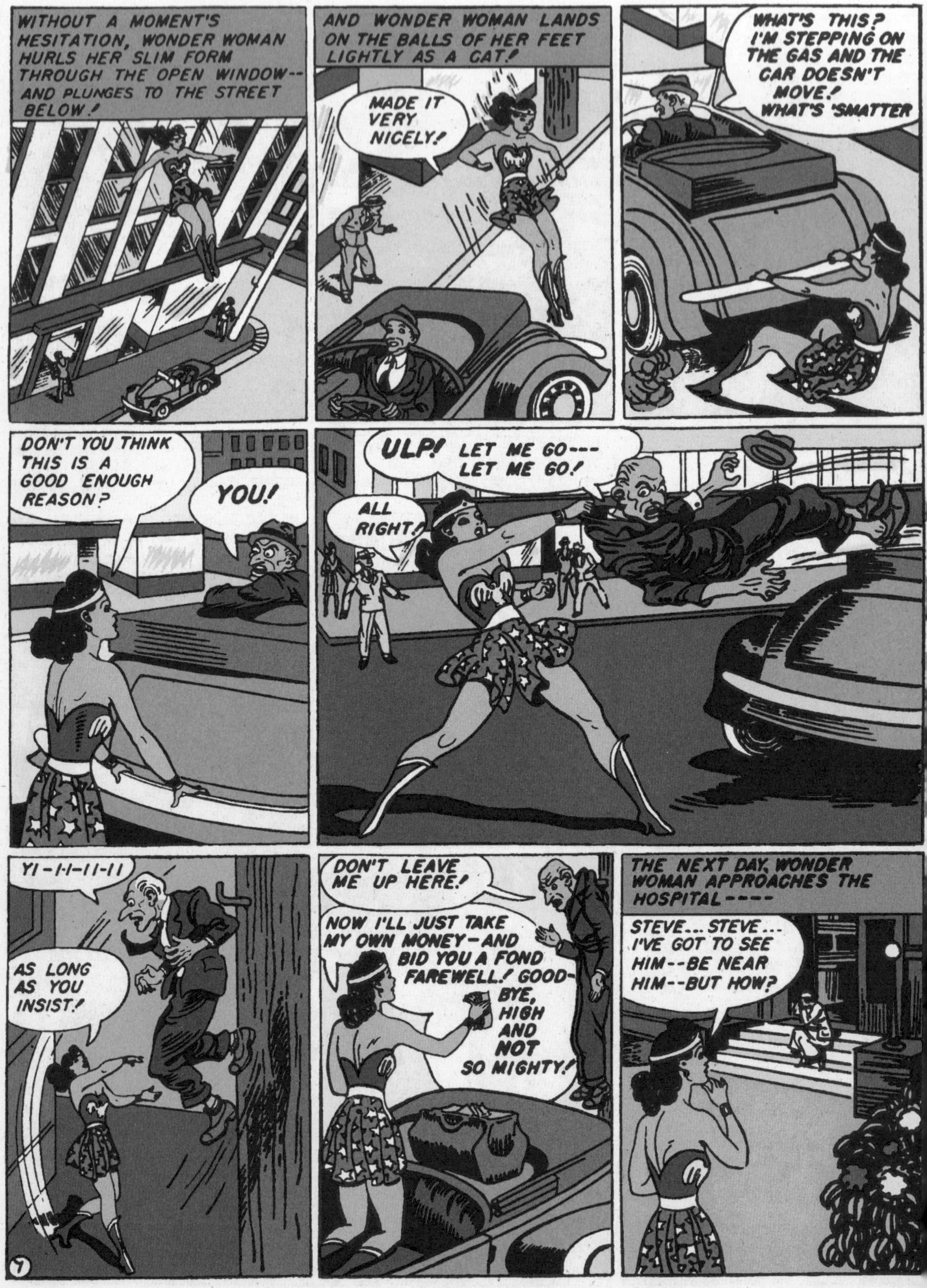
WITHOUT A MOMENT'S HESITATION, WONDER WOMAN HURLS HER SLIM FORM THROUGH THE OPEN WINDOW--AND PLUNGES TO THE STREET BELOW!
AND WONDER WOMAN LANDS ON THE BALLS OF HER FEET LIGHTLY AS A CAT!
MADE IT VERY NICELY!
WHAT'S THIS? I'M STEPPING ON THE GAS AND THE CAR DOESN'T MOVE! WHAT'S 'SMATTER
DON'T YOU THINK THIS IS A GOOD ENOUGH REASON?
YOU!
ULP! LET ME GO---LET ME GO!
ALL RIGHT!
YI-I-I-II-II
AS LONG AS YOU INSIST!
DON'T LEAVE ME UP HERE!
NOW I'LL JUST TAKE MY OWN MONEY-AND BID YOU A FOND FAREWELL! GOOD-BYE, HIGH AND NOT SO MIGHTY!
THE NEXT DAY, WONDER WOMAN APPROACHES THE HOSPITAL----
STEVE... STEVE... I'VE GOT TO SEE HIM--BE NEAR HIM--BUT HOW?
7

Panel 1: AS SHE NEARS THE STEPS, WONDER WOMAN SEES A GIRL HUDDLED AND CRYING THERE---

I DON'T MEAN TO INTRUDE BUT CAN I HELP YOU?

NO ONE CAN HELP ME! BOO—HOO!

Panel 2: THE GIRL TELLS WONDER WOMAN THAT SHE IS AN ARMY NURSE JUST APPOINTED TO THIS HOSPITAL---

AND TODAY MY FIANCÉ JUST GOT A JOB IN SOUTH AMERICA, BUT HE CAN'T SEND FOR ME BECAUSE HIS SALARY IS TOO SMALL AT THE MOMENT!

THAT'S TERRIBLE, AND JUST THINK-- IT ALL WOULD WORK OUT RIGHT IF ONLY YOU HAD A LITTLE MONEY!

Panel 3: I JUST NOTICED — WITH THESE GLASSES OFF, YOU LOOK A LOT LIKE ME! I HAVE AN IDEA! IF I GAVE YOU MONEY WOULD YOU SELL ME YOUR CREDENTIALS?

YOU--YOU MEAN YOU WANT TO TAKE MY PLACE HERE AT THE HOSPITAL? BUT— I CAN'T--- I MEAN--

Panel 4: LOOK— BY TAKING YOUR PLACE I CAN SEE THE MAN I LOVE AND YOU CAN MARRY THE MAN YOU LOVE! NO HARM DONE, FOR I'M A TRAINED NURSE, TOO — JUST A LITTLE MONEY AND A SUBSTITUTION)—

AND WE'D BOTH BE HAPPY! I'LL DO IT! OH— THIS IS WONDERFUL!

Panel 5: OH, BY THE WAY— MY NAME IS DIANA. WHAT'S YOURS?

WHY, THAT'S AN AMAZING COINCIDENCE—I'M DIANA TOO! DIANA PRINCE! AND YOU'D BETTER REMEMBER THAT LAST NAME — BECAUSE IT'LL BE YOURS FROM NOW ON.

Panel 6: AND SO THAT AFTERNOON----

AN ANGEL--- A BEAUTIFUL ANGEL!

OH, CAPTAIN TREVOR —YOU FLATTER ME I'M JUST DIANA PRINCE, YOUR SPECIAL NURSE!

HE REMEMBERED ME--- HE REMEMBERED!

Panel 7: DAYS PASS AND STEVE TREVOR RECOVERS RAPIDLY UNDER HIS NEW NURSE'S TENDER CARE---

YOU'RE PRETTY SWELL TO ME, DIANA! BUT I'M JUST WASTING AWAY HERE. I SHOULD BE BACK ON MY JOB!

I DON'T BELIEVE IT'S YOUR JOB. YOU WANT TO FIND THAT "BEAUTIFUL ANGEL" YOU WERE TALKING ABOUT— THE ONE WHO BROUGHT YOU HERE! BE A GOOD BOY, NOW, AND KEEP QUIET---

Panel 8: GREAT GUNS! NOW I'VE GOT TO GO--- DOCTOR OR NO DOCTOR!

BY THE TIME THEY NOTICE I'M GONE, IT'LL BE TOO LATE TO STOP ME!

HE'S GONE! OVER-EXERTION MAY KILL TREVOR! IT'S YOUR FAULT, NURSE---YOU SHOULD NEVER HAVE LEFT THE ROOM--

"NEW DRAFT QUOTA CALLED TOMORROW. MYSTERIOUS ENEMY THREATENS TO BOMB CAMP MERRICK WITH A NEW POISON GAS WHICH PENETRATES ALL GAS MASKS!

SORRY DOCTOR!

THAT NIGHT, NURSE DIANA PRINCE DARTS TOWARD AN OLD DESERT-ED BARN ON THE OUTSKIRTS OF WASHINGTON----

I HOPE NO ONE'S FOUND THIS HIDEOUT WHILE I'VE BEEN NURSING STEVE TREVOR!

INSIDE THE BARN, THE GIRL TRANSFORMS HERSELF FROM DRAB DIANA PRINCE TO THE EXCITING AMAZON MAIDEN... WONDER WOMAN!

IT FEELS GRAND TO BE MYSELF AGAIN! AND NOW FOR CLEVER STEVE TREVOR... THE IMPETUOUS DARLING!

AT CAMP MERRICK, STEVE TREVOR REPORTS TO THE C.O.!

I'VE GOT AIR PATROLS COVERING THE ENTIRE COAST. BUT THIS MYSTERY BOMBER USES A STRATO-SPHERE PLANE. HE'LL POWER-DIVE ON THE CAMP AND I'M GOING TO WAIT FOR HIM.

WE'RE DEPENDING ON YOU, CAPTAIN!

HIGH OVER CAMP MERRICK, STEVE TREVOR CIRCLES LIKE A BIRD OF PREY--WAITING FOR THE ENEMY!

THEN-- LIKE A DIVING, WINGED COMET--THE MYSTERY BOMBER!

WOW! HE MUST BE DOING 650 M.P.H.! I'VE GOT TO STOP HIM!

JUMPING BLUE BLAZES! THAT GUY'S GOT A FLYING FORT! I CAN'T EVEN DENT HIS POLISH!

THE ONLY THING TO DO -- CRASH HIM! HERE GOES NOTHING!

THE AIR IS SUDDENLY DEAFENED BY A SHATTERING THUNDEROUS EXPLOSION!

I GOT HIM--BUT MY 'CHUTE! IT'S--IT'S RIPPED AWAY! I'M A GONER FOR SURE! KEEP 'EM FLYING BOYS!

LIKE A STREAK OF LIGHT, A SILENT, TRANSPARENT PLANE HURTLES OUT OF THE BLUE WITH WONDER WOMAN AT THE CONTROLS!

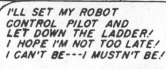

I'LL SET MY ROBOT CONTROL PILOT AND LET DOWN THE LADDER! I HOPE I'M NOT TOO LATE! I CAN'T BE---I MUSTN'T BE!

WONDER WOMAN'S RIGHT ARM GRASPS TREVOR'S FALLING BODY AND TIGHTENS AROUND HIS WAIST WITH THE UNFAILING GRIP OF A BOA CONSTRICTOR! THE SHOCK IS GREAT BUT HER LOVE AND STRENGTH ARE GREATER!

GOT HIM! NOW TO CARRY HIM BACK TO MY PLANE!

YOU---THE BEAUTIFUL ANGEL!

A GUARDIAN ANGEL IS MORE LIKE IT!

10

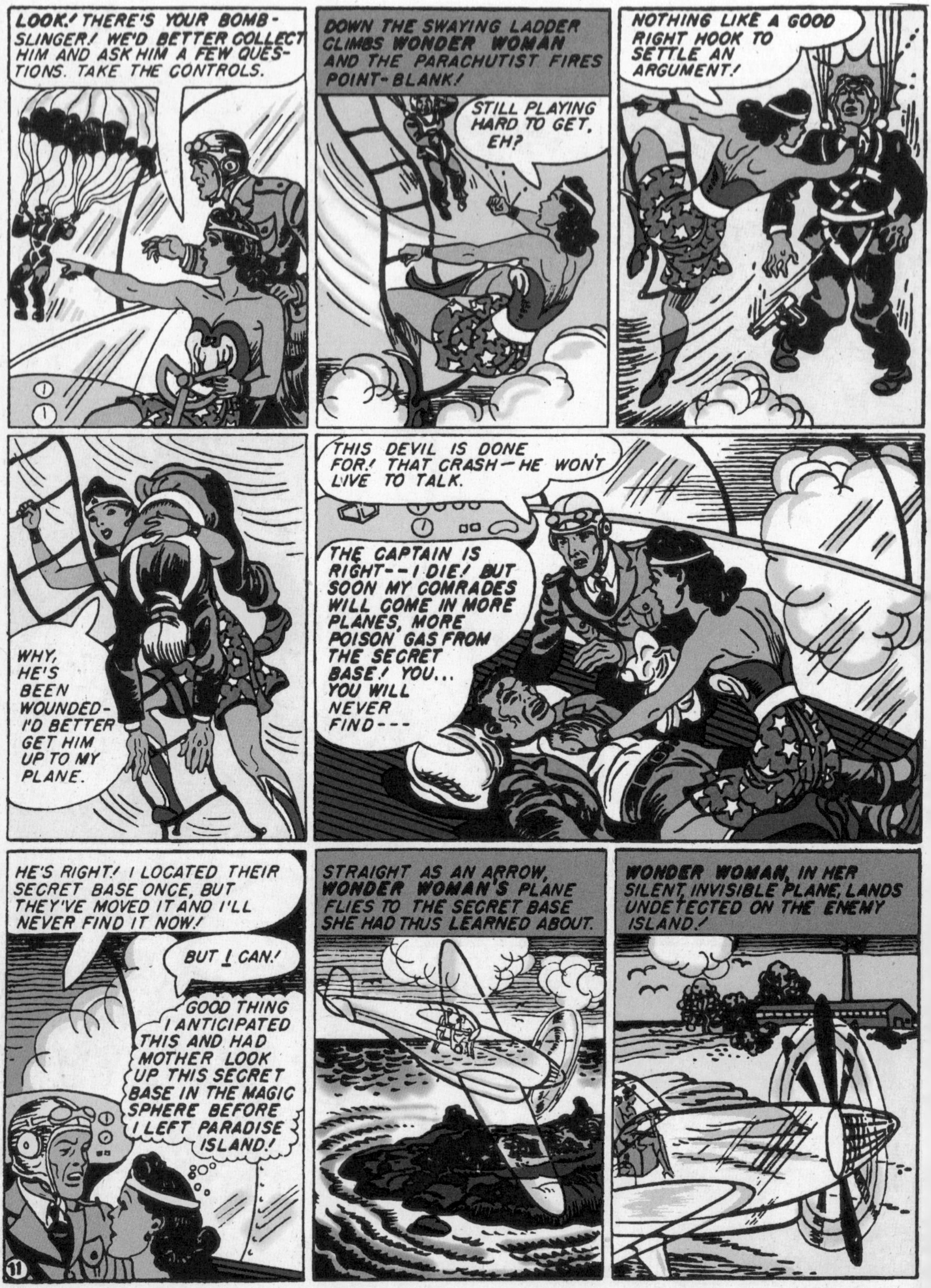
LOOK! THERE'S YOUR BOMB-SLINGER! WE'D BETTER COLLECT HIM AND ASK HIM A FEW QUESTIONS. TAKE THE CONTROLS.
DOWN THE SWAYING LADDER CLIMBS WONDER WOMAN AND THE PARACHUTIST FIRES POINT-BLANK!
STILL PLAYING HARD TO GET, EH?
NOTHING LIKE A GOOD RIGHT HOOK TO SETTLE AN ARGUMENT!
WHY, HE'S BEEN WOUNDED- I'D BETTER GET HIM UP TO MY PLANE.
THIS DEVIL IS DONE FOR! THAT CRASH—HE WON'T LIVE TO TALK.
THE CAPTAIN IS RIGHT--I DIE! BUT SOON MY COMRADES WILL COME IN MORE PLANES, MORE POISON GAS FROM THE SECRET BASE! YOU... YOU WILL NEVER FIND---
HE'S RIGHT! I LOCATED THEIR SECRET BASE ONCE, BUT THEY'VE MOVED IT AND I'LL NEVER FIND IT NOW!
BUT I CAN!
GOOD THING I ANTICIPATED THIS AND HAD MOTHER LOOK UP THIS SECRET BASE IN THE MAGIC SPHERE BEFORE I LEFT PARADISE ISLAND!
11
STRAIGHT AS AN ARROW, WONDER WOMAN'S PLANE FLIES TO THE SECRET BASE SHE HAD THUS LEARNED ABOUT.
WONDER WOMAN, IN HER SILENT, INVISIBLE PLANE, LANDS UNDETECTED ON THE ENEMY ISLAND!

AS TWO GUARDS PATROL THE GROUNDS, TWO SINISTER FIGURES CATAPULT OUT OF THE SHRUBBERY

WHAT.!.!?

SINCE THESE DOORS ARE LOCKED.. WHY, WE'LL HAVE TO LET OURSELVES IN!

WELL I'LL BE.. LOOK AT *HER!*

HOW NICE TO MAKE YOUR ACQUAINTANCE!

HERE—PUT ON THIS MASK!

TREVOR FIRES AT A CONTAINER OF POISON GAS!

THE GAS GATHERS LIKE A MALIGNANT CLOUD ABOUT THE ENEMY BUT THE GAS MASKS PROTECT **WONDER WOMAN** AND TREVOR!

LOOK! THERE'S THEIR LEADER!

LOOK OUT! HE'S THROWING A SWITCH!

FOOLS! I'LL DIE—BUT YOU DIE WITH ME!

THERE IS ONE TERRIBLE, CATACLYSMIC BLAST... AN ETERNAL MOMENT OF SHATTERING RUIN...

WONDER WOMAN EASILY LEAPS CLEAR — BUT STEVE IS BURIED UNDER THE DEBRIS!

WORKING AT A FEVERISH PACE WONDER WOMAN UNCOVERS STEVE TREVOR---

ARE YOU HURT, STEVE? WHY DIDN'T YOU JUMP LIKE I DID?

JUMP LIKE YOU? WHAT AM I — A KANGAROO?

YOUR LEG-- IT'S BROKEN!

MY LEG DOES SEEM BENT A BIT--BUT I'M GLAD OF IT. AT LEAST IT SHOWS YOU CARE!

YOUR LEG WILL BE RIGHT AS NEW IN A SHORT WHILE. ARUMPH.... YOU DID MAGNIFICENT WORK, CAPTAIN.... MAGNIFICENT!

I DIDN'T DO IT!, A BEAUTIFUL ANGEL WAS RESPONSIBLE!

CONGRATULATIONS, CAPTAIN! YOU DID EXCELLENT WORK!

THANKS, CHIEF. BUT FOR HEAVEN'S SAKE, DON'T GIVE ME THE CREDIT. IT BELONGS TO THAT BEAUTIFUL GIRL— WONDER WOMAN!

LATER....

JUST SAW THE GENERAL OUTSIDE. THEY THINK YOU'RE DELIRIOUS, TALKING ABOUT A "BEAUTIFUL ANGEL"— A WONDER WOMAN WHO REALLY BROKE UP THAT NAZI GANG AND SAVED YOUR LIFE!

THAT'S RIGHT! YOU LAUGH, TOO...BUT I'M NOT DELIRIOUS, YOU HEAR ME! THERE IS A WONDER WOMAN! I SAW HER!

ALL RIGHT, I BELIEVE YOU! ANYWAY, CAPTAIN.... YOU DON'T NEED WONDER WOMAN NOW — YOU'VE GOT ME!

LISTEN, DIANA! YOU'RE A NICE KID, AND I LIKE YOU. BUT IF YOU THINK YOU CAN HOLD A CANDLE TO WONDER WOMAN YOU'RE CRAZY!

13

SO I'M MY OWN RIVAL, EH? THAT'S FUNNY... IF MOTHER COULD ONLY SEE ME NOW.... AS A VERY FEMININE WOMAN. .A NURSE, NO LESS, IN A WORLD FULL OF MEN, AND IN LOVE, TOO - WITH MYSELF FOR A RIVAL!

AND SO ENDS THE FIRST EPISODE OF WONDER WOMAN ALIAS DIANA PRINCE, ARMY NURSE! FOLLOW HER EXCITING ADVENTURES AS SHE BESTS THE WORLD'S MOST VILLAINOUS MEN AT THEIR OWN GAME EVERY MONTH IN SENSATION COMICS

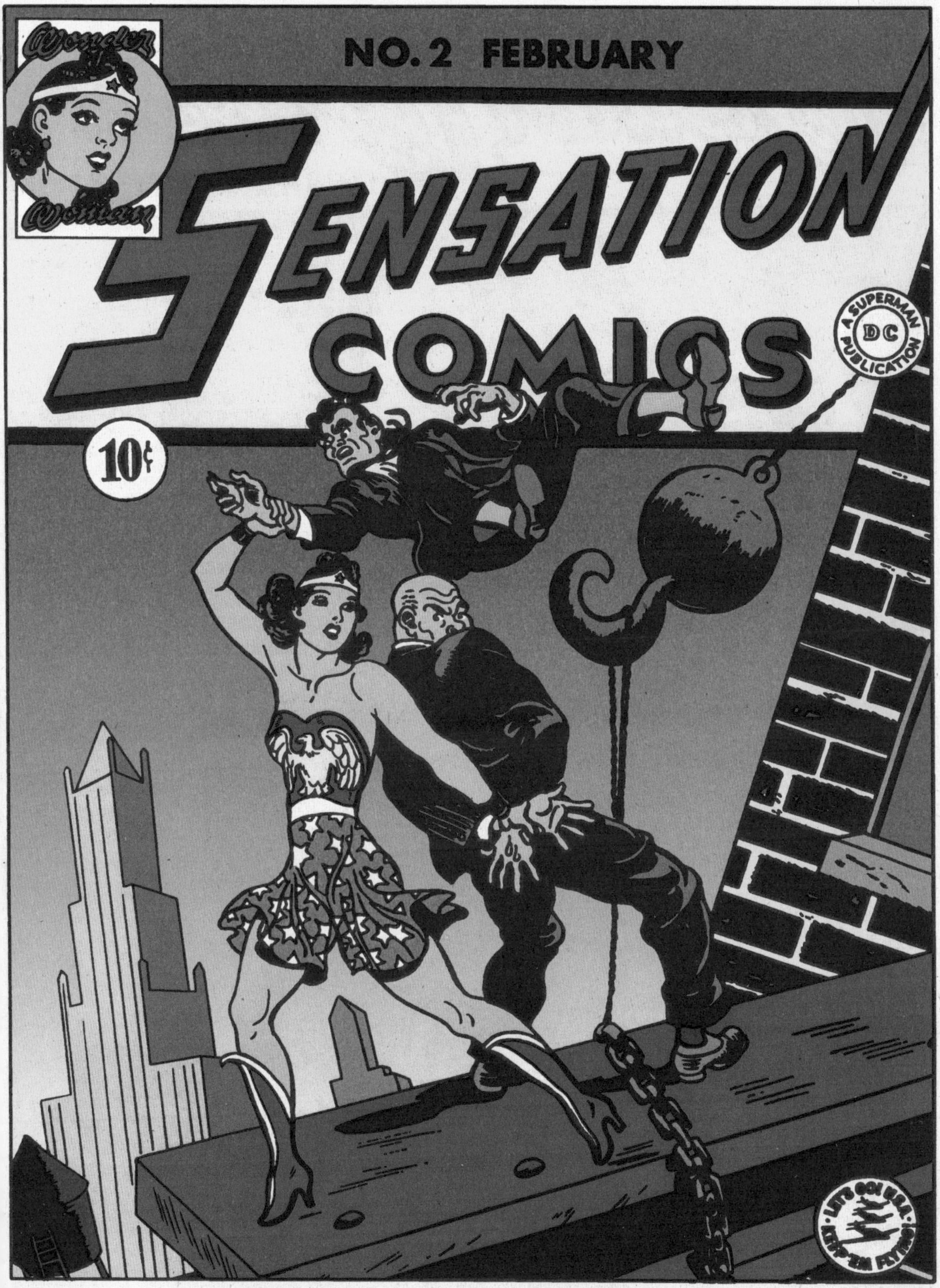

Wonder Woman
NO. 2 FEBRUARY
SENSATION COMICS
A SUPERMAN DC PUBLICATION
10¢

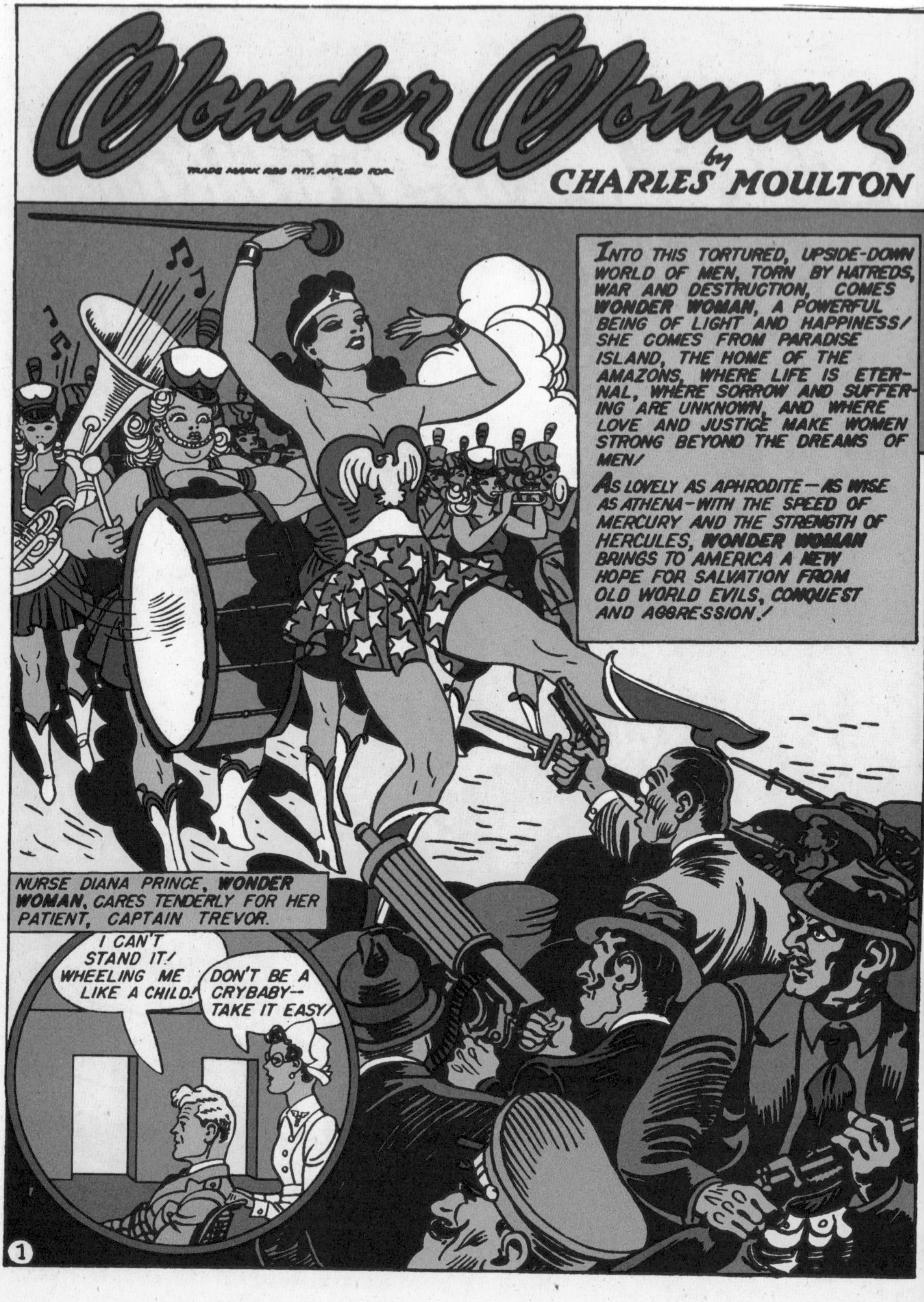
Wonder Woman
TRADE MARK REG PAT. APPLIED FOR
by CHARLES MOULTON
INTO THIS TORTURED, UPSIDE-DOWN WORLD OF MEN, TORN BY HATREDS, WAR AND DESTRUCTION, COMES WONDER WOMAN, A POWERFUL BEING OF LIGHT AND HAPPINESS! SHE COMES FROM PARADISE ISLAND, THE HOME OF THE AMAZONS, WHERE LIFE IS ETERNAL, WHERE SORROW AND SUFFERING ARE UNKNOWN, AND WHERE LOVE AND JUSTICE MAKE WOMEN STRONG BEYOND THE DREAMS OF MEN!
AS LOVELY AS APHRODITE—AS WISE AS ATHENA—WITH THE SPEED OF MERCURY AND THE STRENGTH OF HERCULES, WONDER WOMAN BRINGS TO AMERICA A NEW HOPE FOR SALVATION FROM OLD WORLD EVILS, CONQUEST AND AGGRESSION!
NURSE DIANA PRINCE, WONDER WOMAN, CARES TENDERLY FOR HER PATIENT, CAPTAIN TREVOR.
I CAN'T STAND IT! WHEELING ME LIKE A CHILD!
DON'T BE A CRYBABY—TAKE IT EASY!
1

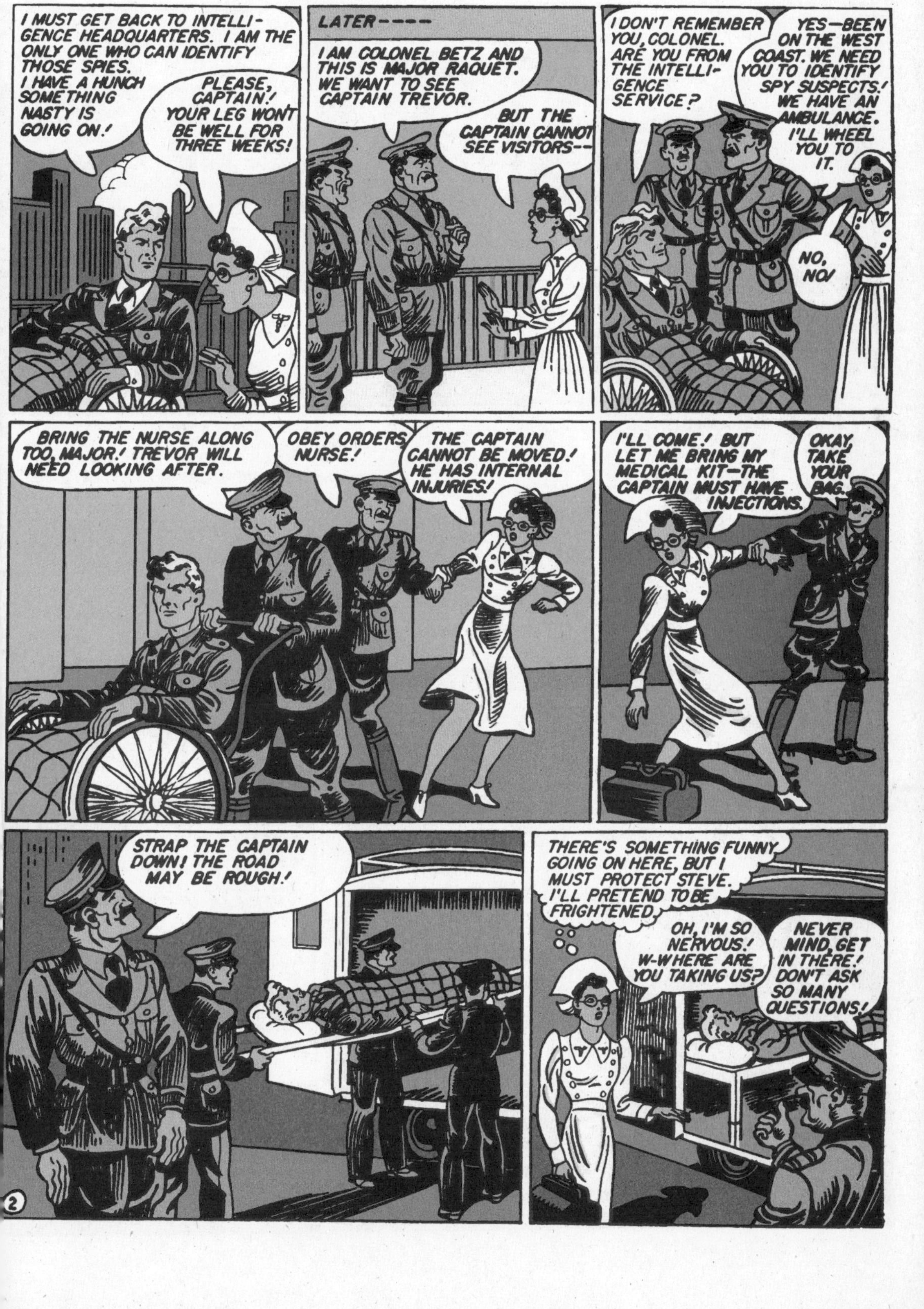
I MUST GET BACK TO INTELLIGENCE HEADQUARTERS. I AM THE ONLY ONE WHO CAN IDENTIFY THOSE SPIES. I HAVE A HUNCH SOMETHING NASTY IS GOING ON!
PLEASE, CAPTAIN! YOUR LEG WON'T BE WELL FOR THREE WEEKS!
LATER----
I AM COLONEL BETZ AND THIS IS MAJOR RAQUET. WE WANT TO SEE CAPTAIN TREVOR.
BUT THE CAPTAIN CANNOT SEE VISITORS--
I DON'T REMEMBER YOU, COLONEL. ARE YOU FROM THE INTELLIGENCE SERVICE?
YES—BEEN ON THE WEST COAST. WE NEED YOU TO IDENTIFY SPY SUSPECTS! WE HAVE AN AMBULANCE. I'LL WHEEL YOU TO IT.
NO, NO!
BRING THE NURSE ALONG TOO, MAJOR! TREVOR WILL NEED LOOKING AFTER.
OBEY ORDERS, NURSE!
THE CAPTAIN CANNOT BE MOVED! HE HAS INTERNAL INJURIES!
I'LL COME! BUT LET ME BRING MY MEDICAL KIT—THE CAPTAIN MUST HAVE INJECTIONS.
OKAY, TAKE YOUR BAG.
STRAP THE CAPTAIN DOWN! THE ROAD MAY BE ROUGH!
2
THERE'S SOMETHING FUNNY GOING ON HERE, BUT I MUST PROTECT STEVE. I'LL PRETEND TO BE FRIGHTENED.
OH, I'M SO NERVOUS! W-WHERE ARE YOU TAKING US?
NEVER MIND, GET IN THERE! DON'T ASK SO MANY QUESTIONS!

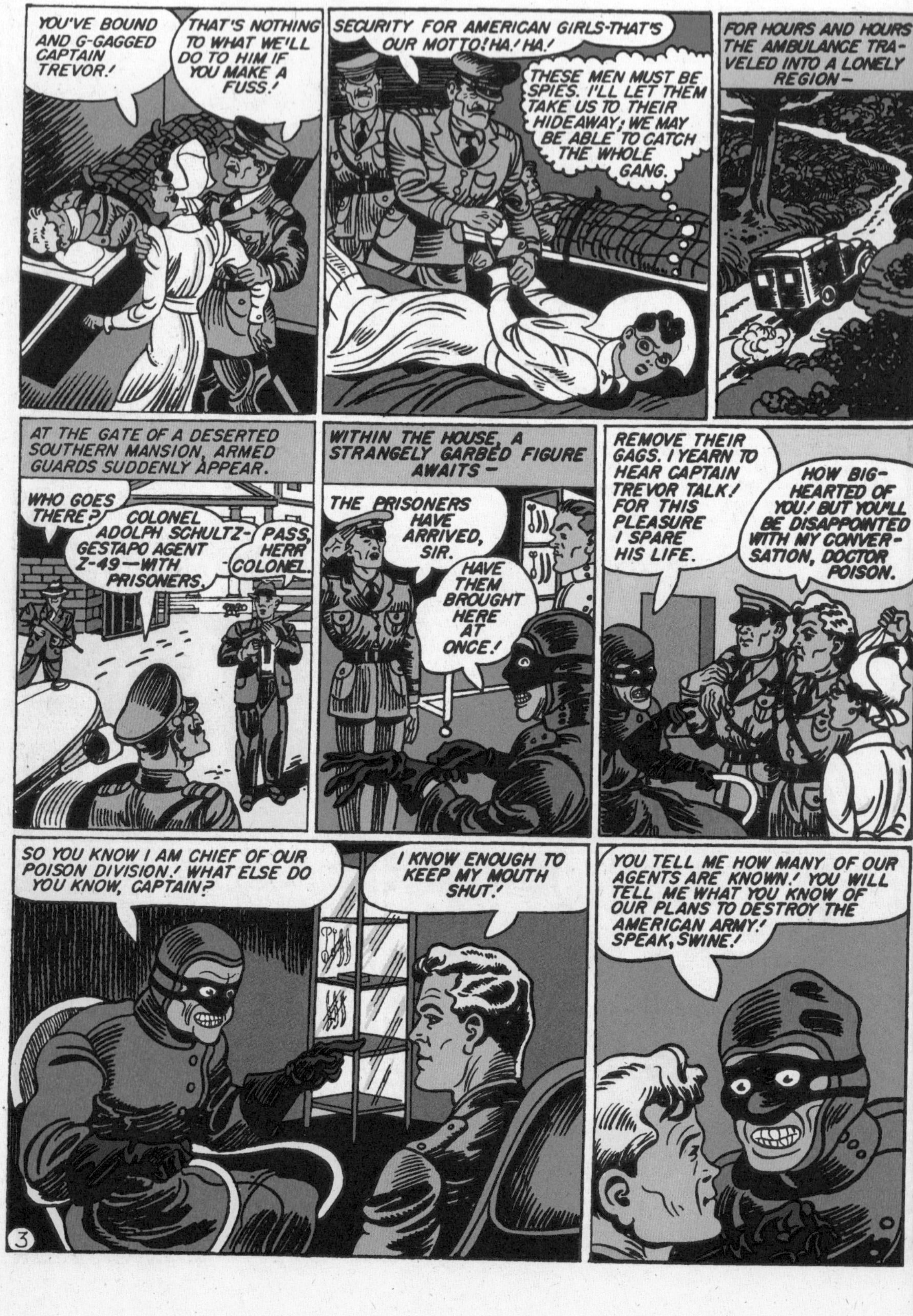
YOU'VE BOUND AND G-GAGGED CAPTAIN TREVOR!
THAT'S NOTHING TO WHAT WE'LL DO TO HIM IF YOU MAKE A FUSS!
SECURITY FOR AMERICAN GIRLS-THAT'S OUR MOTTO! HA! HA!
THESE MEN MUST BE SPIES. I'LL LET THEM TAKE US TO THEIR HIDEAWAY; WE MAY BE ABLE TO CATCH THE WHOLE GANG.
FOR HOURS AND HOURS THE AMBULANCE TRAVELED INTO A LONELY REGION—
AT THE GATE OF A DESERTED SOUTHERN MANSION, ARMED GUARDS SUDDENLY APPEAR.
WHO GOES THERE?
COLONEL ADOLPH SCHULTZ-GESTAPO AGENT Z-49—WITH PRISONERS.
PASS, HERR COLONEL.
WITHIN THE HOUSE, A STRANGELY GARBED FIGURE AWAITS—
THE PRISONERS HAVE ARRIVED, SIR.
HAVE THEM BROUGHT HERE AT ONCE!
REMOVE THEIR GAGS. I YEARN TO HEAR CAPTAIN TREVOR TALK! FOR THIS PLEASURE I SPARE HIS LIFE.
HOW BIG-HEARTED OF YOU! BUT YOU'LL BE DISAPPOINTED WITH MY CONVERSATION, DOCTOR POISON.
SO YOU KNOW I AM CHIEF OF OUR POISON DIVISION! WHAT ELSE DO YOU KNOW, CAPTAIN?
I KNOW ENOUGH TO KEEP MY MOUTH SHUT!
YOU TELL ME HOW MANY OF OUR AGENTS ARE KNOWN! YOU WILL TELL ME WHAT YOU KNOW OF OUR PLANS TO DESTROY THE AMERICAN ARMY! SPEAK, SWINE!
3

THE ONLY THING I'LL TELL YOU, POISON, IS WHERE TO GO.

THE CAPTAIN IS QUITE COCKY! BUT WE'LL MAKE HIM TALK! PUT HIM ON THE OPERATING TABLE!

THIS SYRINGE CONTAINS SCOPOLAMINE AND MORPHINE IN SUITABLE PROPORTIONS. YOU KNOW WHAT THAT IS?

TRUTH SERUM! YOU DEVIL!

DIANA, UNABLE TO RESTRAIN HERSELF, BURSTS HER BONDS—

DON'T YOU DARE GIVE THAT DRUG TO CAPTAIN TREVOR! IT MIGHT KILL HIM!

WOT HIT ME?

SHE'S NO NURSE! SHE'S A JACK DEMPSEY!

BUT THE SPY CHIEF SUBDUES DIANA BY THREATENING STEVE.

STOP! OBEY ME, NURSE, OR I WILL CUT YOUR PATIENT'S THROAT!

OH-H-H! I'LL OBEY YOU—

THEN STERILIZE THIS SYRINGE, NURSE!

YES, DOCTOR.

I ALMOST GAVE MYSELF AWAY THAT TIME—I'LL HAVE TO WATCH MY STEP!

DIANA SECRETLY CHANGES THE TRUTH SERUM FOR A SYRINGE OF HARMLESS SALINE SOLUTION IN HER MEDICAL KIT.

I CHANGED THE HYPODERMICS-- THIS INJECTION WON'T AFFECT YOU. PRETEND THAT TRUTH SERUM IS MAKING YOU TALK!

RIGHT! GOOD GIRL!

THE DRUG IS TAKING EFFECT—HE'LL TALK IN A MINUTE!

UG—WUG—GRU! SPIES—PHLUT—KILL—ARMY—

STEVE GIVES FALSE INFORMATION WHICH THE SPY CHIEF BELIEVES IS TRUTH FORCED BY THE SERUM—

I CANNOT IDENTIFY ANY MORE SPIES! WE SUSPECT TWO SENATORS AND THREE CABINET MEMBERS! WE BELIEVE DR. POISON HAS INVENTED A NEW CYANIDE BOMB—

I HAVE LEARNED ALL I NEED TO KNOW! A WONDERFUL DRUG, THIS TRUTH SERUM! TAKE TREVOR TO A CELL. TWO GUARDS WILL WATCH HIM CONSTANTLY!

OH PLEASE, DOCTOR! RELEASE CAPTAIN TREVOR! LET ME TAKE HIM BACK TO THE HOSPITAL.

CLOSE YOUR MOUTH! IF YOU MAKE THE SLIGHTEST DISTURBANCE, TREVOR WILL BE SHOT INSTANTLY!

DIANA'S GUARDS TAKE NO CHANCES! BEFORE LOCKING HER IN A CELL THEY TIE HER TO THE BED!

DOUBLE KNOT THOSE ROPES-- THIS DAME'S A HOUDINI!

YOU'RE TELLING ME! SHE'S GOT A RIGHT LIKE JOE LOUIS!

BUT AS SOON AS THE GUARDS HAVE LEFT--

THEY SHOULD HAVE USED CHAINS—IT WOULD BE MORE FUN BREAKING THEM!

LUCKY THIS OUTFIT WAS IN MY BAG. I CAN DO BETTER WITH FEWER CLOTHES!

5

TOO BAD TO SMASH THE DOOR, BUT THEY FORGOT TO LEAVE ME THE KEY.

WONDER WOMAN IS PEERING THROUGH A GRATING INTO TREVOR'S CELL.

THEY'LL SHOOT STEVE IF I CRASH THE DOOR. I MUST TRY ANOTHER PLAN---

THIS LOOKS LIKE A GARAGE. I'LL BORROW A CAR. I MAY NEED IT TO BRING REINFORCEMENTS.

I'LL COAST DOWN THE HILL SO THE NOISE OF THE ENGINE WON'T DISTURB MY HOSTS.

THIS IS THE EASIEST WAY TO START A CAR. NOW TO STEP ON THE GAS--

IT'S WONDER WOMAN!

THAT'S RIGHT. I SAW HER ON THE STAGE! LET HER GO, SHE'S PROBABLY DOING SOME PUBLICITY STUNT!

HOLDING TREVOR AS HOSTAGE, "DR. POISON" PREPARES TO DESTROY ARMY MORALE WITH A NEW DRUG.

THESE CYLINDERS CONTAIN REVERSO, THE NEW DRUG I HAVE INVENTED. REVERSO CONFUSES THE BRAIN CENTERS. IT WILL MAKE SOLDIERS DO THE EXACT OPPOSITE OF WHAT THEY ARE TOLD!

THERE IS THE POINT WHERE YOU WILL TAP THE WATER MAIN WHICH SUPPLIES THE ARMY CAMP. YOU WILL EMPTY TWELVE CYLINDERS OF REVERSO INTO THIS PIPE SLOWLY- ONE GALLON PER HOUR. IN 24 HOURS THE WHOLE CAMP WILL BE IN CONFUSION!

6

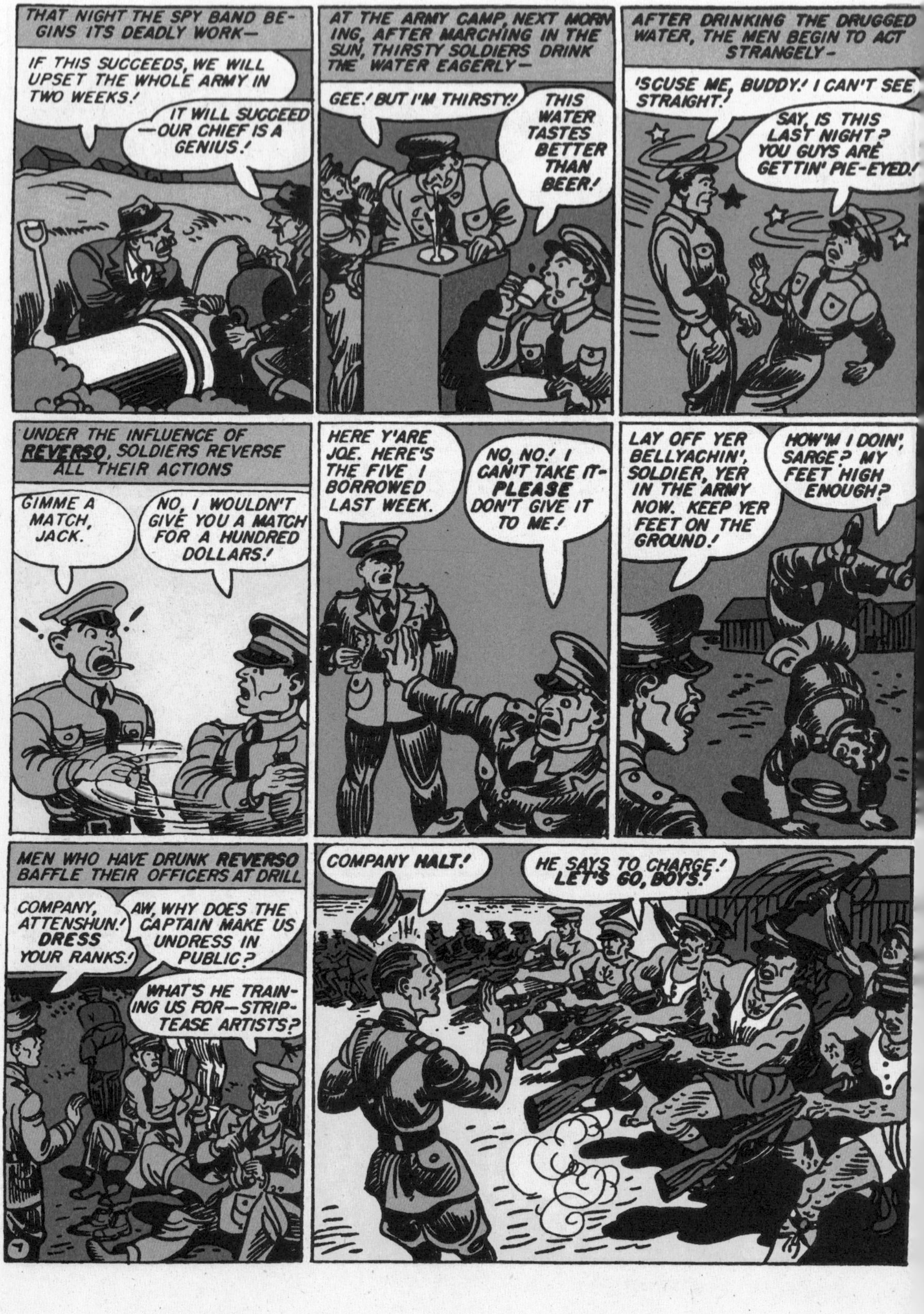
THAT NIGHT THE SPY BAND BEGINS ITS DEADLY WORK—
IF THIS SUCCEEDS, WE WILL UPSET THE WHOLE ARMY IN TWO WEEKS!
IT WILL SUCCEED —OUR CHIEF IS A GENIUS!
AT THE ARMY CAMP, NEXT MORNING, AFTER MARCHING IN THE SUN, THIRSTY SOLDIERS DRINK THE WATER EAGERLY—
GEE! BUT I'M THIRSTY!
THIS WATER TASTES BETTER THAN BEER!
AFTER DRINKING THE DRUGGED WATER, THE MEN BEGIN TO ACT STRANGELY-
'SCUSE ME, BUDDY! I CAN'T SEE STRAIGHT!
SAY, IS THIS LAST NIGHT? YOU GUYS ARE GETTIN' PIE-EYED!
UNDER THE INFLUENCE OF REVERSO, SOLDIERS REVERSE ALL THEIR ACTIONS
GIMME A MATCH, JACK.
NO, I WOULDN'T GIVE YOU A MATCH FOR A HUNDRED DOLLARS!
HERE Y'ARE JOE. HERE'S THE FIVE I BORROWED LAST WEEK.
NO, NO! I CAN'T TAKE IT- PLEASE DON'T GIVE IT TO ME!
LAY OFF YER BELLYACHIN', SOLDIER, YER IN THE ARMY NOW. KEEP YER FEET ON THE GROUND!
HOW'M I DOIN', SARGE? MY FEET HIGH ENOUGH?
MEN WHO HAVE DRUNK REVERSO BAFFLE THEIR OFFICERS AT DRILL
COMPANY, ATTENSHUN! DRESS YOUR RANKS!
AW, WHY DOES THE CAPTAIN MAKE US UNDRESS IN PUBLIC?
WHAT'S HE TRAINING US FOR—STRIP-TEASE ARTISTS?
COMPANY HALT!
HE SAYS TO CHARGE! LET'S GO, BOYS!

THE GENERAL CALLS AN EMERGENCY MEETING OF HIS STAFF — AN ENTIRE ARMY CORPS IS OUT OF CONTROL!

WHAT CAN WE DO?

MORE MEN ARE GOING CRAZY EVERY MINUTE, GENERAL! THEY REVERSE ALL ORDERS! THEY'RE COMPLETELY OUT OF CONTROL!

PUT THESE MADMEN IN THE INTERNMENT CAMP BY REVERSING YOUR COMMANDS. ORDER THEM TO DO THE OPPOSITE OF WHAT YOU WANT!

THOUSANDS OF SOLDIERS WHO HAVE DRUNK REVERSO ARE PUT BEHIND BARBED WIRE BY GIVING OPPOSITE COMMANDS.

BACKWARD MARCH!

FORWARD MARCH, BOYS!

COLUMN LEFT, MARCH!

RIGHT WE GO!

THAT EVIL GENIUS, "DOCTOR POISON," TAUNTS CAPTAIN TREVOR WITH THE SUCCESS OF REVERSO

I THOUGHT YOU MIGHT ENJOY THE MORNING NEWSPAPER, CAPTAIN.

YOU'RE THE PERFECT HOST — WHAT'S THIS! GREAT HOUNDS OF HADES!

DAILY BLADE

MYSTERIOUS MADNESS SEIZES SOLDIERS AT ARMY CAMP. MEN DO OPPOSITE OF EVERYTHING OFFICERS COMMAND — THOUSANDS OF SOLDIERS INTERNED — STRANGE MENTAL DISEASE SPREADING

YOU POISONOUS SNAKE! I'LL KILL —

OH NO! I'LL DO THE KILLING! MY NOVEL EXPERIMENT IN ARMY MORALE IS QUITE AMUSING, DON'T YOU THINK? MY NEW DRINK FOR THIRSTY SOLDIERS IS SO INVIGORATING!

THE NURSE HAS ESCAPED! SHE BROKE HER ROPES AND SMASHED THE CELL DOOR!

FOOL! DO YOU EXPECT ME TO BELIEVE THAT? FIND THIS GIRL AT ONCE, OR YOU SHALL PAY THE PENALTY!

SOUNDS LIKE WONDER WOMAN MIGHT HAVE COME TO DIANA'S RESCUE. BUT HOW COULD SHE HAVE FOUND THIS PLACE?

8

THE SPY BAND ENTRENCHES AGAINST POSSIBLE ATTACK—
DIG TRENCHES ACROSS THIS ROAD AND DEFEND THEM TO THE LAST MAN! I MUST HAVE TIME TO COMPRESS THE *REVERSO* FOR SHIPMENT. SHOULD THE GIRL WHO ESCAPED BRING SOLDIERS, TELL THEM TREVOR WILL BE SHOT IF THEY ATTACK!

WONDER WOMAN KNOWS THAT ATTACK BY FORCE WILL ENDANGER CAPTAIN TREVOR'S LIFE. SO THE WISE AMAZON MAIDEN DEVISES AN AMAZING PLAN—

HOLLIDAY COLLEGE FOR WOMEN

I AM LOOKING FOR MY FRIEND, ETTA CANDY.

ETTA IS REHEARSING WITH THE BAND IN MUSIC HALL..AND IF THAT'S ONE OF THE NEW BAND COSTUMES YOU'RE WEARING, IT'S NO WONDER THE DEAN SAID YOU MUST TAKE THEM OFF!

REGISTRAR

THAT'S A DUCKY COSTUME, MY PET, BUT THE DEAN WON'T LET YOU WEAR IT! SHE INSISTS ON MORE ABOVE THE WAIST!

I AM NOT HERE TO JOIN THE BAND. I SEEK ETTA CANDY.

THIS IS ETTA CANDY.

OH, I'D NEVER HAVE KNOWN YOU, ETTA! ER-THAT IS-MY FRIEND, DIANA PRINCE, THE NURSE, SAID YOU WERE A THIN GIRL WHEN SHE KNEW YOU IN THE HOSPITAL.

I WAS THIN, ALL RIGHT, WHEN I WENT TO THE HOSPITAL. BUT AFTER THEY TOOK OUT MY APPENDIX, I COULD EAT ANYTHING—SO I DID! NURSE DIANA WAS SWELL TO ME—I'D DO ANYTHING FOR HER—EXCEPT DIET!

HELP ME SAVE THE MAN DIANA LOVES! I'LL TELL YOU ABOUT HIM———

SENTIMENTAL ETTA AGREES TO HELP A HANDSOME MAN IN DISTRESS—
BESIDES YOUR BAND, WE NEED A HUNDRED PRETTY GIRLS BRAVE ENOUGH TO CAPTURE DANGEROUS MEN!

SAY! IF YOU'RE OUT TO CATCH *MEN*, EVERY GIRL IN COLLEGE WILL BE GLAD TO HELP! WOO! WOO!

HUNDREDS OF GIRLS VOLUNTEER AND *WONDER WOMAN* PICKS THE PRETTIEST AND STRONGEST—
THIS RECRUIT FILLS OUR QUOTA!

AMERICA'S FIRST WOMEN'S EXPEDITIONARY FORCE! ONE HUNDRED BEAUTIFUL ATHLETIC GIRLS—LIKE ME!

WONDER WOMAN LEADS TWENTY-FIVE CARS FULL OF GIRLS TO A SECLUDED SPOT NEAR THE SPY-BAND HEADQUARTERS.

RAH! RAH! GLAMOUR GIRLS BLAH!

SHOW US A MAN AND WE WON'T TELL MA—UMPH! AND A BATHING SUIT RAH! RAH! RAH!

ON ARRIVAL, THE CARS ARE HIDDEN IN THE WOODS AND WONDER WOMAN DISTRIBUTES WEAPONS—NOT RIFLES, BUT HAND-CUFFS!

HIDE THESE MANACLES WHERE YOU CAN REACH THEM QUICKLY! WHEN I GIVE THE SIGNAL, GET YOUR MAN'S HANDS BEHIND HIM OR CHAIN HIS WRISTS TO HIS ANKLES!

FORWARD—MARCH!

HALT!

PHEU! WUFF! SHERMAN WAS RIGHT!

GIRLS, I WARN YOU! THERE WILL BE GREAT DANGER! THESE MEN ARE KILLERS! WE HAVE TO MARCH INTO THE VERY MUZZLES OF THEIR RIFLES AND MACHINE GUNS! IF ANY GIRL WANTS TO QUIT, THIS IS YOUR LAST CHANCE!

WE'LL NEVER QUIT!

LET'S GO!

WHO'S AFRAID OF A MAN?

IF THEY'RE MEN, WE CAN CATCH THEM!

HOLDING THE TRENCHES AGAINST WONDER WOMAN'S ARMY IS SOMETHING ELSE AGAIN—

WHAT'S THE MATTER, ETTA? AFRAID TO GO ON?

HECK, NO! BUT I'VE FINISHED ALL THE CANDY I BROUGHT. CAN'T WE WAIT TILL I GET SOME MORE?

WAS IST, BLITZKRIEG?

WE CAN HOLD THESE TRENCHES AGAINST AN ARMY! SHOOT TO KILL, MEN!

VAIT, HERR COLONEL! LOOK! THEY ARE WOMEN!

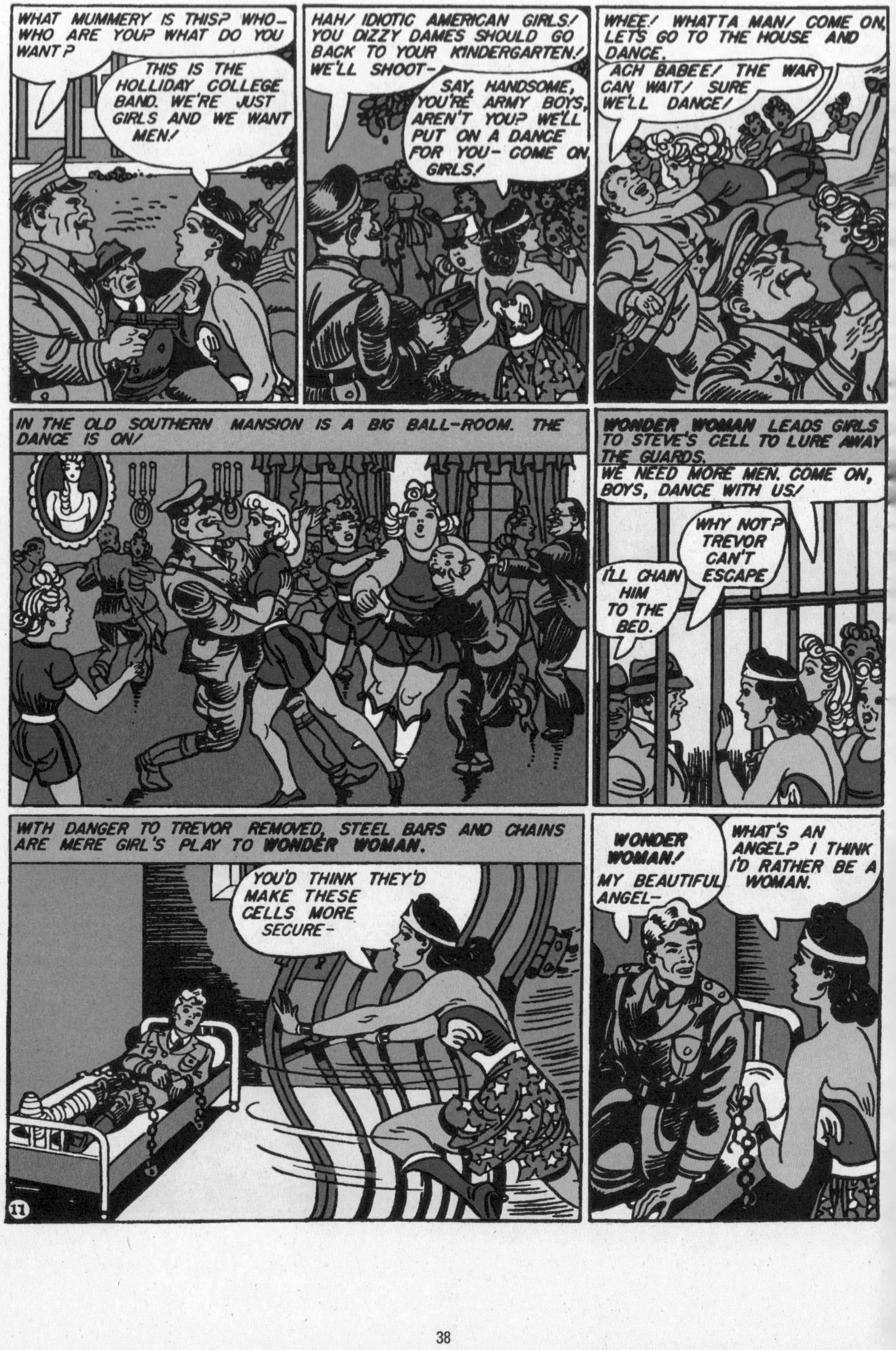

WHAT MUMMERY IS THIS? WHO— WHO ARE YOU? WHAT DO YOU WANT?
THIS IS THE HOLLIDAY COLLEGE BAND. WE'RE JUST GIRLS AND WE WANT MEN!
HAH! IDIOTIC AMERICAN GIRLS! YOU DIZZY DAMES SHOULD GO BACK TO YOUR KINDERGARTEN! WE'LL SHOOT-
SAY, HANDSOME, YOU'RE ARMY BOYS, AREN'T YOU? WE'LL PUT ON A DANCE FOR YOU- COME ON GIRLS!
WHEE! WHATTA MAN! COME ON, LET'S GO TO THE HOUSE AND DANCE.
ACH BABEE! THE WAR CAN WAIT! SURE WE'LL DANCE!
IN THE OLD SOUTHERN MANSION IS A BIG BALL-ROOM. THE DANCE IS ON!
WONDER WOMAN LEADS GIRLS TO STEVE'S CELL TO LURE AWAY THE GUARDS.
WE NEED MORE MEN. COME ON, BOYS, DANCE WITH US!
WHY NOT? TREVOR CAN'T ESCAPE
I'LL CHAIN HIM TO THE BED.
WITH DANGER TO TREVOR REMOVED, STEEL BARS AND CHAINS ARE MERE GIRL'S PLAY TO WONDER WOMAN.
YOU'D THINK THEY'D MAKE THESE CELLS MORE SECURE-
11
WONDER WOMAN! MY BEAUTIFUL ANGEL-
WHAT'S AN ANGEL? I THINK I'D RATHER BE A WOMAN.

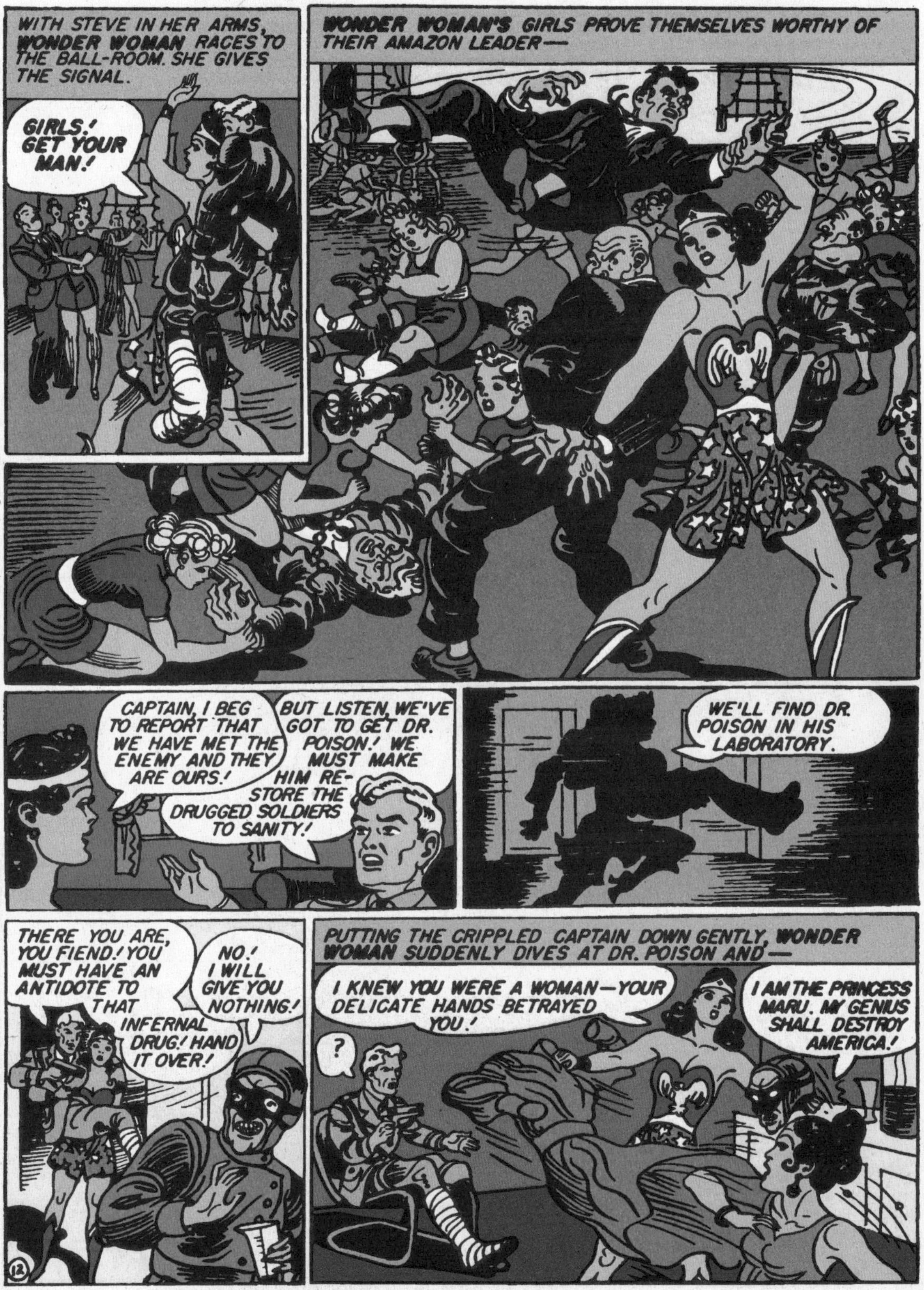
WITH STEVE IN HER ARMS, WONDER WOMAN RACES TO THE BALL-ROOM. SHE GIVES THE SIGNAL.
GIRLS! GET YOUR MAN!
WONDER WOMAN'S GIRLS PROVE THEMSELVES WORTHY OF THEIR AMAZON LEADER—
CAPTAIN, I BEG TO REPORT THAT WE HAVE MET THE ENEMY AND THEY ARE OURS!
BUT LISTEN, WE'VE GOT TO GET DR. POISON! WE MUST MAKE HIM RESTORE THE DRUGGED SOLDIERS TO SANITY!
WE'LL FIND DR. POISON IN HIS LABORATORY.
THERE YOU ARE, YOU FIEND! YOU MUST HAVE AN ANTIDOTE TO THAT INFERNAL DRUG! HAND IT OVER!
NO! I WILL GIVE YOU NOTHING!
12
PUTTING THE CRIPPLED CAPTAIN DOWN GENTLY, WONDER WOMAN SUDDENLY DIVES AT DR. POISON AND—
I KNEW YOU WERE A WOMAN—YOUR DELICATE HANDS BETRAYED YOU!
?
I AM THE PRINCESS MARU. MY GENIUS SHALL DESTROY AMERICA!

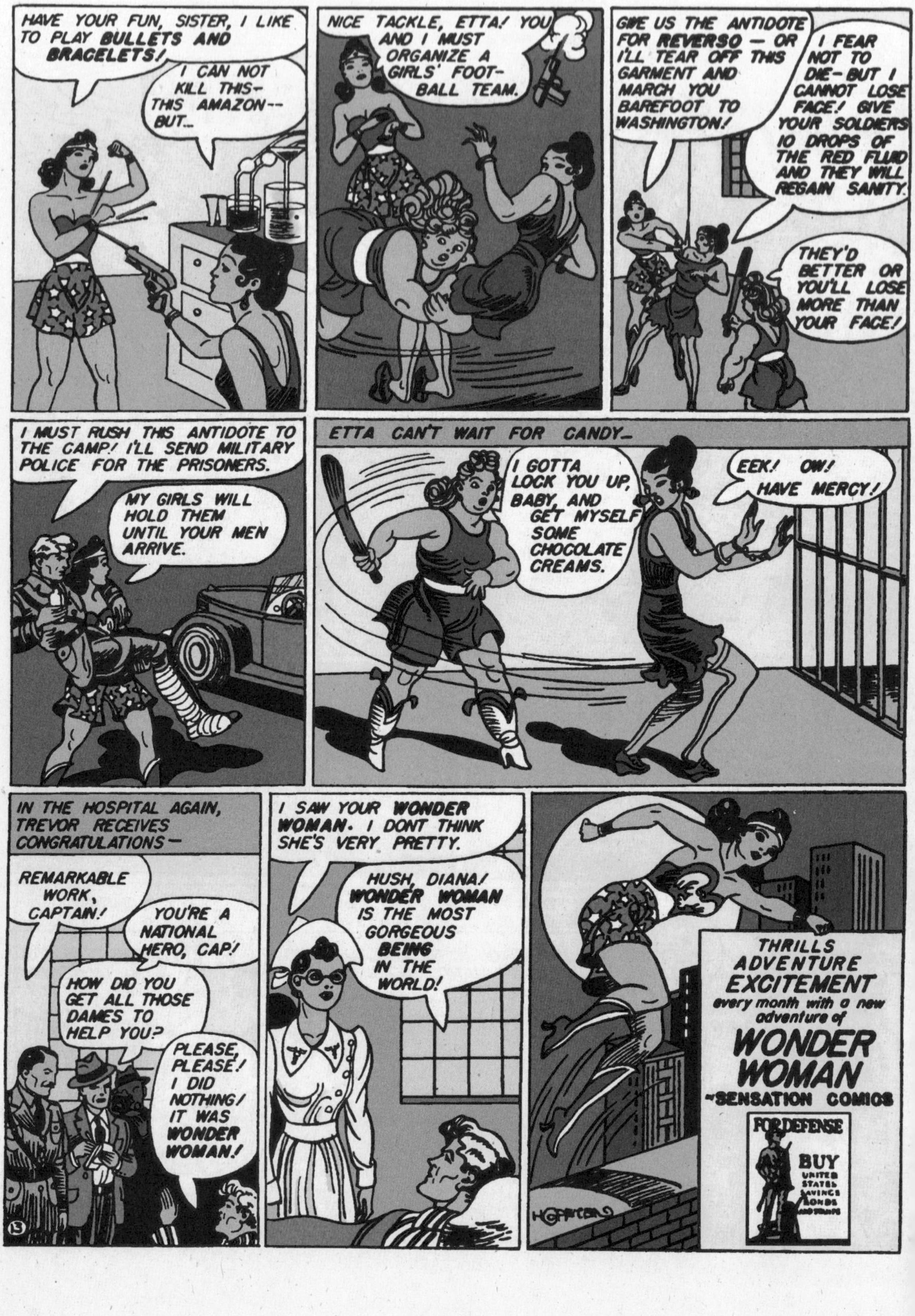
HAVE YOUR FUN, SISTER, I LIKE TO PLAY BULLETS AND BRACELETS!
I CAN NOT KILL THIS- THIS AMAZON-- BUT...
NICE TACKLE, ETTA! YOU AND I MUST ORGANIZE A GIRLS' FOOT-BALL TEAM.
GIVE US THE ANTIDOTE FOR REVERSO — OR I'LL TEAR OFF THIS GARMENT AND MARCH YOU BAREFOOT TO WASHINGTON!
I FEAR NOT TO DIE- BUT I CANNOT LOSE FACE! GIVE YOUR SOLDIERS 10 DROPS OF THE RED FLUID AND THEY WILL REGAIN SANITY.
THEY'D BETTER OR YOU'LL LOSE MORE THAN YOUR FACE!
I MUST RUSH THIS ANTIDOTE TO THE CAMP! I'LL SEND MILITARY POLICE FOR THE PRISONERS.
MY GIRLS WILL HOLD THEM UNTIL YOUR MEN ARRIVE.
ETTA CAN'T WAIT FOR CANDY—
I GOTTA LOCK YOU UP, BABY, AND GET MYSELF SOME CHOCOLATE CREAMS.
EEK! OW! HAVE MERCY!
IN THE HOSPITAL AGAIN, TREVOR RECEIVES CONGRATULATIONS—
REMARKABLE WORK, CAPTAIN!
YOU'RE A NATIONAL HERO, CAP!
HOW DID YOU GET ALL THOSE DAMES TO HELP YOU?
PLEASE, PLEASE! I DID NOTHING! IT WAS WONDER WOMAN!
13
I SAW YOUR WONDER WOMAN. I DONT THINK SHE'S VERY PRETTY.
HUSH, DIANA! WONDER WOMAN IS THE MOST GORGEOUS BEING IN THE WORLD!
THRILLS ADVENTURE EXCITEMENT every month with a new adventure of WONDER WOMAN in SENSATION COMICS
FOR DEFENSE
BUY
UNITED STATES SAVINGS BONDS AND STAMPS
H.G. PETER

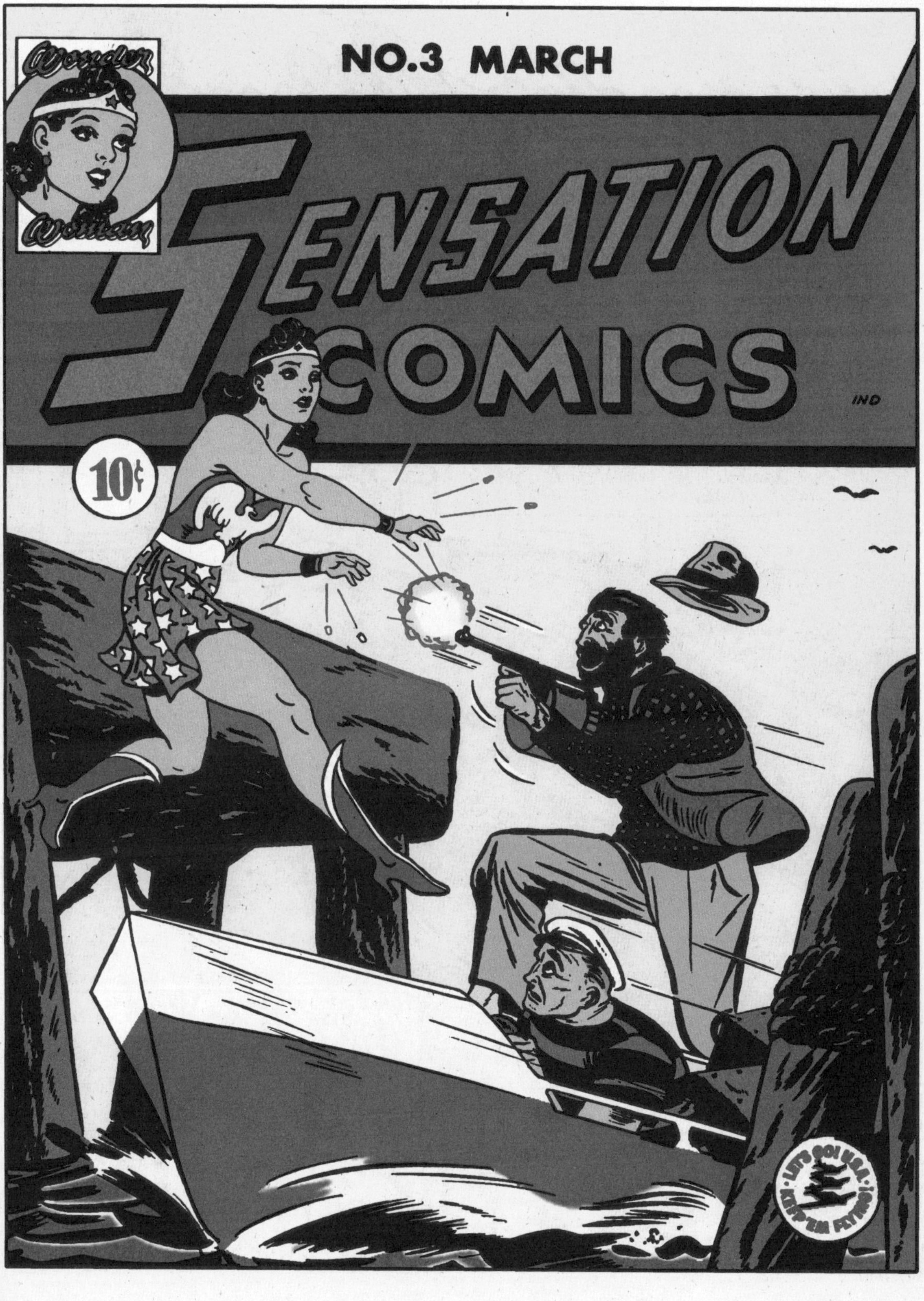
NO.3 MARCH
Wonder Woman
SENSATION COMICS
IND
10¢
LET'S GO! U.S.A.
KEEP 'EM FLYING!

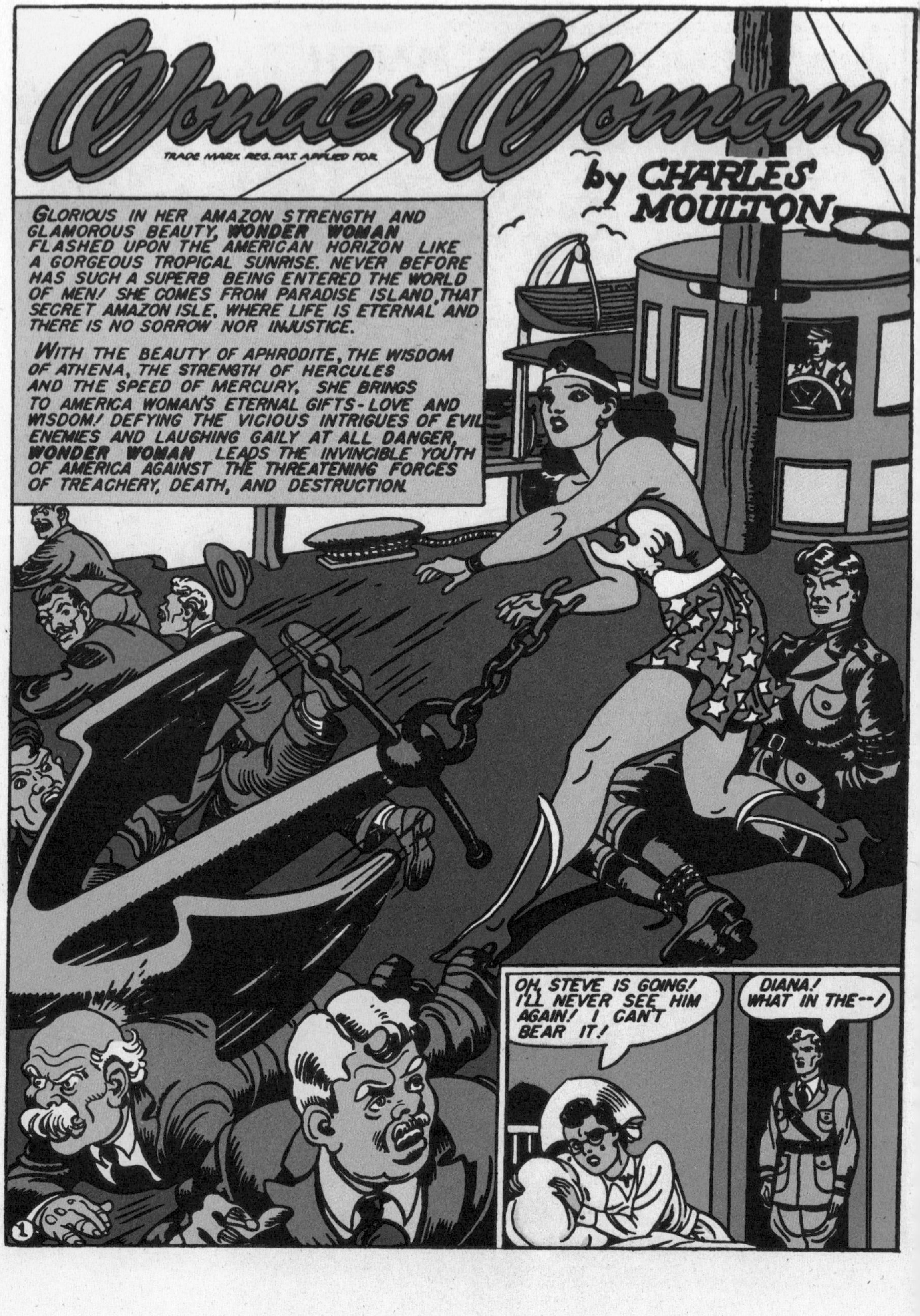
Wonder Woman
TRADE MARK REG. PAT. APPLIED FOR
by CHARLES MOULTON
GLORIOUS IN HER AMAZON STRENGTH AND GLAMOROUS BEAUTY, WONDER WOMAN FLASHED UPON THE AMERICAN HORIZON LIKE A GORGEOUS TROPICAL SUNRISE. NEVER BEFORE HAS SUCH A SUPERB BEING ENTERED THE WORLD OF MEN! SHE COMES FROM PARADISE ISLAND, THAT SECRET AMAZON ISLE, WHERE LIFE IS ETERNAL AND THERE IS NO SORROW NOR INJUSTICE.
WITH THE BEAUTY OF APHRODITE, THE WISDOM OF ATHENA, THE STRENGTH OF HERCULES AND THE SPEED OF MERCURY, SHE BRINGS TO AMERICA WOMAN'S ETERNAL GIFTS - LOVE AND WISDOM! DEFYING THE VICIOUS INTRIGUES OF EVIL ENEMIES AND LAUGHING GAILY AT ALL DANGER, WONDER WOMAN LEADS THE INVINCIBLE YOUTH OF AMERICA AGAINST THE THREATENING FORCES OF TREACHERY, DEATH, AND DESTRUCTION.
OH, STEVE IS GOING! I'LL NEVER SEE HIM AGAIN! I CAN'T BEAR IT!
DIANA! WHAT IN THE--!

DIANA! YOU MUSTN'T FEEL THIS WAY! I'LL DO ANYTHING I CAN TO SHOW MY GRATITUDE FOR YOUR WONDERFUL NURSING.

WILL-(SOB) YOU-(SOB)- LET ME BE YOUR SECRETARY?

I HAVE A GIRL — LILA BROWN. SHE'S A WONDERFUL SECRETARY! BEEN WITH ME FOR YEARS!

I'LL BET I CAN TAKE DICTATION AND TYPE TWICE AS FAST AS YOUR PRECIOUS LILA!

SO! YOU CLAIM YOU ARE A GOOD STENOGRAPHER, EH? COLONEL DARNELL, MY CHIEF, NEEDS A NEW SECRETARY-

OH, STEVE! GET ME THAT POSITION, PLEASE!

I'LL ASK THE COLONEL TO GIVE YOU A TRYOUT. BUT YOU'VE GOT TO BE GOOD!

I'LL SHOW YOU—JUST GIVE ME A CHANCE!

LATER

WHY DO YOU WANT TO GIVE UP NURSING, MISS PRINCE?

WELL—I LOVE NURSING PATIENTS LIKE—ER—CAPTAIN TREVOR! BUT NOW THAT I'VE BEEN ASSIGNED TO SURGERY, I'M FRIGHTENED! I CAN'T STAND THE SIGHT OF BLOOD!

POOR LITTLE GIRL! I'M AFRAID YOU CAN'T TAKE MY DICTATION. BUT I'LL GIVE YOU A TEST!

OH YES, SIR! I'LL GLADLY TAKE A TEST!

ALL RIGHT, TAKE THIS LETTER. DEAR SIR, DISREGARDINGTHELETHAL LASSITUDESUPERINDUCEDBYTOXICINFUSIONSOFCARBONMONOXIDE FOLLOWINGCEREBRALCONCUSSIONSCAUSEDBYINVOLUNTARYABSORP-TIONSOFHYDROCYANICSHELLEXPLOSIONDIFFUSIONS- ETC.,ETC.

THE SMARTY! HE'S THROWING THE DICTIONARY AT ME AT THE RATE OF 160 WORDS A MINUTE, BUT I'LL SHOW HIM!

ER—AM I DICTATING TOO FAST?

OH NO, SIR! I GOT EVERY WORD! I'LL TYPE IT FOR YOU.

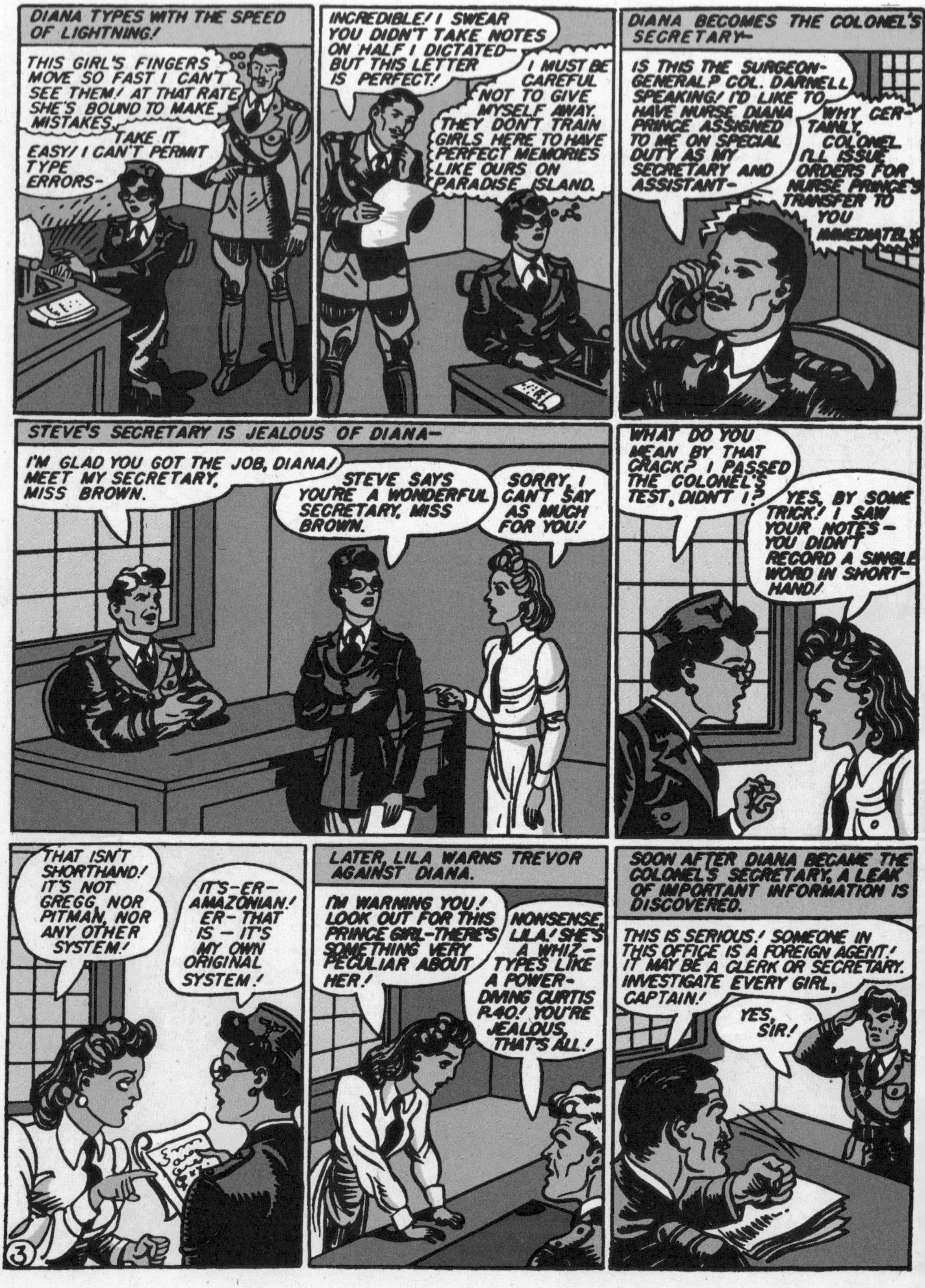
DIANA TYPES WITH THE SPEED OF LIGHTNING!
THIS GIRL'S FINGERS MOVE SO FAST I CAN'T SEE THEM! AT THAT RATE SHE'S BOUND TO MAKE MISTAKES.
TAKE IT EASY! I CAN'T PERMIT TYPE ERRORS-
INCREDIBLE! I SWEAR YOU DIDN'T TAKE NOTES ON HALF I DICTATED- BUT THIS LETTER IS PERFECT!
I MUST BE CAREFUL NOT TO GIVE MYSELF AWAY. THEY DON'T TRAIN GIRLS HERE TO HAVE PERFECT MEMORIES LIKE OURS ON PARADISE ISLAND.
DIANA BECOMES THE COLONEL'S SECRETARY-
IS THIS THE SURGEON-GENERAL? COL. DARNELL SPEAKING! I'D LIKE TO HAVE NURSE DIANA PRINCE ASSIGNED TO ME ON SPECIAL DUTY AS MY SECRETARY AND ASSISTANT-
WHY CERTAINLY, COLONEL I'LL ISSUE ORDERS FOR NURSE PRINCE'S TRANSFER TO YOU IMMEDIATELY
STEVE'S SECRETARY IS JEALOUS OF DIANA-
I'M GLAD YOU GOT THE JOB, DIANA! MEET MY SECRETARY, MISS BROWN.
STEVE SAYS YOU'RE A WONDERFUL SECRETARY, MISS BROWN.
SORRY, I CAN'T SAY AS MUCH FOR YOU!
WHAT DO YOU MEAN BY THAT CRACK? I PASSED THE COLONEL'S TEST, DIDN'T I?
YES, BY SOME TRICK! I SAW YOUR NOTES- YOU DIDN'T RECORD A SINGLE WORD IN SHORTHAND!
THAT ISN'T SHORTHAND! IT'S NOT GREGG NOR PITMAN, NOR ANY OTHER SYSTEM!
IT'S-ER- AMAZONIAN! ER- THAT IS - IT'S MY OWN ORIGINAL SYSTEM!
3
LATER, LILA WARNS TREVOR AGAINST DIANA.
I'M WARNING YOU! LOOK OUT FOR THIS PRINCE GIRL-THERE'S SOMETHING VERY PECULIAR ABOUT HER!
NONSENSE, LILA! SHE'S A WHIZ- TYPES LIKE A POWER-DIVING CURTIS P-40! YOU'RE JEALOUS, THAT'S ALL!
SOON AFTER DIANA BECAME THE COLONEL'S SECRETARY, A LEAK OF IMPORTANT INFORMATION IS DISCOVERED.
THIS IS SERIOUS! SOMEONE IN THIS OFFICE IS A FOREIGN AGENT! IT MAY BE A CLERK OR SECRETARY. INVESTIGATE EVERY GIRL, CAPTAIN!
YES, SIR!

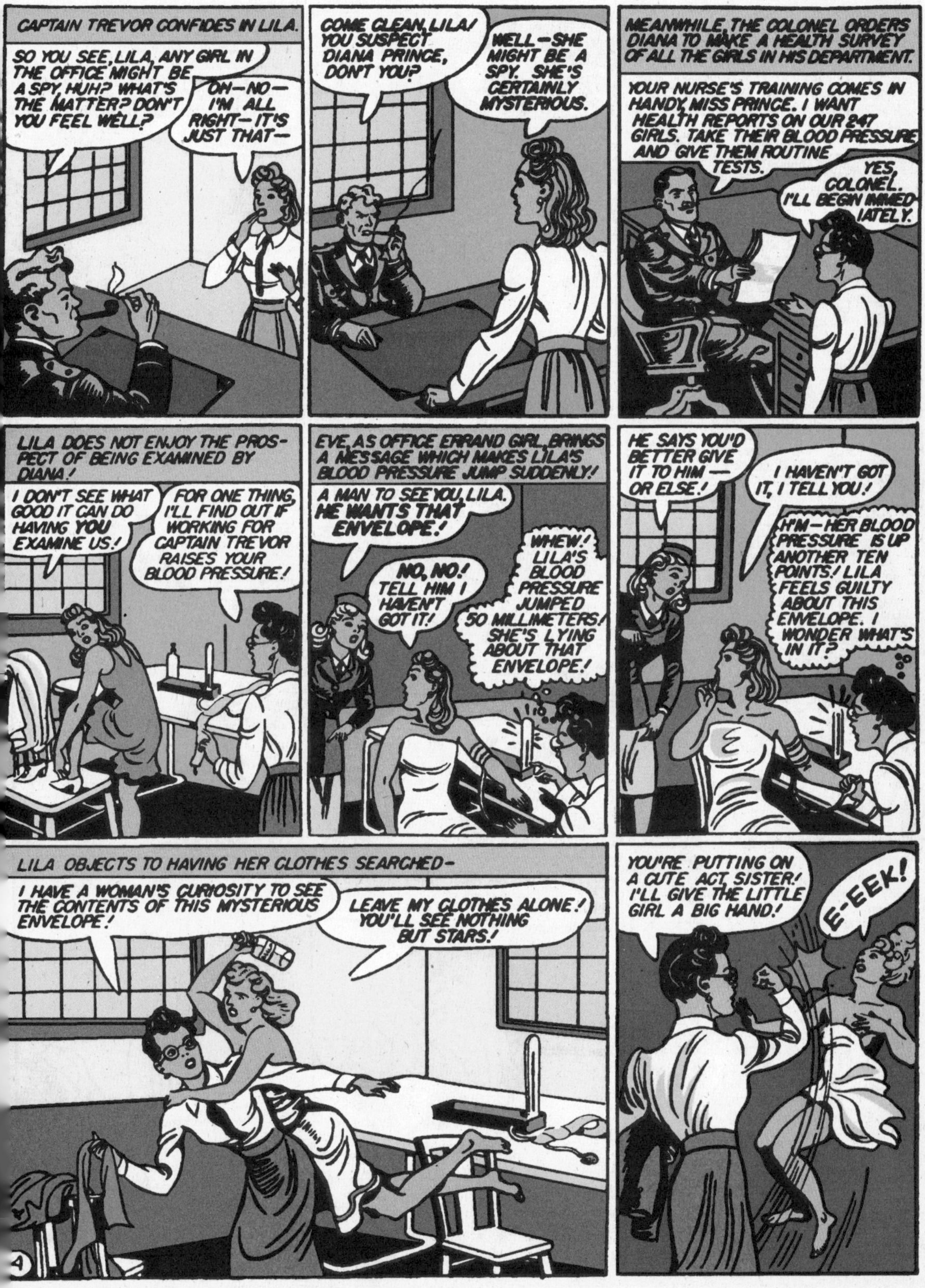
CAPTAIN TREVOR CONFIDES IN LILA.
SO YOU SEE, LILA, ANY GIRL IN THE OFFICE MIGHT BE A SPY, HUH? WHAT'S THE MATTER? DON'T YOU FEEL WELL?
OH—NO—I'M ALL RIGHT—IT'S JUST THAT—
COME CLEAN, LILA! YOU SUSPECT DIANA PRINCE, DON'T YOU?
WELL—SHE MIGHT BE A SPY. SHE'S CERTAINLY MYSTERIOUS.
MEANWHILE, THE COLONEL ORDERS DIANA TO MAKE A HEALTH SURVEY OF ALL THE GIRLS IN HIS DEPARTMENT.
YOUR NURSE'S TRAINING COMES IN HANDY, MISS PRINCE. I WANT HEALTH REPORTS ON OUR 247 GIRLS. TAKE THEIR BLOOD PRESSURE AND GIVE THEM ROUTINE TESTS.
YES, COLONEL. I'LL BEGIN IMMEDIATELY.
LILA DOES NOT ENJOY THE PROSPECT OF BEING EXAMINED BY DIANA!
I DON'T SEE WHAT GOOD IT CAN DO HAVING YOU EXAMINE US!
FOR ONE THING, I'LL FIND OUT IF WORKING FOR CAPTAIN TREVOR RAISES YOUR BLOOD PRESSURE!
EVE, AS OFFICE ERRAND GIRL, BRINGS A MESSAGE WHICH MAKES LILA'S BLOOD PRESSURE JUMP SUDDENLY!
A MAN TO SEE YOU, LILA. HE WANTS THAT ENVELOPE!
NO, NO! TELL HIM I HAVEN'T GOT IT!
WHEW! LILA'S BLOOD PRESSURE JUMPED 50 MILLIMETERS! SHE'S LYING ABOUT THAT ENVELOPE!
HE SAYS YOU'D BETTER GIVE IT TO HIM — OR ELSE!
I HAVEN'T GOT IT, I TELL YOU!
H'M—HER BLOOD PRESSURE IS UP ANOTHER TEN POINTS! LILA FEELS GUILTY ABOUT THIS ENVELOPE. I WONDER WHAT'S IN IT?
LILA OBJECTS TO HAVING HER CLOTHES SEARCHED—
I HAVE A WOMAN'S CURIOSITY TO SEE THE CONTENTS OF THIS MYSTERIOUS ENVELOPE!
LEAVE MY CLOTHES ALONE! YOU'LL SEE NOTHING BUT STARS!
4
YOU'RE PUTTING ON A CUTE ACT, SISTER! I'LL GIVE THE LITTLE GIRL A BIG HAND!
E-EEK!

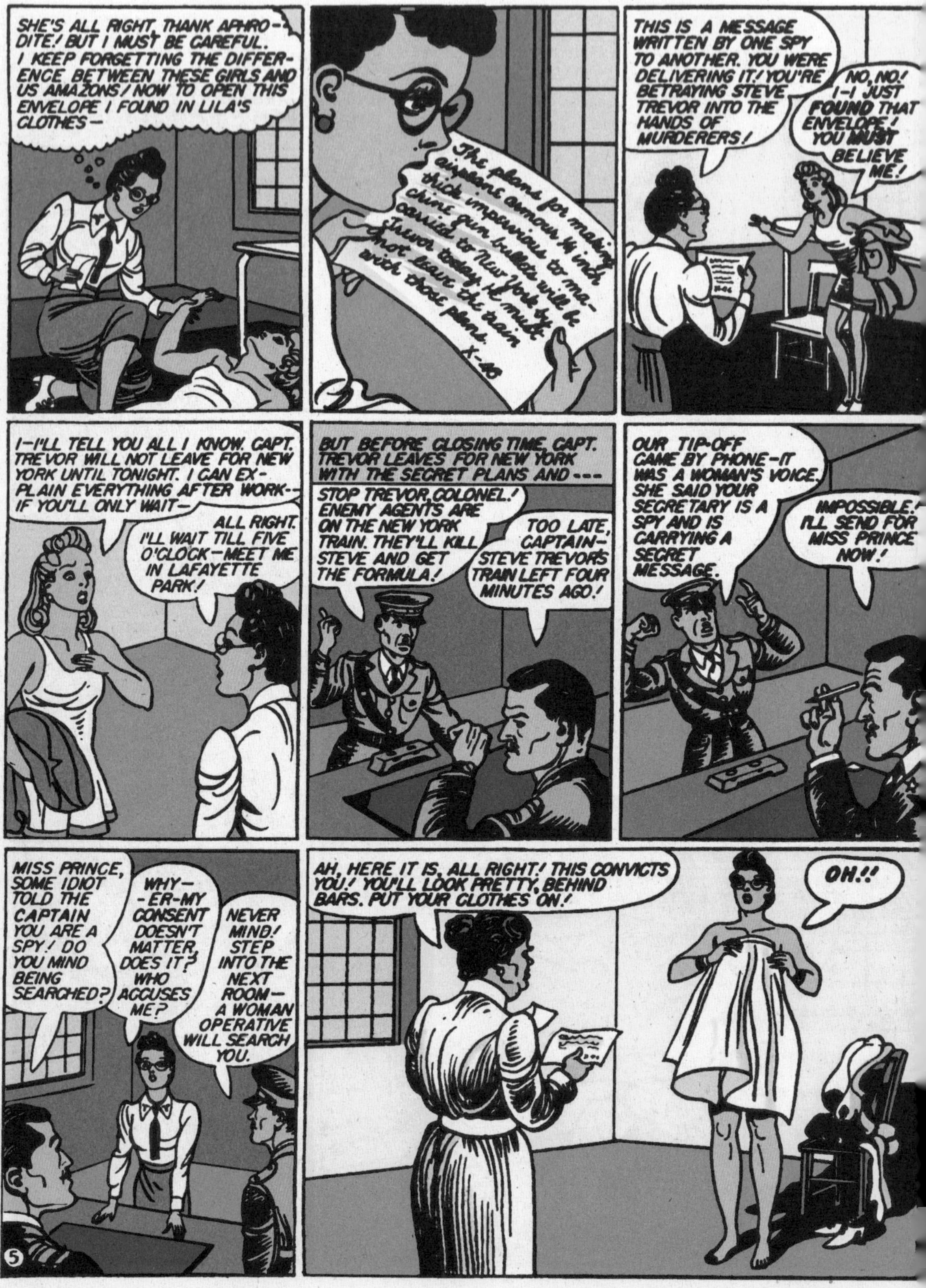
SHE'S ALL RIGHT, THANK APHRODITE! BUT I MUST BE CAREFUL. I KEEP FORGETTING THE DIFFERENCE BETWEEN THESE GIRLS AND US AMAZONS! NOW TO OPEN THIS ENVELOPE I FOUND IN LILA'S CLOTHES—
The plans for making airplane armour inch thick impervious to machine gun bullets will be carried to New York by Trevor today. He must not leave the train with those plans.
THIS IS A MESSAGE WRITTEN BY ONE SPY TO ANOTHER. YOU WERE DELIVERING IT! YOU'RE BETRAYING STEVE TREVOR INTO THE HANDS OF MURDERERS!
NO, NO! I-I JUST FOUND THAT ENVELOPE! YOU MUST BELIEVE ME!
I-I'LL TELL YOU ALL I KNOW. CAPT. TREVOR WILL NOT LEAVE FOR NEW YORK UNTIL TONIGHT. I CAN EXPLAIN EVERYTHING AFTER WORK—IF YOU'LL ONLY WAIT—
ALL RIGHT. I'LL WAIT TILL FIVE O'CLOCK—MEET ME IN LAFAYETTE PARK!
BUT BEFORE CLOSING TIME, CAPT. TREVOR LEAVES FOR NEW YORK WITH THE SECRET PLANS AND ---
STOP TREVOR, COLONEL! ENEMY AGENTS ARE ON THE NEW YORK TRAIN. THEY'LL KILL STEVE AND GET THE FORMULA!
TOO LATE, CAPTAIN—STEVE TREVOR'S TRAIN LEFT FOUR MINUTES AGO!
OUR TIP-OFF CAME BY PHONE—IT WAS A WOMAN'S VOICE. SHE SAID YOUR SECRETARY IS A SPY AND IS CARRYING A SECRET MESSAGE.
IMPOSSIBLE! I'LL SEND FOR MISS PRINCE NOW!
MISS PRINCE, SOME IDIOT TOLD THE CAPTAIN YOU ARE A SPY! DO YOU MIND BEING SEARCHED?
WHY—ER-MY CONSENT DOESN'T MATTER, DOES IT? WHO ACCUSES ME?
NEVER MIND! STEP INTO THE NEXT ROOM—A WOMAN OPERATIVE WILL SEARCH YOU.
5
AH, HERE IT IS, ALL RIGHT! THIS CONVICTS YOU! YOU'LL LOOK PRETTY, BEHIND BARS. PUT YOUR CLOTHES ON!
OH!!

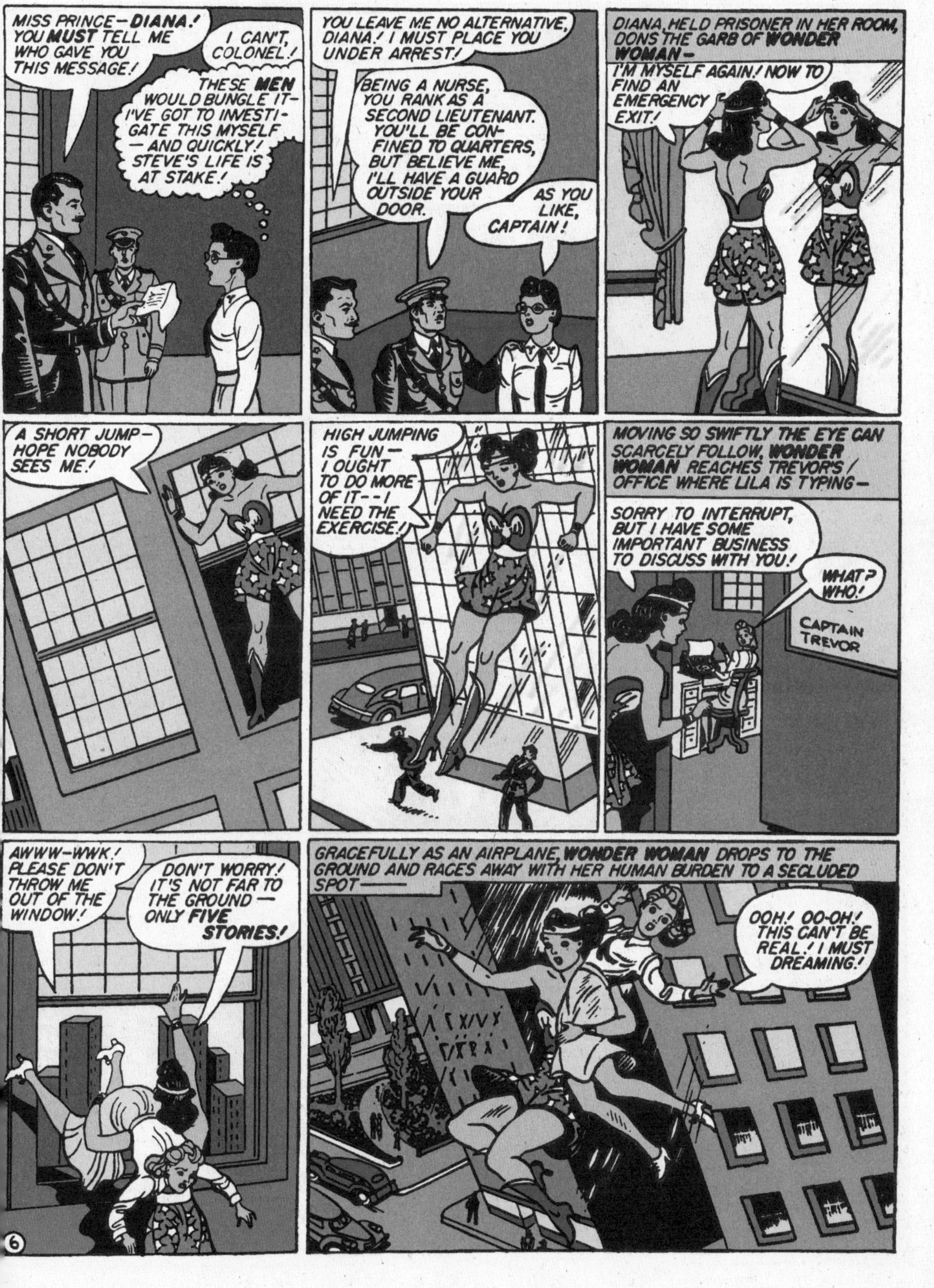
MISS PRINCE—DIANA! YOU MUST TELL ME WHO GAVE YOU THIS MESSAGE!
I CAN'T, COLONEL!
THESE MEN WOULD BUNGLE IT—I'VE GOT TO INVESTIGATE THIS MYSELF—AND QUICKLY! STEVE'S LIFE IS AT STAKE!
YOU LEAVE ME NO ALTERNATIVE, DIANA! I MUST PLACE YOU UNDER ARREST!
BEING A NURSE, YOU RANK AS A SECOND LIEUTENANT. YOU'LL BE CONFINED TO QUARTERS, BUT BELIEVE ME, I'LL HAVE A GUARD OUTSIDE YOUR DOOR.
AS YOU LIKE, CAPTAIN!
DIANA, HELD PRISONER IN HER ROOM, DONS THE GARB OF WONDER WOMAN—
I'M MYSELF AGAIN! NOW TO FIND AN EMERGENCY EXIT!
A SHORT JUMP—HOPE NOBODY SEES ME!
HIGH JUMPING IS FUN—I OUGHT TO DO MORE OF IT--I NEED THE EXERCISE!
MOVING SO SWIFTLY THE EYE CAN SCARCELY FOLLOW, WONDER WOMAN REACHES TREVOR'S OFFICE WHERE LILA IS TYPING—
SORRY TO INTERRUPT, BUT I HAVE SOME IMPORTANT BUSINESS TO DISCUSS WITH YOU!
WHAT? WHO!
CAPTAIN TREVOR
AWWW-WWK! PLEASE DON'T THROW ME OUT OF THE WINDOW!
DON'T WORRY! IT'S NOT FAR TO THE GROUND—ONLY FIVE STORIES!
6
GRACEFULLY AS AN AIRPLANE, WONDER WOMAN DROPS TO THE GROUND AND RACES AWAY WITH HER HUMAN BURDEN TO A SECLUDED SPOT——
OOH! OO-OH! THIS CAN'T BE REAL! I MUST DREAMING!

COME CLEAN, LILA! YOU'RE THE ONLY ONE WHO CAN SAVE STEVE TREVOR'S LIFE! YOU TALK — AND TALK FAST!

I—I'LL TELL YOU EVERYTHING!

LILA CONFESSES ALL TO WONDER WOMAN

I'M NOT A SPY. IT'S MY YOUNGER SISTER, EVE. EVE FELL HARD FOR A HANDSOME MAN NAMED GROSS, A NAZI AGENT. SHE DIDN'T KNOW THAT AND GAVE HIM INFORMATION WITHOUT REALIZING IT. GROSS HELD IT OVER HER—THREATENED TO GIVE HER AWAY. IT WOULD MEAN DISGRACE AND PRISON FOR HER.

WHAT ABOUT THE MESSAGE YOU HAD?

GROSS MADE EVE GET HIM INFORMATION ABOUT STEVE'S TRIP TO NEW YORK. GROSS IS X-46. HE WROTE THE MESSAGE WHICH EVE WAS TO DELIVER TO ANOTHER SPY. BUT I FOUND IT IN EVE'S STOCKING AND TOOK IT AWAY FROM HER. WHEN THE ENEMY AGENT CALLED FOR IT, I REFUSED TO GIVE IT TO HIM—

THAT WAS WHEN I WAS TAKING LILA'S BLOOD PRESSURE!

GO ON!

A TERRIBLE WOMAN—DIANA PRINCE—TOOK THE MESSAGE FROM ME. I TOLD EVE AND BEGGED HER TO CONFESS ALL, BUT SHE RAN AWAY! I DON'T KNOW WHERE SHE IS!

GROSS IS THE ONLY ENEMY SPY YOU KNOW BY SIGHT. WE'VE GOT TO FIND *HIM* TO SAVE STEVE!

GROSS HAS A SPEED BOAT IN THE POTOMAC RIVER.

COME ON — WHAT ARE WE WAITING FOR? WE'LL CATCH GROSS ON HIS BOAT!

THAT'S GROSS'S SPEED BOAT!

HE'S PULLING UP ANCHOR — DIVE IN! WE'VE GOT TO GET HIM!

WOW! THE WATER IS LIKE ICE!

SWIM FASTER AND WARM YOURSELF UP!

HE'S STARTING THE BOAT—WE CAN'T MAKE IT!

CAN'T MAKE WHAT— EXCUSES? HOLD ON TIGHT!

7

48

CHURNING THE WATER TO FOAM, WONDER WOMAN GAINS RAPIDLY ON THE SPEED BOAT—

DONNERWETTER! WHAT'S CHASING ME— A HUMAN TORPEDO?

MY BOAT'S DOING 50 MILES AN HOUR AND THAT GIRL IS OVERTAKING ME AS THOUGH I WERE STANDING STILL!

IS THAT ANY WAY TO GREET A LADY? I'M COMING ABOARD ANYWAY!

DONNER BLITZEN! SHE CATCHES EVERY BULLET ON HER BRACELET!

BANG BANG

WONDER WOMAN PERSUADES HERR GROSS TO TALK

THERE'S A TIME FOR PLAY, PRETTY BOY, BUT THIS ISN'T IT. I'M THROUGH WITH OUR BULLETS AND BRACELETS GAME. LILA, IS THIS YOUR NASTY AGENT X-46?

LEMME GO!

YES, THAT'S GROSS!

COME, COME, LITTLE MAN! TELL ME ALL ABOUT THE PLOT TO KILL CAPT. TREVOR— OR I'LL DUNK YOU LIKE A DOUGHNUT!

I'LL TELL YOU NOTHING, YOU BLITZING SHE-MONSTER!

I SAID I'D DUNK YOU! ARE YOU READY TO TALK?

GLUB-BLUB. I'LL GLUB-TELL EVERY-BLUB EVERY- BLUB-THING!

3

I'LL SIT HERE TO PRESS THE SEA WATER OUT OF YOU. TALK FAST!

AFTER MY MESSAGE WAS INTERCEPTED— I CHANGED OUR PLANS. SENT EVE ON TRAIN. SHE'LL TRICK TREVOR OFF— ULP-BALTIMORE. MY AGENTS WILL GET-ULP-FORMULA— TAKE TREVOR ON YACHT. I'M-UGH-MEETING YACHT IN CHESAPEAKE BAY.

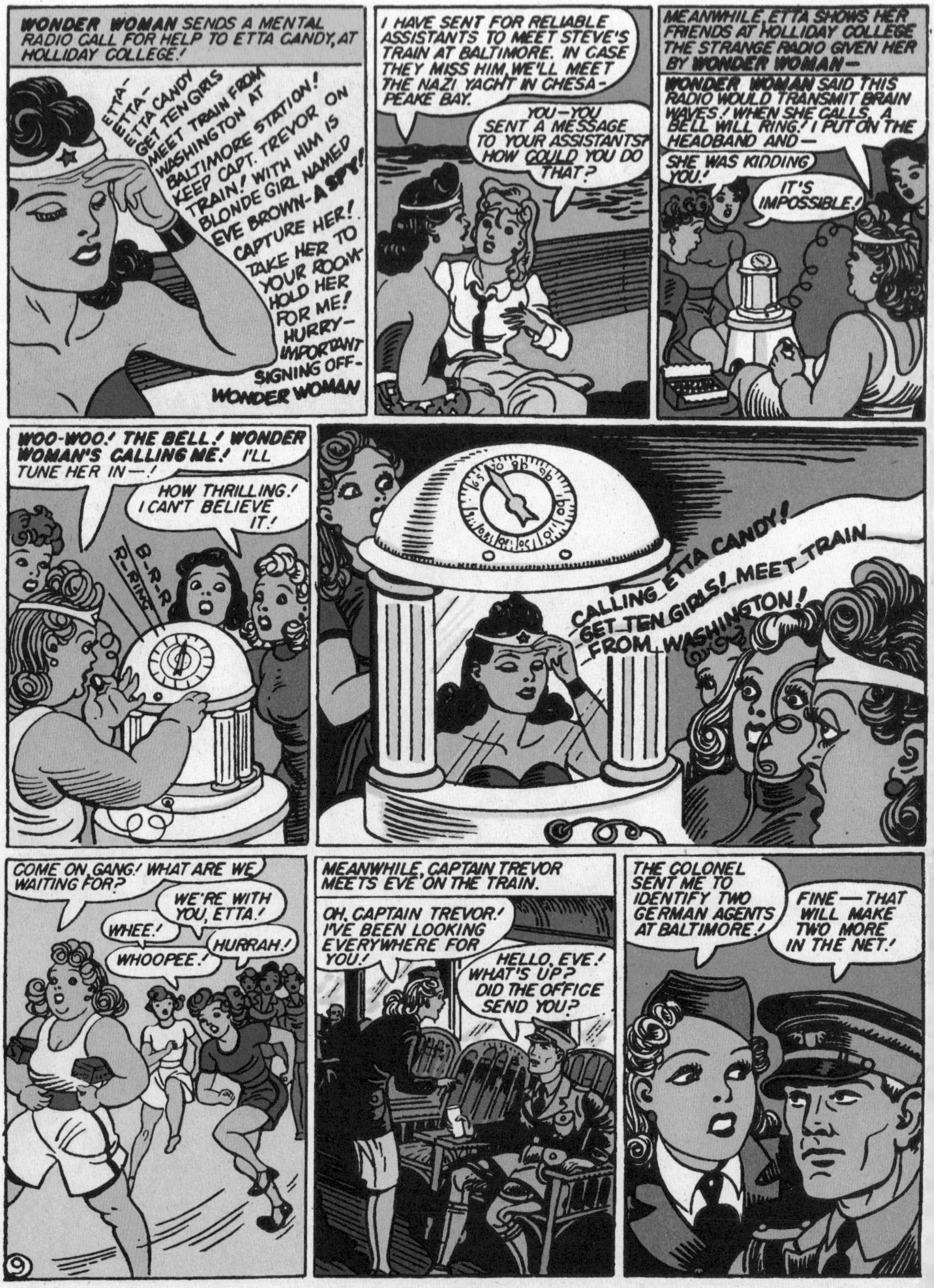
WONDER WOMAN SENDS A MENTAL RADIO CALL FOR HELP TO ETTA CANDY, AT HOLLIDAY COLLEGE!
ETTA- ETTA CANDY GET TEN GIRLS MEET TRAIN FROM WASHINGTON AT BALTIMORE STATION! KEEP CAPT. TREVOR ON TRAIN! WITH HIM IS BLONDE GIRL NAMED EVE BROWN-A SPY! CAPTURE HER! TAKE HER TO YOUR ROOM-HOLD HER FOR ME! HURRY-IMPORTANT SIGNING OFF-WONDER WOMAN
I HAVE SENT FOR RELIABLE ASSISTANTS TO MEET STEVE'S TRAIN AT BALTIMORE. IN CASE THEY MISS HIM, WE'LL MEET THE NAZI YACHT IN CHESA-PEAKE BAY.
YOU—YOU SENT A MESSAGE TO YOUR ASSISTANTS? HOW COULD YOU DO THAT?
MEANWHILE, ETTA SHOWS HER FRIENDS AT HOLLIDAY COLLEGE THE STRANGE RADIO GIVEN HER BY WONDER WOMAN—
WONDER WOMAN SAID THIS RADIO WOULD TRANSMIT BRAIN WAVES! WHEN SHE CALLS, A BELL WILL RING! I PUT ON THE HEADBAND AND—
SHE WAS KIDDING YOU!
IT'S IMPOSSIBLE!
WOO-WOO! THE BELL! WONDER WOMAN'S CALLING ME! I'LL TUNE HER IN—!
HOW THRILLING! I CAN'T BELIEVE IT!
B-R-R R-RING
CALLING ETTA CANDY! GET TEN GIRLS! MEET TRAIN FROM WASHINGTON!
COME ON, GANG! WHAT ARE WE WAITING FOR?
WE'RE WITH YOU, ETTA!
WHEE!
HURRAH!
WHOOPEE!
9
MEANWHILE, CAPTAIN TREVOR MEETS EVE ON THE TRAIN.
OH, CAPTAIN TREVOR! I'VE BEEN LOOKING EVERYWHERE FOR YOU!
HELLO, EVE! WHAT'S UP? DID THE OFFICE SEND YOU?
THE COLONEL SENT ME TO IDENTIFY TWO GERMAN AGENTS AT BALTIMORE!
FINE—THAT WILL MAKE TWO MORE IN THE NET!

AT BALTIMORE, CAPTAIN TREVOR UNSUSPECTINGLY GETS OFF THE TRAIN WITH EVE.

HURRY, CAPTAIN! I SEE THE MEN WE'RE AFTER!

O.K., GAL! LEAD ON!

CAPTAIN TREVOR FOLLOWS EVE HURRIEDLY TO A DARK BAGGAGE ROOM AND THEN—

AS STEVE FALLS, HE THROWS AWAY THE FORMULA TO SAVE IT FROM THE ENEMY.

BUT EVE SEES THE ENVELOPE—QUICKLY SHE SNATCHES IT—

WE'VE GOT TREVOR—WHERE'S THE GIRL? ORDERS ARE TO LIQUIDATE HER TOO!

SHE GOT WISE—SHE'S RUNNING LIKE A RABBIT!

AND LIKE A RABBIT SHE RUNS BLINDLY INTO A TRAP.

HEY, WHO ARE YOU? WHERE ARE YOU GOING IN SUCH A RUSH? GRAB HER, GIRLS—SHE MUST BE THE BLONDE WE'RE AFTER!

YOU'RE EVE BROWN, AREN'T YOU? WHERE'S CAPTAIN TREVOR?

WHERE YOU'LL NEVER FIND HIM! YOU'RE TOO LATE!

AIN'T YOU HAZING THIS GAL PRETTY ROUGH?

WE'RE INITIATING HER INTO THE BEETA LAMBA SORORITY. HAVE SOME CANDY.

10

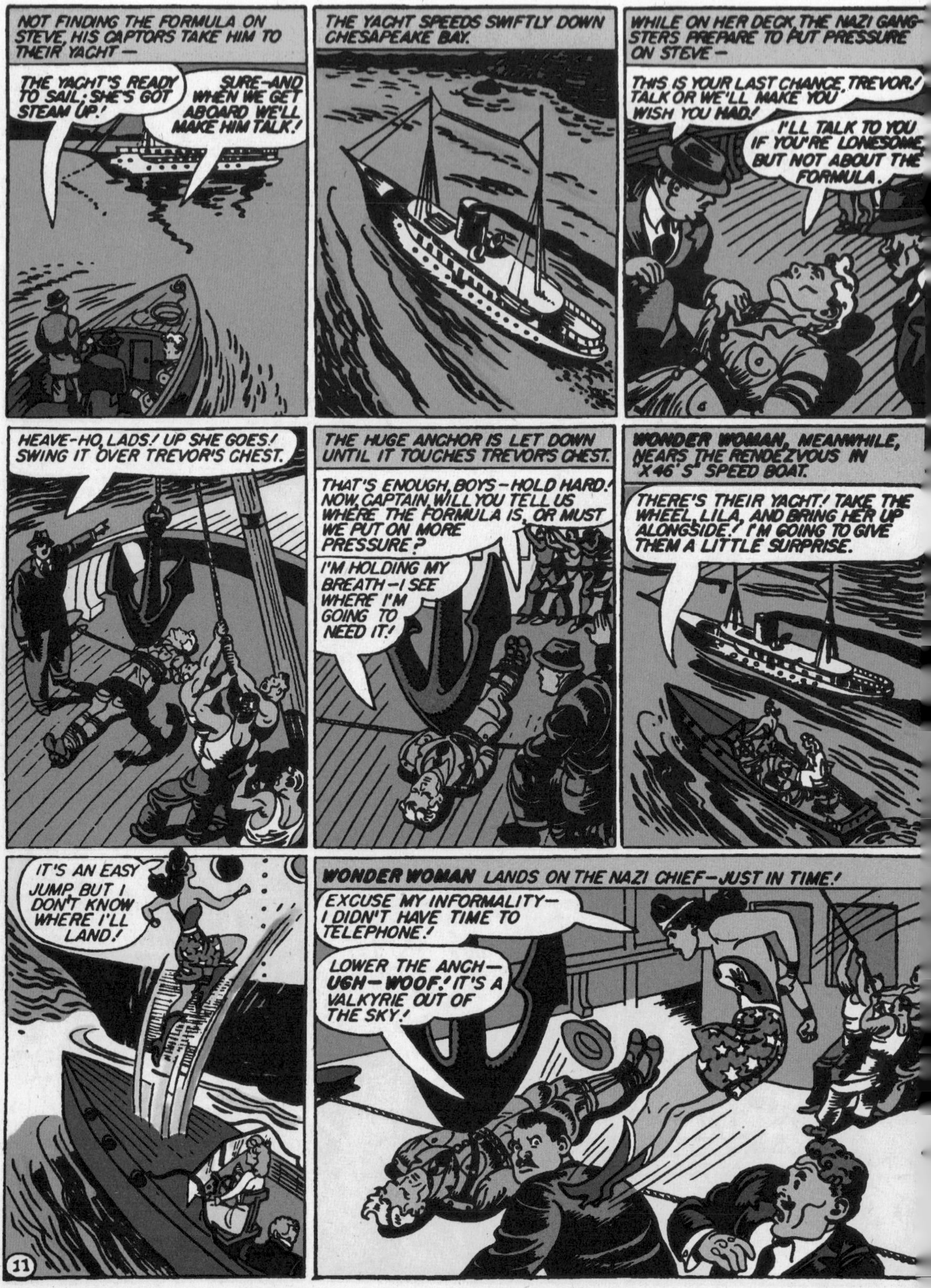
NOT FINDING THE FORMULA ON STEVE, HIS CAPTORS TAKE HIM TO THEIR YACHT —
THE YACHT'S READY TO SAIL; SHE'S GOT STEAM UP!
SURE—AND WHEN WE GET ABOARD WE'LL MAKE HIM TALK!
THE YACHT SPEEDS SWIFTLY DOWN CHESAPEAKE BAY.
WHILE ON HER DECK THE NAZI GANGSTERS PREPARE TO PUT PRESSURE ON STEVE —
THIS IS YOUR LAST CHANCE, TREVOR! TALK OR WE'LL MAKE YOU WISH YOU HAD!
I'LL TALK TO YOU IF YOU'RE LONESOME, BUT NOT ABOUT THE FORMULA.
HEAVE-HO, LADS! UP SHE GOES! SWING IT OVER TREVOR'S CHEST.
THE HUGE ANCHOR IS LET DOWN UNTIL IT TOUCHES TREVOR'S CHEST.
THAT'S ENOUGH, BOYS—HOLD HARD! NOW, CAPTAIN, WILL YOU TELL US WHERE THE FORMULA IS, OR MUST WE PUT ON MORE PRESSURE?
I'M HOLDING MY BREATH—I SEE WHERE I'M GOING TO NEED IT!
WONDER WOMAN, MEANWHILE, NEARS THE RENDEZVOUS IN "X 46' S" SPEED BOAT.
THERE'S THEIR YACHT! TAKE THE WHEEL, LILA, AND BRING HER UP ALONGSIDE! I'M GOING TO GIVE THEM A LITTLE SURPRISE.
IT'S AN EASY JUMP BUT I DON'T KNOW WHERE I'LL LAND!
11
WONDER WOMAN LANDS ON THE NAZI CHIEF—JUST IN TIME!
EXCUSE MY INFORMALITY—I DIDN'T HAVE TIME TO TELEPHONE!
LOWER THE ANCH—UGH—WOOF! IT'S A VALKYRIE OUT OF THE SKY!

LIFTING THE GREAT ANCHOR LIKE A BASKET-BALL AND WRENCHING IT FROM ITS CABLE, WONDER WOMAN HURLS THE PONDEROUS METAL AT THE STUPEFIED SPY BAND!

THIS IS A NEW GAME—GLAD I GOT HERE IN TIME TO PLAY!

IT LOOKS TO ME LIKE A STRIKE, AS THEY SAY IN BOWLING!

DID THEY HURT YOU, STEVE?

NO. BUT THEY'D HAVE CRUSHED ME LIKE A LEMON SQUASH IF YOU HAD ARRIVED ONE SECOND LATER!

CREEPING UP BEHIND WONDER WOMAN, THE YACHT CREW OPENS FIRE!

LOOK OUT BEHIND YOU!

MORE PLAYMATES!

DON'T SHOOT THEM, STEVE! IT'S MORE FUN TO CAPTURE THEM ALIVE!

HA! SHE SHOWS MERCY! MAYBE SHE'S A REAL WOMAN AFTER ALL!

LET'S PILE 'EM UP, STEVE! IT'LL BE EASIER TO COUNT OUR PRISONERS.

WHAT A WOMAN!

WELL, THE PRISONERS ARE SECURED. BUT I'M WORRIED ABOUT THAT FORMULA I THREW AWAY.

AND I'M WORRIED ABOUT MY POOR FOOLISH SISTER.

COME— WE'LL LOOK FOR EVE AND THE FORMULA AT HOLLIDAY COLLEGE.

2

TURNING OVER YACHT AND PRISONERS TO ARMY AUTHORITIES AT BALTIMORE, THEY HURRY TO HOLLIDAY COLLEGE. ETTA CANDY'S ROOM IS IN THAT DORMITORY.

ETTA AND HER FRIENDS CONTINUE EVE'S INITIATION INTO BEETA LAMDA SORORITY.

YOU'RE A BUM SPY, BLONDIE! YOU CAN'T EVEN LOCATE A PIECE OF CANDY!

YOU MISSED AGAIN!

LET'S GIVE HER THE HITLER CURE!

WONDER WOMAN! WONDER WOMAN!

THAT'S ENOUGH NONSENSE, GIRLS! RELEASE YOUR PRISONER!

THERE'S YOUR FORMULA CAPTAIN! I DIDN'T KNOW THEY WERE GOING TO HURT YOU—HONEST! WHEN I SAW WHAT HAPPENED, I GRABBED THE ENVELOPE AND RAN—

I'LL SAY SHE RAN! RIGHT INTO OUR ARMS!

I DID NOT TELL YOU TO TORTURE THIS GIRL!

THESE GIRLS DID NOT HURT ME, WONDER WOMAN. THEY MADE A FOOL OF ME, AND I SAW HOW SILLY I'D BEEN. I LOVE MY COUNTRY AS MUCH AS ANYONE, BUT I WAS SCARED AND DIDN'T REALIZE WHAT I WAS DOING. NOW I'M READY TO TAKE MY MEDICINE! PUT ON THE HANDCUFFS!

COLONEL DARNELL AND CAPTAIN TREVOR APOLOGIZE TO DIANA PRINCE.

IF I HAD BEEN HERE, YOU'D NEVER HAVE BEEN ARRESTED!

PLEASE FORGIVE ME, DIANA! I'LL DO ANYTHING YOU SAY — ANYTHING TO ATONE FOR MY STUPIDITY!

I'LL TAKE YOUR WORD, COLONEL. RELEASE EVE AND LET HER GO HOME AND ATTEND HOLLIDAY COLLEGE! ALL SHE NEEDS IS A LITTLE EDUCATION!

CONGRATULATIONS, CAPTAIN!

WONDERFUL WORK!

YOU MUST BE A SUPERMAN!

HOW DO YOU DO IT?

I'M TELLING YOU— I DID NOTHING! IT WAS WONDER WOMAN, MY BEAUTIFUL ANGEL!

I CERTAINLY DO GET THE WORST OF THIS DEAL, EVERY TIME! THEY SUSPECT ME OF BEING A SPY AND ARREST ME, AND STEVE TREVOR IS SO BUSY TALKING ABOUT THIS "BEAUTIFUL ANGEL" WONDER WOMAN THAT HE PAYS NO ATTENTION TO ME WHATSOEVER! I WONDER IF I AM GETTING JEALOUS OF MY OTHER SELF.

13

Follow WONDER WOMAN every month in SENSATION COMICS

APRIL NO. 4

Sensation Comics

Wonder Woman

A SUPERMAN PUBLICATION

10¢

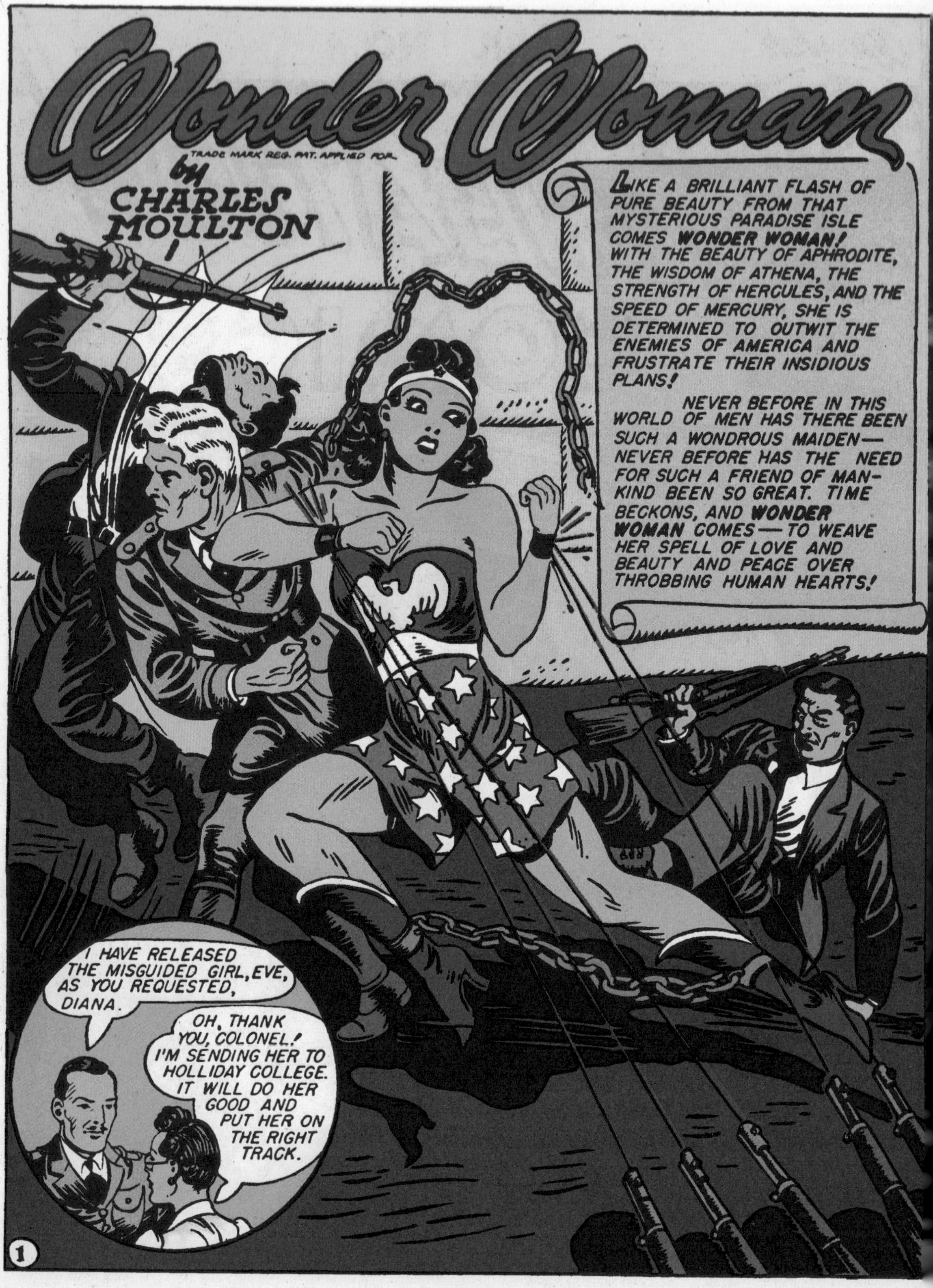
Wonder Woman
TRADE MARK REG. PAT. APPLIED FOR
by CHARLES MOULTON
LIKE A BRILLIANT FLASH OF PURE BEAUTY FROM THAT MYSTERIOUS PARADISE ISLE COMES WONDER WOMAN! WITH THE BEAUTY OF APHRODITE, THE WISDOM OF ATHENA, THE STRENGTH OF HERCULES, AND THE SPEED OF MERCURY, SHE IS DETERMINED TO OUTWIT THE ENEMIES OF AMERICA AND FRUSTRATE THEIR INSIDIOUS PLANS!
NEVER BEFORE IN THIS WORLD OF MEN HAS THERE BEEN SUCH A WONDROUS MAIDEN— NEVER BEFORE HAS THE NEED FOR SUCH A FRIEND OF MAN-KIND BEEN SO GREAT. TIME BECKONS, AND WONDER WOMAN COMES—TO WEAVE HER SPELL OF LOVE AND BEAUTY AND PEACE OVER THROBBING HUMAN HEARTS!
I HAVE RELEASED THE MISGUIDED GIRL, EVE, AS YOU REQUESTED, DIANA.
OH, THANK YOU, COLONEL! I'M SENDING HER TO HOLLIDAY COLLEGE. IT WILL DO HER GOOD AND PUT HER ON THE RIGHT TRACK.
1

I'M SO GLAD THE COLONEL SEES EVE MY WAY—I THINK HE LIKES ME! WOULDN'T IT BE FUN TO MAKE STEVE TREVOR JEALOUS!

NEXT DAY CAPTAIN TREVOR STOPS AT DIANA'S DESK—

SO THE COLONEL RELEASED THAT GIRL, EVE, JUST BECAUSE YOU ASKED HIM TO!

YES, WASN'T THAT SWEET OF HIM?

STEVE IS JEALOUS—HOW PRICELESS!

THAT "SWEET" COLONEL PUT YOU IN CHARGE OF GIRLS' WELFARE, DIDN'T HE? YOU'D BETTER WARN THE GIRLS THERE'S A MANIAC LOOSE. READ THIS!

WHAT? ENID MURDERED! I CAN'T BELIEVE IT!

The Daily Blade
ANOTHER GOVT. GIRL FOUND M...
POLICE SEEKING...
ESCAPED FROM...

The Daily Blade

ANOTHER GOVERNMENT GIRL FOUND MURDERED ★★★★
POLICE SEEKING MANIAC REC
ESCAPED FROM INSANE ASYL

THE BODY OF PRETTY ENID HARPER WAS FOUND TODAY NEAR GEORGE-TOWN BRIDGE BRUTALLY MUR-DERED. MISS HARPER WAS A VALUED EM-PLOYEE OF THE ARMY INTELLIGENCE SERVICE.

I DON'T BELIEVE ENID WAS KILLED BY A MANIAC! I'LL BET SHE HAD AN IM-PORTANT MESSAGE THAT ENEMY AGENTS WANTED!

POSITIVELY NOT! ENID HAD NO SECRET DOCUMENTS—SHE'S BEEN OUT SICK FOR A WEEK!

"SICK" FOR A WEEK AND THEN MURDERED---THAT'S QUEER! CAPTAIN TREVOR—STEVE, WON'T YOU PLEASE INVESTIGATE ENID'S MURDER?

SORRY, DIANA. CAN'T DO IT—IT'S FOR THE DISTRICT POLICE AND I CAN'T BUTT IN.

DIANA ISN'T AFRAID OF HURTING THE POLICE DEPARTMENT'S FEELINGS; SHE DETERMINES TO INVESTIGATE.

BRING ME THE ATTENDANCE RECORDS FOR EVERY GIRL IN THIS SERVICE FOR THE LAST MONTH!

YES, MISS PRINCE.

AHA! GARLA SWANSON— SECRETARY TO OUR CHIEF ESPIONAGE OFFICER—REPORTED "SICK" THIS MORNING! MAY BE NOTHING TO IT, BUT I'M GOING TO INVESTIGATE!

②

DIANA CALLS CARLA'S LAND-LADY.

MRS. O'GRADY, IS CARLA STILL ROOMING WITH YOU?

SURE, SHE LEFT ME BOARDIN' HOUSE LAST EVENIN', SHE DID! WINT TO STAY WID A SASSIETY FRIND, BARONESS VON GUNTHER OR SOMETHIN'!

VON GUNTHER, BARONESS PAULA—HM! THAT MUST BE CARLA'S "SASSIETY FRIEND." I BELIEVE I'LL CALL ON THE BARONESS.

DIRECTORY DISTRICT OF COLUMBIA

HAF YOU AN APPOINTMENT MIT DIE FRAU BARONESS?

NO, FRITZIE. BUT TELL YOUR MADAM I'M LOOKING FOR CARLA SWANSON. SHE'LL SEE ME, I'M SURE!

THE BARONESS KNOWS NO ORDINARY PEOPLE.

I AM DIANA PRINCE. I WORK IN THE INTELLIGENCE OFFICE AND—

I DO NOT KNOW YOU. DID YOU BRING A MESSAGE, PERHAPS?

I WANT TO SEE MY FRIEND, CARLA SWANSON! I UNDERSTAND SHE'S STAYING WITH YOU—

MY DEAH! I NEVER HEARD OF SUCH A PERSON. WHY SHOULD I KNOW A WRETCHED LITTLE TYPIST?

BUT I MUST SEE CARLA! I KNOW SHE CAME HERE.

HA! IF YOU HAD NEVER HEARD OF SUCH A PERSON, HOW WOULD YOU KNOW SHE'S A TYPIST?

SIGFRIED, SHOW THIS PERSON OUT!

IT IS A BLEASURE! COME, FRAULEIN CLOWN, ZISS VAY OUDT!

YOU—YOU BRUTE!

THIS BARONESS IS A PHONEY! SHE KNOWS WHERE CARLA IS. I MUST SAVE CARLA, IF IT ISN'T TOO LATE!

BE CAREFUL MIT YOUR STEP!

STEVE, MEANWHILE, GETS A NEW LEAD—

YOU SENT FOR ME, COLONEL?

YES, CAPTAIN. YOUNG EVE BROWN REGISTERED AT HOLLIDAY COLLEGE TODAY—THE GESTAPO GANG TRAILED HER OUT THERE. THIS IS HER STORY—

WHILE PASSING AN EMPTY CLASS-ROOM, EVE WAS SEIZED BY A MYSTERIOUS HAND.

BE QUIET! IF YOU SCREAM, I'LL KILL YOU. COME IN HERE!

E-E-E-K! LET ME GO!

SO! YOU GOT OUT OF PRISON AND NOW YOU WANT TO GO TO SCHOOL. GOODT! YOU SHALL GO TO SCHOOL — BUT NOT HOLLI-DAY COLLEGE!

WH—WHAT DO YOU MEAN?

YOU VILL GO TO OUR SCHOOL OF ESPIONAGE! THERE VE TRAIN GIRLS TO BE SPIES FOR US IN EVERY GOVERNMENT OFFICE! YOU LEARN SHORT-WAVE, SECRET CODES, PHOTOGRAPHY, HEIN?

NO—NO — I WON'T DO IT!

MEET US TONIGHT BY THE COLLEGE LAKE AT 9 O'CLOCK. PROMISE OR I KILL YOU!

ER—GLUG! I PROMISE!

CAPTAIN TREVOR DETERMINES TO LOCATE THE SPY SCHOOL.

I HATE TO ASK THIS OF YOU, EVE! IF ANY-THING GOES WRONG—

IT'S GOOD-BYE LITTLE EVIE! BUT I'M NOT AFRAID, I'LL DO ANY-THING YOU SAY!

KEEP YOUR APPOINTMENT WITH THE GESTAPO AGENTS TO-NIGHT AT COLLEGE LAKE. LET THEM TAKE YOU TO THEIR SCHOOL OF ESPIONAGE. WE MUST FIND THAT SCHOOL!

COUNT ON ME, CAPTAIN—I'LL DO IT!

BUT EVE FORGETS THAT AS A PLEDGE OF BEETA LAMDA SORORITY SHE MUST OBEY HER SISTERS' ORDERS.

'BEETA LAMDA'

NEOPHYTE EVE, YOU WILL GO TO YOUR ROOM AND, STUDY TILL 11 O'CLOCK.

OH! PLEASE, I-OO-UF!

THE BEETAS MAKE SURE THAT EVE OBEYS ORDERS—

NOT A WORD OUT OF YOU, NEOPHYTE EVE, UNTIL 11 O'CLOCK.

OH, WHAT CAN I DO? I MUST MEET THOSE NAZI AGENTS AT NINE!

I'LL NEVER MAKE IT! AND CAPTAIN TREVOR WILL THINK I GOT SCARED AND FAILED HIM AGAIN! DARN THIS DOG-COLLAR ANYWAY!

WHEN EVE FAILS TO APPEAR ON TIME THE GESTAPO AGENTS BECOME SUSPICIOUS—

EVE LOST HER NERVE! I'D BETTER PITCH INTO THESE CHAPS BEFORE THEY MAKE A BREAK FOR IT.

THE GIRL HAS BETRAYED US!

IT'S A TRAP!

LET'S GET AWAY FROM HERE QUICK!

ALL RIGHT, YOU MEN — I'VE GOT THE DROP ON YOU — PUT UP YOUR HANDS AND COME QUIETLY.

VAS?

QUICK, MEN! GRAB HIM!

BANG!

SO YOU BOYS WANT A FIGHT, EH!

UGGF!

I HATE TO GET ROUGH WITH YOU BOYS, BUT YOU ASKED FOR IT!

AR-RCH OW-W-W!

MOTORCYCLE POLICE, HEARING THE SHOT, ARRIVE WHEN THE FIGHT IS OVER.

GREAT SIZZLING FISH, CAPTAIN! DID YOU KNOCK ALL THOSE GUYS OUT?

YES, BUT ONE SEEMS TO HAVE GOTTEN AWAY. I'M GOING AFTER HIM. HOLD THESE PRISONERS FOR ME.

⑤

EVE, FREEING HERSELF AT LAST, HURRIES TO KEEP HER APPOINTMENT AT COLLEGE LAKE.

IF ONLY I'M NOT TOO LATE! WHAT WILL CAPTAIN TREVOR THINK OF ME?

BUT THE ALERT BEETA GIRLS DISCOVER EVE'S ESCAPE AND START IN PURSUIT—

WOO-WOO! EVE GOT AWAY! COME ON, GIRLS! BRING YOUR ROPES AND PADDLES.

WHEE-EE! BETCHA EVE'S GONE TO MEET A MAN! WAIT'LL WE GET HER!

AS THEY REACH THE STREET, THE GIRLS SEE CAPTAIN TREVOR CHASING THE ESCAPED SPY.

LOOK, GIRLS! IT'S CAPTAIN TREVOR!

SAY, IF STEVE'S AFTER HIM, THE GUY DESERVES TO BE CAUGHT! C'MON!

THE GESTAPO AGENT GETS AWAY IN STEVE'S CAR.

I'LL HAVE TO WARN THEM AT OUR SECRET SCHOOL!

STEVE GRABS ONE OF THE POLICEMEN'S MOTORCYCLES AND SPEEDS IN PURSUIT.

I'M GLAD HE GOT AWAY — HE MAY LEAD ME TO THEIR SECRET SPY SCHOOL-I HOPE SO!

ETTA CANDY FOLLOWS STEVE ON THE OTHER MOTORCYCLE!

WHEE-EES UMP! THERE GOES MY CANDY! I HOPE THOSE BOYS ARE HEADING FOR A SWEET SHOP!

THE COLLEGE GIRLS GET THEIR FAVORITE JALOPIES AND FOLLOW ETTA.

ETTA, ETTA! LET'S GO GET HER. SHE'S AFTER STEVE TREVOR AND SHE OUGHT TO KNOW BETTER!

BLONDES PREFER GENTLEMEN

THIS CAR IS PAID FOR — IS YOURS?

WHILE THE SPY CHASE GOES MERRILY ON, LET US FOLLOW THE UNHAPPY FATE OF CARLA, WHO WAS INVITED TO VISIT THE BARONESS VON GUNTHER

I'M CARLA-

ENTER, BLEASE! DER BARONESS EXPECTS YOU!

IT'S WONDERFUL OF YOU, BARONESS, TO INVITE ME! BUT I CAN'T SEE WHY-

MY DEAH! I HAVE HEARD SO MUCH ABOUT YOUR CLEVER WORK FROM-ER-MUTUAL FRIENDS-

I CAN RECOMMEND THESE DAIQUIRIS, MY DEAH!

NO THANK YOU, BARONESS, I NEVER DRINK COCKTAILS BUT I'LL TAKE SOME TEA.

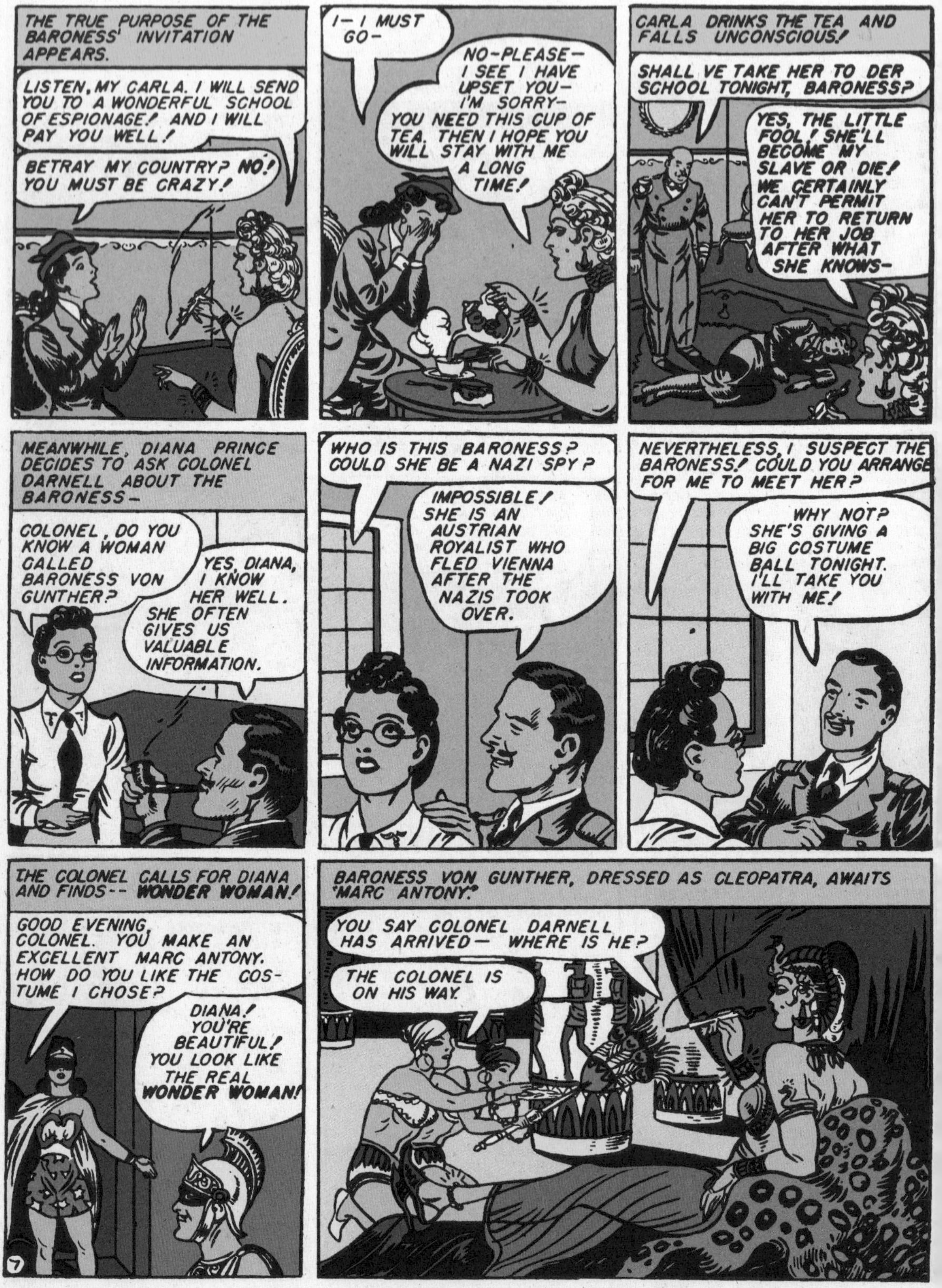
THE TRUE PURPOSE OF THE BARONESS' INVITATION APPEARS.
LISTEN, MY CARLA. I WILL SEND YOU TO A WONDERFUL SCHOOL OF ESPIONAGE! AND I WILL PAY YOU WELL!
BETRAY MY COUNTRY? NO! YOU MUST BE CRAZY!
I-- I MUST GO-
NO-PLEASE- I SEE I HAVE UPSET YOU- I'M SORRY- YOU NEED THIS CUP OF TEA. THEN I HOPE YOU WILL STAY WITH ME A LONG TIME!
CARLA DRINKS THE TEA AND FALLS UNCONSCIOUS!
SHALL VE TAKE HER TO DER SCHOOL TONIGHT, BARONESS?
YES, THE LITTLE FOOL! SHE'LL BECOME MY SLAVE OR DIE! WE CERTAINLY CAN'T PERMIT HER TO RETURN TO HER JOB AFTER WHAT SHE KNOWS-
MEANWHILE, DIANA PRINCE DECIDES TO ASK COLONEL DARNELL ABOUT THE BARONESS-
COLONEL, DO YOU KNOW A WOMAN CALLED BARONESS VON GUNTHER?
YES, DIANA, I KNOW HER WELL. SHE OFTEN GIVES US VALUABLE INFORMATION.
WHO IS THIS BARONESS? COULD SHE BE A NAZI SPY?
IMPOSSIBLE! SHE IS AN AUSTRIAN ROYALIST WHO FLED VIENNA AFTER THE NAZIS TOOK OVER.
NEVERTHELESS, I SUSPECT THE BARONESS! COULD YOU ARRANGE FOR ME TO MEET HER?
WHY NOT? SHE'S GIVING A BIG COSTUME BALL TONIGHT. I'LL TAKE YOU WITH ME!
THE COLONEL CALLS FOR DIANA AND FINDS-- WONDER WOMAN!
GOOD EVENING, COLONEL. YOU MAKE AN EXCELLENT MARC ANTONY. HOW DO YOU LIKE THE COSTUME I CHOSE?
DIANA! YOU'RE BEAUTIFUL! YOU LOOK LIKE THE REAL WONDER WOMAN!
7
BARONESS VON GUNTHER, DRESSED AS CLEOPATRA, AWAITS "MARC ANTONY."
YOU SAY COLONEL DARNELL HAS ARRIVED— WHERE IS HE?
THE COLONEL IS ON HIS WAY.

CLEOPATRA RECEIVES MARC ANTONY -- AND LOOKS DAGGERS AT HIS COMPANION!

THY BEAUTY, O QUEEN, IS DIVINE!

OR WOULD YOU SAY DEVILISH?

THE BARONESS TALKS PRIVATELY WITH **WONDER WOMAN**—

WHO ARE YOU? AND WHY DO YOU COME HERE?

THEY CALL ME **WONDER WOMAN.** I CAME TO WARN YOU. YOU ARE SUSPECTED. YOU'D BETTER MOVE THE GIRLS TONIGHT!

WONDER WOMAN'S PLAN SUCCEEDS--- THE BARONESS KIDNAPS HER MYSTERIOUS INFORMANT!

THANK YOU FOR THE INFORMATION. I WILL REWARD YOU—

WONDER WOMAN PERMITS HERSELF TO BE BOUND—

CARRY THIS GIRL TO MY PLANE. I WILL TELL COLONEL DARNELL SHE WENT OFF WITH ANOTHER MAN. I WILL JOIN YOU LATER.

HURRY BARONESS! I FEEL DANGER!

THE BARONESS LANDS HER PLANE SKILLFULLY NEAR AN ABANDONED COAL MINE IN WEST VIRGINIA—

THERE ARE NO DANGER SIGNALS— THIS GIRL IS LYING!

I DON'T KNOW THIS GIRL - BUT I'LL MAKE HER TALK. CHAIN HER WITH CARLA AT THE 1000-FOOT LEVEL. I'LL HIDE THE PLANE AND BE DOWN PRESENTLY.

WONDER WOMAN FINDS CARLA IN A STRANGE MENTAL STATE.

GET UP, CARLA! QUICK! I'VE COME TO RESCUE YOU!

I AM THE BARONESS PAULA'S SLAVE. ONLY SHE CAN RELEASE ME.

WHAT DO YOU MEAN, THE BARONESS' SLAVE? HOW DID SHE DO THIS TO YOU?

I WILL TELL YOU. SHE WILL DO THE SAME TO YOU.

 I AM THE SLAVE OF THE BARON-ESS—SHE IS MY MISTRESS—SHE COMMANDS, I OBEY—

POOR GIRL—SHE'S BEEN DRUGGED AND HYPNOTIZED! HOW CLEVER!

 I AM A *KINDER* MISTRESS—I AM *STRONGER* THAN BARON-ESS PAULA. I WILL BREAK YOUR CHAINS!

YOU--COULD? —I WILL NO LONGER BE ENSLAVED?

 SEE, IT'S EASY. I CAN BREAK ALL YOUR CHAINS THE SAME WAY!

WONDERFUL! CAN YOU REALLY *FREE* ME FROM THE BARONESS?

 THE MISTRESS COMES! OH, *PLEASE*, MEND MY CHAIN—IF *SHE* SEES IT BROKEN, SHE WILL BEAT ME!

THIS IS PITIFUL! I MUST FREE CARLA'S MIND OR SHE WILL BE INSANE FOR LIFE!

 TO FREE CARLA AND THE OTHER CAPTIVES, *WONDER WOMAN* AGREES TO BECOME THE BARONESS' SLAVE—

YOU TRIED TO TRICK ME! YOU KNEW I HOLD THESE GIRLS—YES?

THAT'S TRUE. SO WHAT?

 SO THIS! YOU BECOME MY SLAVE—LEARN ESPIONAGE IN OUR SCHOOL, THEN I SPARE YOUR LIFE. OTHER-WISE YOU DIE LIKE ENID AND THE OTHERS!

SO *SHE'S* OUR MANIAC MURDERER.

I SUBMIT! CHAIN ME.

 A WEIRD, TERRIFYING FEELING SWEEPS OVER *WONDER WOMAN* AS CHAINS ARE ATTACHED TO HER AMAZON BRACELETS.

WELD HER FETTERS TO THOSE WRIST BANDS; THEY ARE STRONG AND HEAVY!

I FEEL WEAK—APHRODITE, HELP ME!

 STILL BELIEVING THAT SHE CAN BREAK HER BONDS AT WILL, *WONDER WOMAN* ENTERS THE SPY SCHOOL.

I WILL CONDUCT MY NEW SLAVE PERSONALLY THROUGH OUR SCHOOL.

THANK YOU, BARONESS! YOUR AMAZING ORGANI-ZATION FASCI-NATES ME!

STEP HIGHER! POINT TOES DOWN! BACKS STRAIGHT!

THIS TEACHES GIRLS DISCIPLINE. TOMORROW YOU WILL JOIN THEIR RANKS!

WON'T I HAVE FUN?

YOU WILL SPEND 6 HOURS A DAY STUDYING CODE WITH THESE GIRLS.

HOW EXCITING!

STRAIGHTEN THOSE KNEES, SLAVE! THIS GIRL IS BEING PUNISHED FOR STUPIDITY IN HER RADIO WORK!

POOR THING! I MUST FREE THESE GIRLS QUICKLY!

ISN'T THAT BRENDA LEE, WHO "DISAPPEARED" THREE MONTHS AGO?

YES! THIS IS A MINE OF MISSING GIRLS! I COLLECT THEM FROM EVERY STATE. AS MY SLAVES THEY WILL WORK UNDER NEW IDENTITIES.

I HAVE A FAVOR TO ASK—MAY I SHARE CARLA'S CELL?

SO—CARLA IS YOUR FRIEND! WELL, I SEE NO HARM—SHE WILL TEACH YOU TO SUBMIT!

BUT **WONDER WOMAN**, WITH THE PSYCHOLOGICAL KNOWLEDGE OF AMAZONS, SOON RESTORES CARLA'S MIND TO NORMAL—

OH! I FEEL **FREE** AGAIN. YOU ARE MARVELOUS, **WONDER WOMAN!**

BUT WHEN **WONDER WOMAN** TRIES TO BREAK HER CHAINS, SHE MAKES A TERRIBLE DISCOVERY—

GREAT APHRODITE! MY STRENGTH IS GONE—I CANNOT BREAK THIS LITTLE CHAIN!

WONDER WOMAN, IN DESPAIR, REMEMBERS TOO LATE THE QUEEN'S WARNING—

DAUGHTER, IF ANY MAN WELDS CHAINS ON YOUR BRACELETS, YOU WILL BECOME WEAK AS WE AMAZONS WERE WHEN WE SURRENDERED TO HERCULES AND HIS GREEKS.

10

DAWN IS BREAKING AS THE GESTAPO AGENT TRAILED BY TREVOR REACHES THE MINE—

WHERE'S THAT DOD-GASTED BOOB GO-ING NOW? LOOKS LIKE A DESERTED MINE.

SUFFERING RABBITS! HE'S GONE DOWN THE MINE SHAFT! WHAT'S DOWN THERE? I'LL HAVE TO SEE!

STEVE WALKS INTO A TRAP—

STICK 'EM UP, SMART BOY! HENKEL TOLD US YOU WERE ON HIS TRAIL!

SO MY PAL'S NAME IS HENKEL, EH? NICE OF YOU TO INTRODUCE US!

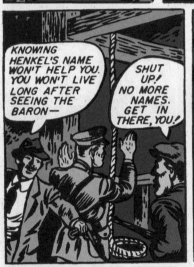

KNOWING HENKEL'S NAME WON'T HELP YOU. YOU WON'T LIVE LONG AFTER SEEING THE BARON—

SHUT UP! NO MORE NAMES. GET IN THERE, YOU!

STEVE IS BROUGHT TO THE BARONESS.

AH, MY DEAR BARONESS! THIS IS AN UNEXPECTED PLEASURE!

BUT A SADNESS ALSO, CAPTAIN! SINCE YOU HAVE RECOGNIZED ME, WE MUST PART, I FEAR, FOREVER!

AT LEAST, CAPTAIN, I WILL ESCORT YOU ON YOUR LAST— WHAT YOU SAY— MILE!

THANK YOU, I'D LIKE TO DO THE SAME FOR YOU, BARONESS!

AT DAWN EACH DAY, THE GIRLS ARE DRAWN UP FOR INSPECTION—

AS STEVE IS LED PAST THE GIRLS, HE RECOG-NIZES WONDER WOMAN.

WONDER WOMAN! HOW—WHAT—

STEVE! OH, WHAT ARE THEY DOING TO YOU?

YOU CAN CLEAN UP THIS CROWD WITH ONE HAND AND I'LL HELP-- LET'S GO!

I--I CAN'T--STEVE-- I CAN'T--

I MUSTN'T LET STEVE KNOW THAT MY STRENGTH IS GONE--NO MAN MUST KNOW THE SECRET OF MY STRENGTH!

SO IT WAS YOU WHO SENT THIS WONDER WOMAN TO SPY ON ME, CAPTAIN!

NO, NO! I SWEAR I DID NOT KNOW SHE WAS HERE--

YOU LIE, CAPTAIN TREVOR! GUARDS, TAKE THEM BOTH TO THE EXECUTION-CHAMBER!

WHAT A GHASTLY FOOL I WAS! AFTER ALL YOU'VE DONE FOR ME, I LET YOU IN FOR THIS--

IT WASN'T YOUR FAULT, STEVE! YOU DIDN'T KNOW I WAS HELPLESS.

AT LEAST, MY BEAUTIFUL ANGEL, WE DIE TOGETHER!

NOT IF I CAN HELP IT!

READY, AIM--

BUT WHAT IS THAT WILD COMMOTION OUTSIDE THE MINE CHAMBER? TO UNDERSTAND ITS CAUSE WE MUST RETURN TO ETTA CANDY

PFEU! THERE'S STEVE'S MOTORCYCLE! HE MUST BE IN THAT SHACK. IN WE GO, GIRLS!

WE'RE WITH YOU, ETTA!

ETTA'S GIRLS CAPTURE THE MINE SHAFT GUARDS

UMPH! GET OFF OF ME, FAT GIRL!

FIRST COMFORTABLE SEAT I'VE HAD SINCE GOT ON THAT MOTORCYCLE.

THE GIRLS DESCEND THE SHAFT--

NO GIGGLES, GIRLS WE GOTTA TAKE THESE FELLOWS BY SURPRISE.

IN THE GREAT MINE CHAMBER GIRLS AND GUARDS CLASH—WHAT A RIOT!

WOO-WOO!

EEEK! WHEE! WOW!

ACH! VE KILL YUH!

IN THE EXECUTION CHAMBER THE BARONESS HESITATES—THEN GIVES THE SIGNAL!

FIRE!

QUICKER THAN A GUN FLASH, WONDER WOMAN LEAPS IN FRONT OF STEVE, CATCHING THE BULLETS ON HER BRACELETS.

MY STRENGTH IS GOING—I MUST MAKE THE BULLETS CUT OFF MY CHAINS!

AH-H! THIS IS MORE LIKE IT! KEEP 'EM FLYING, STEVE!

LOOK OUT! THE DEVIL'S LOOSE! SHE'S A HUMAN CAT!

LED BY WONDER WOMAN AND STEVE, THE GIRLS QUICKLY SUBDUE THE SPIES, AND FREE THE BARONESS' SLAVES.

THE GIRLS, NOW FREE, THANK STEVE!

YOU WERE WONDERFUL, CAPTAIN!

YOU WERE BRAVE!

YOU SAVED US!

AND YOU SAVED WONDER WOMAN!

I DID NOTHING, GIRLS— WONDER WOMAN DID IT ALL!

13

AT 9 O'CLOCK WONDER WOMAN CALLS COLONEL DARNELL—

HELLO, COLONEL! THIS IS DIANA PRINCE. MAY I HAVE TODAY OFF? LAST NIGHT'S PARTY WAS-ER- STRENUOUS!

CERTAINLY, MY DEAR GIRL! YOU MUST HAVE HAD A GAY TIME!

OH, I HAD A GAY TIME, ALL RIGHT! THESE BRACELETS—THEY'RE AN AMAZON'S GREATEST STRENGTH AND WEAKNESS! WHAT A FOOL I WAS TO LET A MAN WELD CHAINS UPON THEM! IT JUST MAKES A GIRL REALIZE HOW SHE HAS TO WATCH HERSELF IN THIS MAN'S WORLD!

WONDER WOMAN'S ADVENTURES ARE DIFFERENT— UNPREDICTABLE! READ A NEW ONE EVERY MONTH IN SENSATION COMICS

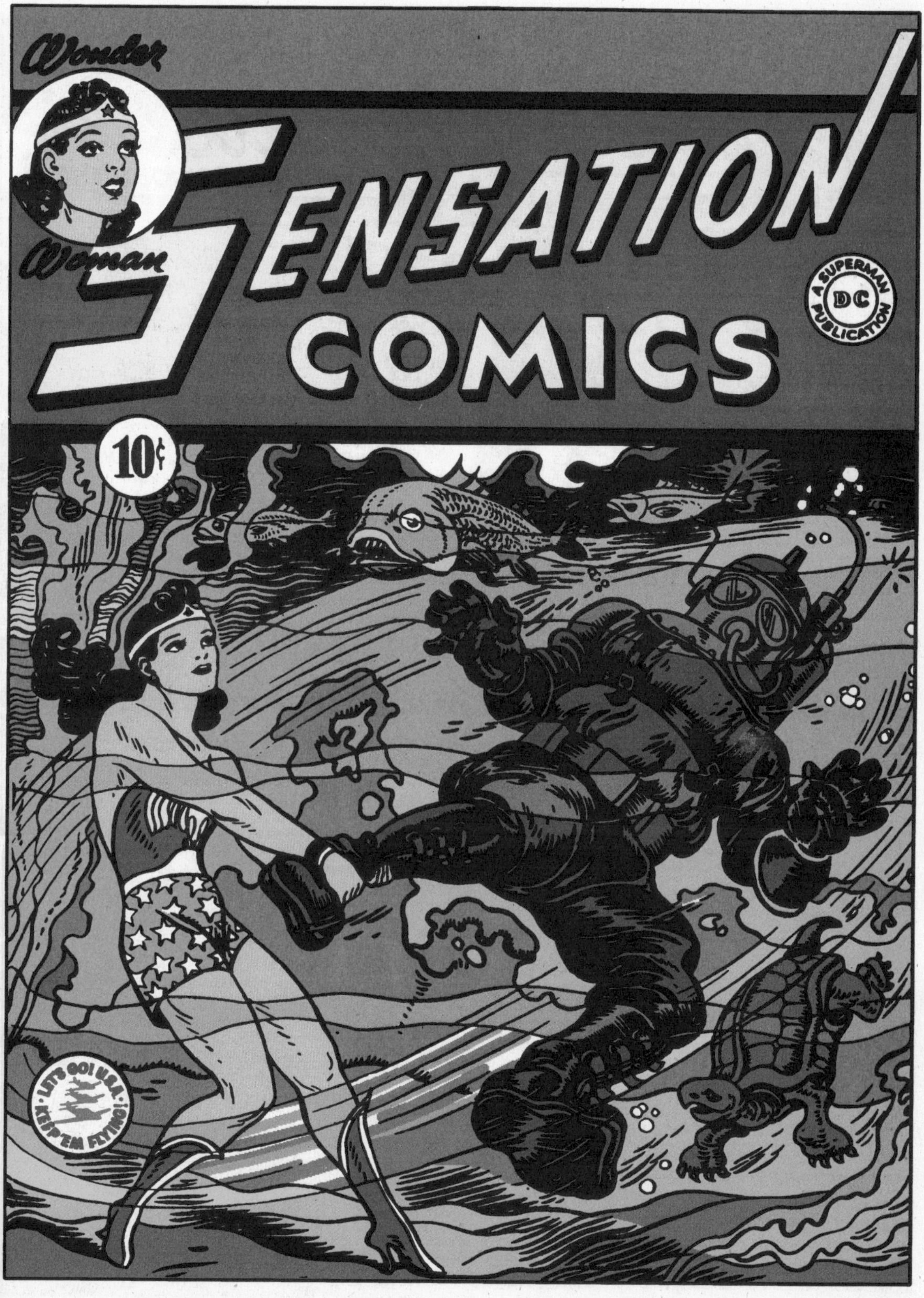
Wonder Woman
SENSATION
COMICS
A SUPERMAN
DC
PUBLICATION
10¢
LET'S GO! U.S.A.
KEEP 'EM FLYING!

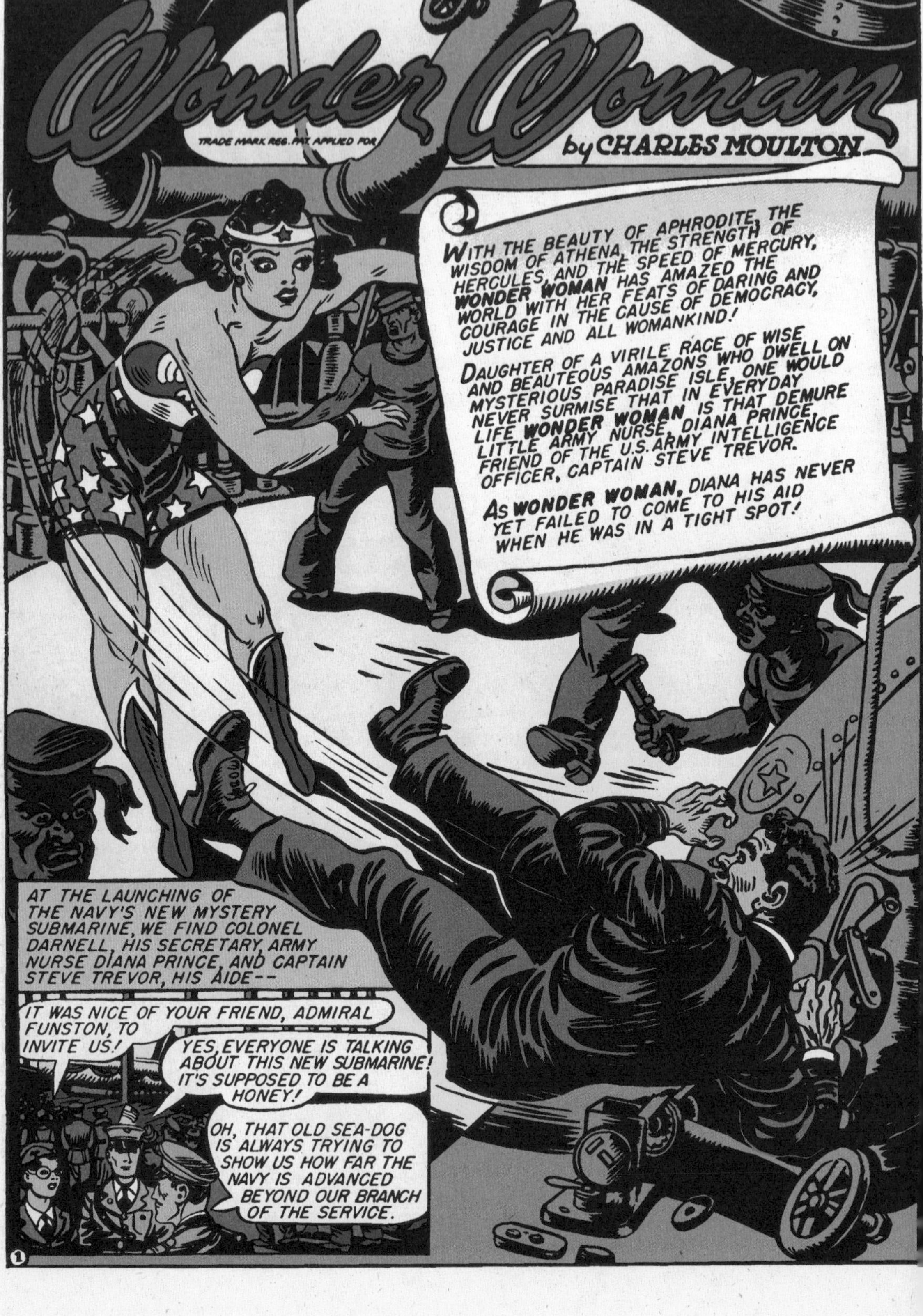
Wonder Woman
TRADE MARK REG. PAT. APPLIED FOR
by CHARLES MOULTON
WITH THE BEAUTY OF APHRODITE, THE WISDOM OF ATHENA, THE STRENGTH OF HERCULES, AND THE SPEED OF MERCURY, WONDER WOMAN HAS AMAZED THE WORLD WITH HER FEATS OF DARING AND COURAGE IN THE CAUSE OF DEMOCRACY, JUSTICE AND ALL WOMANKIND!
DAUGHTER OF A VIRILE RACE OF WISE AND BEAUTEOUS AMAZONS WHO DWELL ON MYSTERIOUS PARADISE ISLE, ONE WOULD NEVER SURMISE THAT IN EVERYDAY LIFE WONDER WOMAN IS THAT DEMURE LITTLE ARMY NURSE, DIANA PRINCE, FRIEND OF THE U.S. ARMY INTELLIGENCE OFFICER, CAPTAIN STEVE TREVOR.
AS WONDER WOMAN, DIANA HAS NEVER YET FAILED TO COME TO HIS AID WHEN HE WAS IN A TIGHT SPOT!
AT THE LAUNCHING OF THE NAVY'S NEW MYSTERY SUBMARINE, WE FIND COLONEL DARNELL, HIS SECRETARY, ARMY NURSE DIANA PRINCE, AND CAPTAIN STEVE TREVOR, HIS AIDE--
IT WAS NICE OF YOUR FRIEND, ADMIRAL FUNSTON, TO INVITE US!
YES, EVERYONE IS TALKING ABOUT THIS NEW SUBMARINE! IT'S SUPPOSED TO BE A HONEY!
OH, THAT OLD SEA-DOG IS ALWAYS TRYING TO SHOW US HOW FAR THE NAVY IS ADVANCED BEYOND OUR BRANCH OF THE SERVICE.
1

WHILE NEARBY, THE ADMIRAL SPEAKS TO DR. SANDS, INVENTOR OF THE NEW CRAFT---

MY DREAM HAS COME TRUE!

IF IT DOES ALL YOU PROMISE, IT'LL DOUBLE OUR SEAPOWER.

WIRE FOR YOU, SIR!

THE GOVERNOR'S WIFE HAS BEEN DELAYED--WON'T BE ABLE TO CHRISTEN THE BOAT! WONDER IF YOUR CHARMING SECRETARY WOULD DO THE HONORS, COLONEL?

HA! WHAT WOULD THE NAVY DO WITHOUT US!

OH! I'VE NEVER CHRISTENED A BOAT.

YOU JUST SAY: I CHRISTEN THEE THE OCTOPUS—AND WHAMO! THAT'S ALL THERE IS TO IT!

THIS IS SO THRILLING!

SURROUNDED BY THE LEADERS OF AMERICA'S NAVAL DEFENSE, DIANA DRAWS BACK THE BOTTLE-A SUDDEN FEAR SEIZES HER!

THIS BOTTLE DOESN'T CONTAIN CHAMPAGNE--IT'S TOO HEAVY! SOMETHING'S WRONG!

GO AHEAD, DIANA! SHOW THEM WHAT AN ARMY WALLOP IS LIKE!

WITH HER MORE THAN NORMAL SENSES, DIANA IS ABLE TO IDENTIFY SUBSTANCES BY THEIR WEIGHT----

WHY, THIS BOTTLE CONTAINS A HIGH EXPLOSIVE! I'LL HAVE TO TRY A FAST RUSE!

WITH A QUICK MOTION OF HER POWERFUL WRISTS, DIANA TEARS THE BOTTLE LOOSE AND HURLS IT FAR INTO THE WATER-----

OH! THE RIBBON BROKE! IT—IT SLIPPED OUT OF MY HAND—HOW CLUMSY OF ME!

AN ILL OMEN!

WITH A DEAFENING ROAR, THE BOTTLE EXPLODES ON A NEARBY SHOAL.

BOOM!

WHEW! IT WOULD HAVE BEEN A WORSE OMEN IF IT HAD EXPLOD-ED HERE!

I THINK I'M GOING TO FAINT—

OR AT LEAST I OUGHT TO MAKE BELIEVE I AM—

POOR CHILD—SHE'S FAINTING!

TO MAINTAIN HER POSE AS AN ORDINARY HUMAN, DIANA PRETENDS TO FAINT----

EVERYTHING IS ALL RIGHT, DIANA!

THAT EXPLOSION WAS MEANT TO KILL US!

YES! TO DESTROY THE SUBMARINE AND DESTROY THE ONLY ONES WHO FULLY UNDERSTAND HER SECRETS!

MEANWHILE, IN A SEA-GOING TUG OFF SHORE—LOOKING THROUGH GLASSES AS HE TALKS—

WE WILL DRINK REAL CHAMPAGNE WHILE— HEY, VOT'S HAPPENED?

IT'S NOT THE GOVERNOR'S WIFE AND SHE'S---THROWING THE BOTTLE!

WHAT'S THIS? AN AMERICAN OFFICER PLAYING TRAITOR?

THAT VENT WRONG— BUT VE GOT ODDER TRICKS YET! VE VILL MAKE THEM THINK THE SUBMARINE IS NO GOOD—AND THEN—

I GET IT! WE USE IT FOR OURSELVES! MIGHT AS WELL GET RID OF THIS ENSIGN'S UNIFORM! I WON'T NEED IT ANY MORE!

MEANWHILE, THE ADMIRAL ISSUES A STERN ORDER—

WE HAVE SEARCHED EVERYWHERE, SIR. ENSIGN MARTIN CAN'T BE FOUND—

ARREST HIM ON SIGHT!

BUT, SIR. I KNOW MARTIN WELL—AN OLD FRIEND OF MINE AND THE MOST LOYAL—

HIS DISAPPEARANCE AFTER BRINGING THAT BOTTLE HERE LOOKS MIGHTY BAD. BUT COME, WE MUST GET ON WITH THE LAUNCHING!

BUT, SIR—

THE LAUNCHING GOES ON—

DON'T BE AFRAID, MISS PRINCE. THIS BOTTLE HAS BEEN CAREFULLY EXAMINED—

I CHRISTEN THEE OCTOPUS!

I'LL HAVE TO WATCH STEVE—HE MIGHT GET INTO TROUBLE TRYING TO HELP HIS FRIEND.

"THE OCTOPUS" GLIDES GRACEFULLY INTO THE WATER—

SHE'LL STRIKE BACK AT THE ENEMIES OF DEMOCRACY!

SHE CERTAINLY LOOKS GOOD!

THIS WILL BE INTERESTING! THE SUB-COMMANDER IS GOING TO REPORT OVER THAT LOUD SPEAKER—AFTER SUBMERGING—

HOW FASCINATING!

BUT IMMEDIATELY UPON SUBMERGING, THERE IS TROUBLE BELOW--

WHY AREN'T WE MOVING?

I DON'T KNOW, SIR! THE ENGINES ARE GOING FULL SPEED!

WE'RE HAVING SOME DIFFICULTY. SHE SEEMS STUCK AT THE BOTTOM!

I THOUGHT THIS COULDN'T HAPPEN TO YOUR INVENTION!

IT CAN'T! SHE HAS ENOUGH POWER TO CUT RIGHT THROUGH RIVER MUD!

THIS IS TERRIBLE. HAVE ALL EMERGENCY CRAFT STAND BY!

YES, SIR!

FEAR SPREADS AMONG THE ONLOOKERS--

OH! MY HUSBAND'S DOWN THERE --

COME, NOW, I'M SURE THEY'LL BE ALL RIGHT.

DON'T CRY. DADDY WILL COME BACK TO US.

WHOEVER IS RESPONSIBLE FOR THIS "ACCIDENT" COULD EXPLAIN MARTIN'S DISAPPEARANCE --

COME, STEVE, WE MIGHT BE OF SOME USE.

BUT SUDDENLY SOMETHING CATCHES STEVE'S EYE--

WAIT A MINUTE!

WHAT IS IT, STEVE?

MEANWHILE, LOCKED IN THE CABIN OF THE SEA-GOING TUG--- THE FRIEND WHOM STEVE TRUSTS!

IT'S NO USE! BEEN TRYING AN HOUR--GUESS THIS TIN CAN ISN'T SHINY ENOUGH TO SEND FLASH SIGNALS.

DIANA SEES AND READS THE SIGNALS AS WELL AS STEVE-- BUT HE DOESN'T KNOW THAT.

BUT STEVE! WHERE ARE YOU GOING?

THAT WAS AN S.O.S. FROM HIS FRIEND AND STEVE'S HEADING FOR TROUBLE!

I'LL EXPLAIN LATER! YOU'D BETTER GO BACK TO THE COLONEL!

SPURRED TO ACTION BY STEVE'S IMMINENT DANGER, THE DEMURE LITTLE ARMY NURSE BECOMES ONCE AGAIN THAT GLORIOUS CREATURE OF STRENGTH AND BEAUTY---THE *WONDER WOMAN!*

IF I KNOW STEVE, HE'LL HEAD RIGHT FOR THAT BOAT! AND SO WILL I - AS THE *WONDER WOMAN!*

IN MIDSTREAM---

I'LL GET MARTIN OUT OF THIS JAM IF IT'S THE LAST THING I DO! *SAY,* THAT SPEED BOAT IS HEADED STRAIGHT FOR ME!

I THINK WE'RE GOING TO THE SAME PLACE, SO HOP IN!

WONDER WOMAN!

WHILE ON THE TUG---

VELL, VE GOT THAT SUB IN TROUBLE - AND VE MAKE MORE YET! GIFF AN ORDER TO ATTACK THEIR AIR SUPPLY!

SWELL, CHIEF! THAT WILL MAKE THEM THINK THAT INVENTOR DIDN'T DO SO GOOD!

BUT EVEN AS THE GHASTLY ORDER IS GIVEN-

THOSE RATS! THEY'LL SUFFOCATE THE MEN DOWN THERE! HAVE TO MAKE A DESPERATE EFFORT TO STOP THEM!

YOU WORMS!

PROCEED AS ORDERED - HEY!

THAT ENSIGN! HE'S LOOSE! STOP HIM!

THIS WILL STOP HIM!

ACH! THESE AMERICANS ARE SO STUBBORN THEY DON'T KNOW WHEN THEY'RE BEATEN!

VE HAVE TO GET RID OF HIM. DESE VEIGHTS WILL TAKE HIM DOWN TO DAVY JONES' LOCKER!

YEAH— AND THEY'LL NEVER FIND OUT IT WASN'T HIM WHO SPIKED THAT CHAMPAGNE!

⑤

GOOD RIDDANCE, AMERICAN FOOL!

'S'LONG, DOPE! THANKS FOR THE USE OF THE UNIFORM!

HELP!

BUT NEARBY---STEVE AND THE WONDER WOMAN!

DID YOU SEE THAT? THEY THREW SOMEONE OVER THE SIDE!

YES! JUST WAIT HERE!

WITH THE GRACE OF A MERMAID AND THE SPEED OF A BARRACUDA, WONDER WOMAN CLEAVES THE WATER AND SWIMS FAR BELOW THE SURFACE—!

MUST REACH HIM IN TIME! THESE PUNY MEN CAN'T STAY UNDER WATER AS LONG AS I CAN.

A WOMAN! I MUST BE SEEING THINGS!

NOTHING LIKE A NICE COOL DIP ON A WARM DAY!

BURDENED WITH THE MAN AND THE HEAVY WEIGHTS, WONDER WOMAN'S SPEED IS UNSTINTED.

HE'LL BE ALL RIGHT!

IT'S MARTIN! THOSE RATS WERE TRYING TO KILL HIM!

WE'LL PAY OUR FRIENDS A VISIT! MEANWHILE, SUPPOSE YOU TELL US WHAT THIS IS ALL ABOUT!

ALL I KNOW IS THAT I WAS TAKING A BOTTLE OF CHAMPAGNE TO THE ADMIRAL WHEN A BUNCH OF THUGS ATTACKED ME AND THEN ONE OF THEM MADE HIM-SELF UP TO LOOK LIKE ME!

SO THAT WAS IT!

BUT AS THE SPEEDBOAT NEARS THE TUG—

DOT BOAT! IT'S COMING OVER HERE.

A DOSE OF THIS WILL SCARE THEM AWAY!

SHOTS RAIN ACROSS THE SPEED BOAT—

DUCK! YOU'LL BE HURT!

HOW ABOUT YOURSELF?

WITH AN EYE FASTER THAN THE SPEED OF BULLETS, WONDER WOMAN WARDS OFF THE DEADLY HAIL WITH HER BRACELETS!

I'LL TAKE CARE OF MYSELF! JUST STAY HERE TILL I CALL FOR YOU!—AND KEEP 'EM FLYING!

THE PARTY'S OVER, BOYS—TURN IN YOUR TICKETS AND GET OFF THE MERRY-GO-ROUND!

HIMMEL! BULLETS DON'T HURT HER!

SHE'S LIKE SOMETHING YOU READ ABOUT!

YOU'RE RIGHT! AND WHILE YOU'RE AT IT, TRY READING ABOUT THIS!

MEANWHILE, STEVE DECIDES TO PITCH IN—

I CAN'T JUST WAIT HERE—I WANT TO GET MY HANDS ON THOSE BABIES!

DROP THAT GUN! THEY'RE BAD THINGS TO PLAY WITH!

BANG!

THE CREW IS TERRIFIED BY THE ONSLAUGHT OF STEVE AND WONDER WOMAN!

ENOUGH! WE'VE HAD ENOUGH!

ALL RIGHT, THAT'S BETTER! DROP YOUR GUNS AND GIVE UP!

BUT TREACHERY IS STILL IN THE SPY LEADER'S HEART---

COME ON, YOU—GET ON YOUR FEET—

HIM I GET, ANYWAY!

BUT JUST THEN ENSIGN MARTIN, HIS STRENGTH RECOVERED, JOINS THE PARTY—

SAY! IF THERE'S A FIGHT, I WANT TO BE IN IT!

AGH! A GHOSTER!

SAY! YOU ARE SUPPOSED TO BE DROWNED!

I'M PRETTY HARD TO CONVINCE!

I'M GETTING OFF THIS TUG!

GHOSTERS ARE MORE DANGEROUS AS SHE-DEVILS!

THIS BOAT IS HAUNTED!

OUR FRIENDS HAVE ALL JUMPED OVERBOARD!

WELL! I TOLD YOU TWO TO WAIT OUT THERE FOR ME!

NOW WE'LL HAVE TO START ALL OVER AGAIN AND ROUND THEM UP!

BUT THEY'VE GOT A GOOD START—

AND THEY'RE SWIMMING IN ALL DIRECTIONS!

BUT STEVE AND MARTIN DO NOT NOTICE WHAT WONDER WOMAN SEES—A SAILING PARTY OF GIRLS FROM HOLLIDAY COLLEGE, HEADED BY THEIR CHUBBY LEADER, ETTA CANDY!

YO! HO! LASSIES! ADVENTURE AHEAD! OR I DON'T KNOW FLASH SIGNALS FROM WONDER WOMAN'S BRACELETS WHEN I SEE THEM!

FLICKING HER SHINY BRACELETS IN THE SUN, WONDER WOMAN INSTRUCTS HER ALLIES FROM HOLLIDAY COLLEGE!

SAY, WHAT ARE YOU DOING, ANYWAY?

YOU'D BE SURPRISED!

8

THOSE MEN IN THE WATER, GIRLS! UP-ER—**DOWN AND AT 'EM!**

BEETA LAMBDA

LIKE A SCHOOL OF INFURIATED MERMAIDS, THE HOLLIDAY GIRLS LASH OUT FOR THEIR VICTIMS!

SHOULD HAVE LEFT THIS CANDY ON DECK—NOW I'LL HAVE TO KEEP IT DRY!

THE MEN FIND THEMSELVES SURROUNDED ON ALL SIDES.

ACH! FIRST SHE-DEVILS--THEN GHOSTERS--NOW **MERMAIDS!**

WHO'S THEM DAMES?

ETTA GIVES A COMMAND—

SUBMERGE AND ATTACK!

AND THE GIRLS GO INTO ACTION!

THIS IS LOTS OF FUN!

JUST LIKE WATER POLO!

BLUB BLUB

BLUB-B

UNABLE TO STAND THE UNDER-WATER ANTICS OF THE GIRLS, THE MEN PROVE EASY VICTIMS!

REMEMBER OUR LIFE-SAVING COURSE, GIRLS! ROLL OUT THE BARRELS! THESE EGGS ARE BAD ENOUGH **ALIVE!**

⑨

BUT A REAL CATASTROPHE HAS BEFALLEN THE BON BON-LOVING ETTA CANDY!

OH! MY CANDY! IT WAS DUNKED!

BUT HER SORROW TURNS TO JOY!

HAVE TO EAT IT, ANYWAY—IT'S ALL I HAVE ABOARD.

OHH! IT TASTES LIKE SALTWATER TAFFY.

MEANWHILE, BACK ON SHORE, THINGS HAVEN'T BEEN GOING SO WELL—

SAFETY BUOYS JAMMED— SEND HELP QUICK— OXYGEN FAILING

EVERYTHING'S GOING WRONG! SOMETHING'S RESPONSIBLE FOR THIS! YOU MUST DO SOMETHING TO SAVE THE MEN ABOARD THE "OCTOPUS"!

I CAN'T UNDERSTAND IT! THAT SUB WAS FOOLPROOF! PERHAPS WE'D BETTER SEND ANOTHER DIVER. I CAN'T IMAGINE WHAT HAPPENED TO THE OTHER TWO!

WHILE ON THE TUG—

TOO BAD THOSE MEN GOT AWAY!

MAYBE THEY DID NOT—SH—LISTEN TO THAT!

STILL HAVE SUB GROUNDED— UNDER MAGNETIC CONTROL— HAVE PUMPED CARBON DIOXIDE— WILL BOARD AND TAKE OVER WHEN CREW IS UNCONSCIOUS—

YOU WAIT HERE AND DON'T TRY TO BE HEROES! I'LL BE RIGHT BACK!

SAY, WHERE ARE YOU GOING? BLAZES! SHE'S GONE AGAIN!

DEEPER— DEEPER— DEEPER— THE WONDER WOMAN DIVES STRAIGHT TO THE SCENE OF THE DISTRESSED SUBMARINE!

ONE MORE DIVER HAS ATTEMPTED THE DANGEROUS TASK—

THAT DIVER NEEDS MY PROTECTION!

WHILE THE DIVER DISCOVERS AND DETACHES THE DEADLY CARBON DIOXIDE LINE, A STRANGE CRAFT NEARBY DISGORGES AN UNDERSEA BOARDING PARTY WHICH PREPARES TO ATTACK THE GROUNDED SUBMARINE———

ADVANCE SCOUTS ATTACK THE LONE DIVER.

THIS CALLS FOR ACTION— HOPE MY BREATH HOLDS OUT!

THEY'VE SEVERED HIS AIR LINE! I'LL HAVE TO GET THIS MAN TO THE SURFACE!

WITH HER LAST BREATH **WONDER WOMAN** MANAGES TO BRING THE DIVER TO THE SURFACE——

HE'LL BE ALL RIGHT! WHEW! JUST ABOUT MADE IT!

SAY! WHAT'S GOING ON HERE? WHO ARE YOU? WHAT HAPPENED TO THIS DIVER?

CAN'T ANSWER NOW! THERE'S MORE WORK TO DO!

IT'S THE **WONDER WOMAN!** SHE'LL SAVE MY SUBMARINE!

LIKE A HUGE FISH—THE STRANGE UNDERSEA CRAFT OF THE ENEMIES OF DEMOCRACY—

THIS IS THE THING FROM WHICH THOSE UNDERSEA SOLDIERS ARE OPERATING! I HAVE TO DESTROY IT!

OH! I'M CAUGHT! I COULD BREAK LOOSE, BUT PERHAPS I'D BETTER SEE WHAT HAPPENS—

WONDER WOMAN IS DRAWN INSIDE THE STRANGE CRAFT—

WHOEVER YOU ARE, YOU'RE OUR PRISONER!

WELL, I'M IN!

NOW TO FIGHT MY WAY OUT AGAIN!

THEY DON'T MAKE BULLETS AS GOOD AS THEY USED TO!

I HAVE TO SMASH THESE CONTROLS! I GUESS THIS HEAVY OBJECT WILL DO—

11

HOW DO YOU LIKE **THOSE** APPLES?

HIMMEL! I SEE IT BUT I DON'T BELIEVE IT! THE CONTROLS! THEY ARE SMASHED!

THIS WILL MAKE GOOD JUNK WHEN I'M THROUGH WITH IT!

HELP!

I'M AGAINST WAR FROM NOW ON!

MEANWHILE, THE BOARDING PARTY IS ATTACKING THE AMERICAN SUBMARINE—

BUT WITH THE DESTRUCTION OF THE ENEMY CRAFT, WHICH HELD THE SUBMARINE IN PLACE BY MAGNETIC FORCE, THE SUBMARINE GLIDES EASILY AWAY—

SHE'S GETTING AWAY!

ACH!

AND ABOARD THE AMERICAN SUBMARINE HOPE COMES AT THE LAST MINUTE

WE WON'T BE ABLE TO HOLD OUT MUCH LONGER— WHAT'S THAT? SHE'S RISING!

WONDER WOMAN, HAVING DISABLED THE CRAFT, PREPARES TO LEAVE—

ARE YOU GOING TO LEAVE US HERE TO DIE LIKE RATS IN A TRAP?

THAT'S WHAT YOU PLANNED TO DO TO THE MEN IN "THE OCTOPUS"! BUT DON'T WORRY— I'LL HAVE A SALVAGE CREW CALL FOR YOU. JUST DON'T OPEN THIS DOOR AFTER I SHUT IT, AND YOU'LL BE SAFE ENOUGH!

IN THE NEXT COMPARTMENT—

THIS STEEL BENDS SO EASILY!

AGAINST THE IN-RUSHING WATER WONDER WOMAN MAKES HER EXIT—

TIME TO GET BACK! I MIGHT BE NEEDED— AS DIANA PRINCE.

"THE OCTOPUS" AFLOAT AGAIN! MUST HURRY NOW—

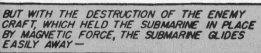

WHILE CHANGING TO HER EVERY DAY GUISE, *WONDER WOMAN* MAKES A HURRIED CALL TO THE ADMIRAL—

WHAT! YES, YES, YES, I'LL DO EVERYTHING YOU SAY- BUT *WONDER WOMAN- WONDER WOMAN!* SHE'S HUNG UP!

THEN, AS DIANA PRINCE, SHE HURRIES TO BE IN ON THINGS!

YOU'RE A NURSE, MISS PRINCE! GET ON THAT TENDER! CAPTAIN TREVOR AND ENSIGN MARTIN MIGHT NEED SOME FIRST AID!

STEVE DOESN'T KNOW HOW CLOSE HE IS TO THE REAL *WONDER WOMAN!*

STEVE, ARE YOU ALL RIGHT?

YES—THANKS TO THAT WONDERFUL *WONDER WOMAN!*

YES! SHE HELPED TO CLEAR MY NAME!

WHILE BACK ON SHORE, ETTA CANDY HAS ARRIVED WITH HER CAPTIVES...

WONDER WOMAN TOLD US TO HAND THEM OVER TO YOU!

THAT WOMAN AGAIN! SAY! WHO'S RUNNING THIS NAVY ANYWAY?

THEN MY SUBMARINE IS A SUCCESS AFTER ALL!

YES! WITH THE AID OF AMERICAN COURAGE, IT WITHSTOOD EVERYTHING THE ENEMIES OF DEMOCRACY COULD OFFER!

AND OUT IN THE BAY A NAVAL SALVAGE CREW DOES SOME STRANGE FISHING...

DOT VONDER WOMAN! ACH!

SAY, WHAT'S THE LOWDOWN ON THIS *WONDER WOMAN?*

DUNNO. BUT I'D SURE LIKE TO HAVE HER RESCUE ME!

WELL, THE LAUNCHING WAS EXCITING, WASN'T IT?

LAUNCHING? OH, YES...

I WONDER IF I'LL SEE HER AGAIN- THAT WONDERFUL, WONDERFUL *WONDER WOMAN*

POOR DIANA DOESN'T RATE WHEN STEVE'S THINKING ABOUT *WONDER WOMAN!* FOLLOW HER AMAZING ADVENTURES EVERY MONTH IN *SENSATION COMICS!*

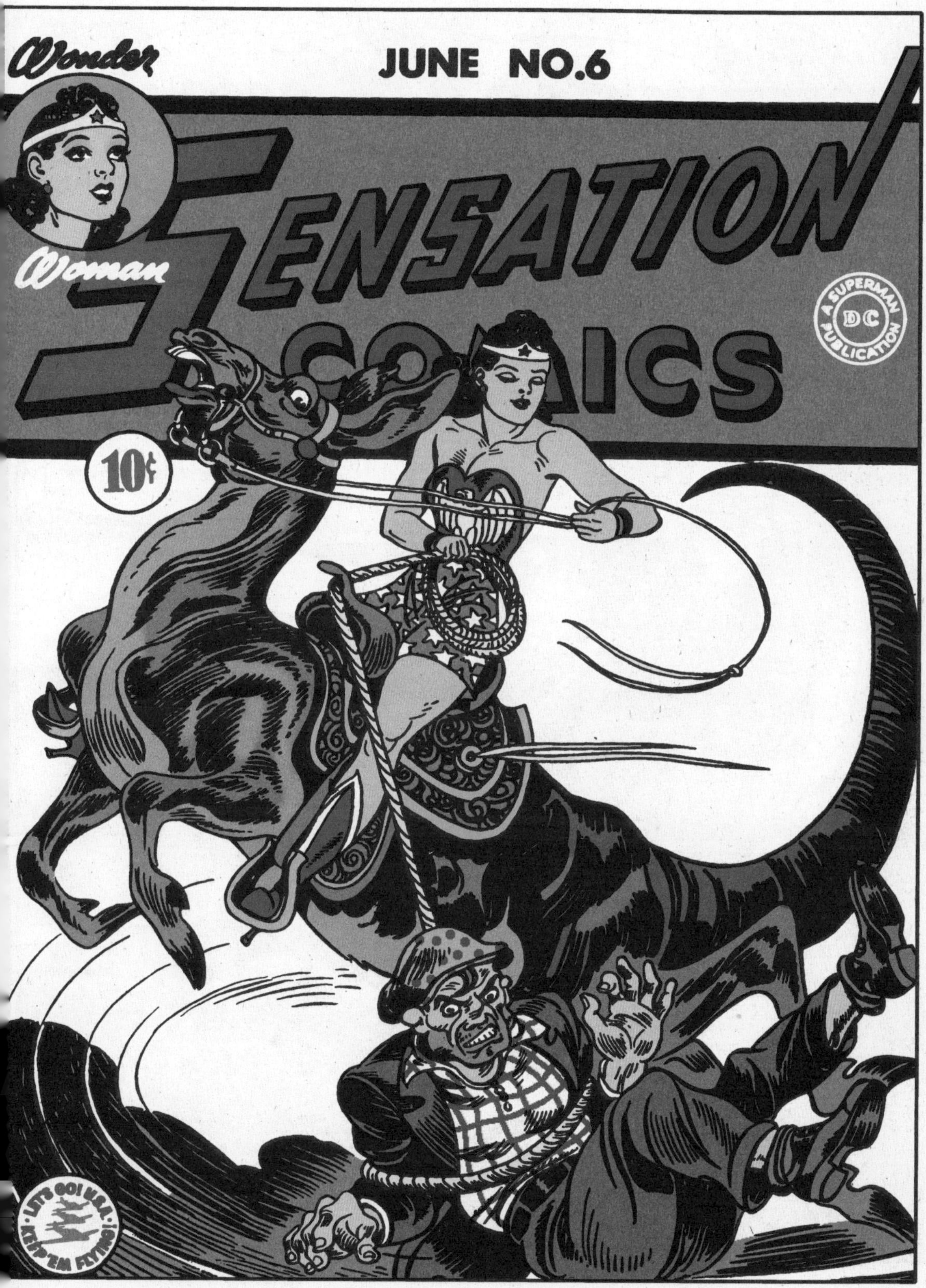
Wonder Woman
JUNE NO.6
SENSATION COMICS
10¢
A SUPERMAN DC PUBLICATION
LET'S GO! U.S.A. KEEP 'EM FLYING!

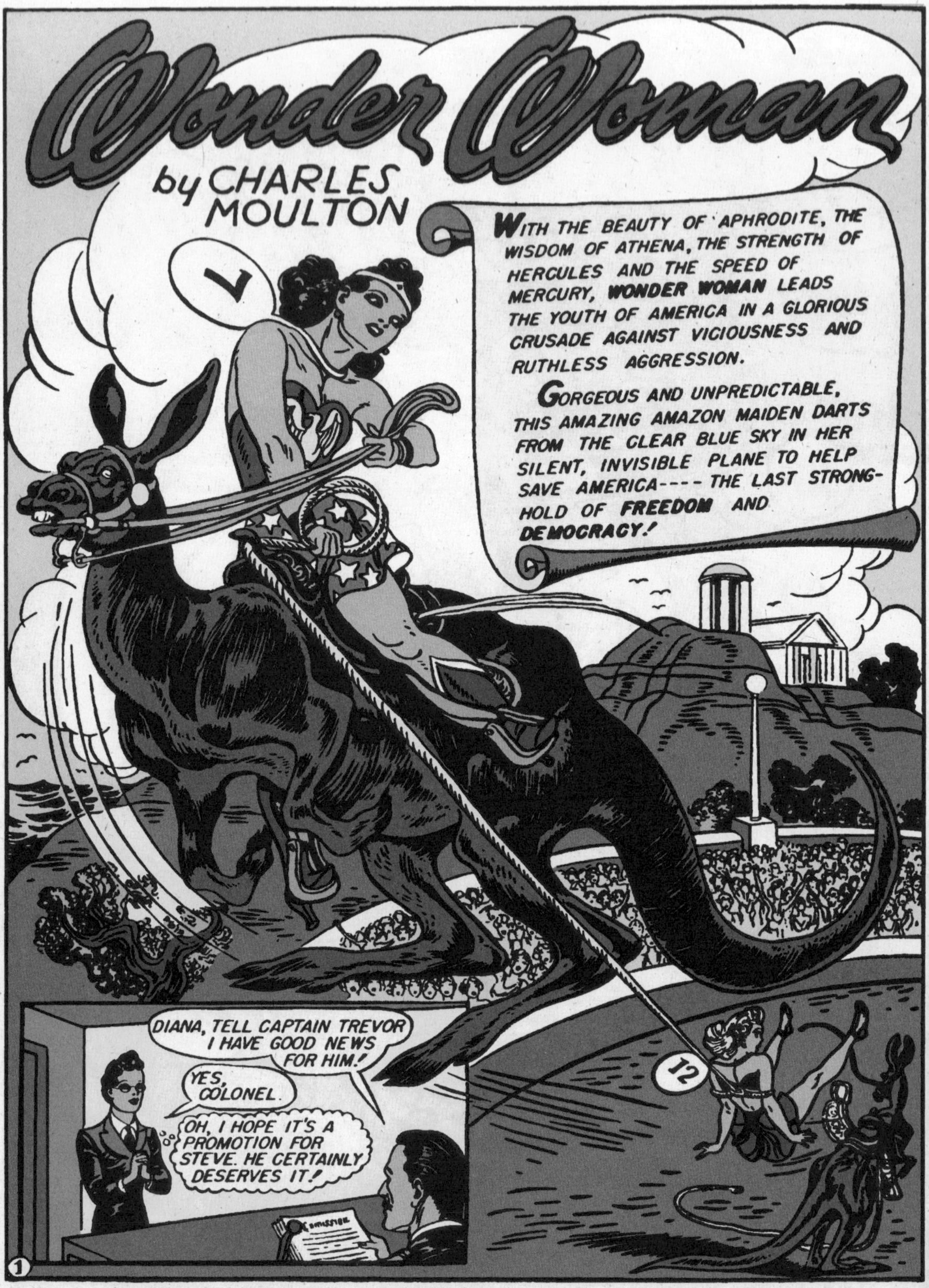

Wonder Woman
by CHARLES MOULTON
WITH THE BEAUTY OF APHRODITE, THE WISDOM OF ATHENA, THE STRENGTH OF HERCULES AND THE SPEED OF MERCURY, WONDER WOMAN LEADS THE YOUTH OF AMERICA IN A GLORIOUS CRUSADE AGAINST VICIOUSNESS AND RUTHLESS AGGRESSION.
GORGEOUS AND UNPREDICTABLE, THIS AMAZING AMAZON MAIDEN DARTS FROM THE CLEAR BLUE SKY IN HER SILENT, INVISIBLE PLANE TO HELP SAVE AMERICA---- THE LAST STRONG-HOLD OF FREEDOM AND DEMOCRACY!
7
12
DIANA, TELL CAPTAIN TREVOR I HAVE GOOD NEWS FOR HIM!
YES, COLONEL.
OH, I HOPE IT'S A PROMOTION FOR STEVE. HE CERTAINLY DESERVES IT!
1

YOU ARE PROMOTED TO THE RANK OF MAJOR — CONGRATU-LATIONS! YOU HAVE DONE SPLENDID WORK BREAKING UP SPY-PLOTS!

THANKS, COLONEL! BUT I REALLY DON'T DESERVE THIS-ALL THE CREDIT BELONGS TO WONDER WOMAN!

CONFIDENTIALLY, MAJOR, I AM GOING TO ENGLAND ON A MISSION OF THE UTMOST IMPORTANCE! SAILING PLANS MUST BE KEPT ABSOLUTELY SECRET!

THEY SHALL BE, SIR!

DURING MY ABSENCE THE GENERAL HAS APPOINTED YOU ACTING COMMANDING OFFICER OF THE INTELLIGENCE SERVICE.

I'LL DO MY BEST, COLONEL!

YOU'LL NEED ME AS YOUR SECRETARY WHILE THE COLONEL IS AWAY! I UNDERSTAND HIS WORK.

YOU UNDERSTAND HOW TO WORK THE COLO-NEL! BUT I AM MAJOR TREVOR'S SECRETARY.

NOW GIRLS-DON'T QUARREL!

IN FAIRNESS TO LILA, I MUST KEEP HER AS MY SECRETARY. YOU, DIANA, MAY TAKE A TWO-WEEKS VACATION UNTIL THE COLONEL RETURNS.

YOU'RE RIGHT—I'M SORRY I SPOKE!

THAT'LL SHOW HER—THE CHISELER.

WHILE CLEANING OUT LILA'S DESK, DIANA FINDS A LETTER THREATENING STEVE—

WHAT'S THIS LETTER DOING IN LILA'S DESK? I'D BETTER READ IT!

To Captain Trevor
So you thought you could have me executed! Bah! For that I shall kill you - as I have killed all the others! Baroness Paula von Gunther

WHY DIDN'T YOU GIVE THIS LETTER TO MAJOR TREVOR?

I DID -- HE ONLY LAUGHED! HE TOLD ME TO FORGET IT. BUT I KEPT THE LETTER!

THE BARONESS IS AS DANGEROUS AS A RATTLESNAKE! WHY ISN'T SHE IN PRISON?

SHE ESCAPED FROM THE POLICE. THEY MADE A NATIONWIDE SEARCH FOR HER, BUT COULDN'T FIND A SINGLE CLUE!

LATER IN THE EVENING, DIANA FEELS A STRONG CONTACT WITH PARADISE ISLAND, THE HOME OF HER PEOPLE, THE AMAZONS.

I MUST FIND THE BARONESS BEFORE SHE MURDERS STEVE! BUT SOMEHOW I KEEP EXPECTING A MENTAL RADIO MESSAGE FROM MOTHER!

QUEEN HYPOLYTE, MEANWHILE, IS FOLLOWING HER DAUGHTER'S CAREER IN THE MAGIC SPHERE.

DIANA IS DOING WELL IN THE WORLD OF MEN! BUT I SEE SHE NEEDS HELP. I WILL CONSULT THE GODDESSES!

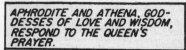

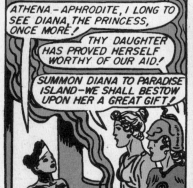

APHRODITE AND ATHENA, GODDESSES OF LOVE AND WISDOM, RESPOND TO THE QUEEN'S PRAYER.

ATHENA—APHRODITE, I LONG TO SEE DIANA THE PRINCESS, ONCE MORE!

THY DAUGHTER HAS PROVED HERSELF WORTHY OF OUR AID!

SUMMON DIANA TO PARADISE ISLAND—WE SHALL BESTOW UPON HER A GREAT GIFT!

OVER THE MENTAL RADIO TO DIANA COMES HER MOTHER'S MESSAGE.

DAUGHTER, RETURN IMMEDIATELY TO PARADISE ISLAND!

OH! HOW WONDERFUL! HOME — I CAN GO TO PARADISE ISLAND FOR MY VACATION!

IN THE OLD BARN, WHERE HER AMAZON AIRPLANE IS HIDDEN, NURSE DIANA BECOMES WONDER WOMAN.

THIS COSTUME FEELS GRAND! THE AMAZON GIRLS HAVE NEVER SEEN ME IN IT; THEY WON'T KNOW ME!

LIKE A RAY OF SUNLIGHT, WONDER WOMAN'S INVISIBLE PLANE DARTS OVER THE OCEAN AT 2000 MILES AN HOUR!

③

MY LOCASCOPE SHOWS I'M OVER PARADISE ISLAND, BUT IT'S COMPLETELY HIDDEN BY CLOUDS! I'LL TURN ON MY ELECTRONIC MIST BEAM.

A POWERFUL LIGHT RAY FROM WONDER WOMAN'S PLANE PENETRATES THE DENSE CLOUD FORMATIONS AND MAKES A RAINBOW PATH TO THE AMAZON LANDING FIELD.

OH! THE AMAZON GIRLS ARE HAVING AN ATHLETIC MEET! I'LL ENTER THE NEXT CONTEST INCOGNITO WITH A MASK ON. NO ONE WILL KNOW ME.

WONDER WOMAN'S SILENT, INVISIBLE PLANE ENABLES HER TO LAND SECRETLY NEAR THE STADIUM.

I'LL GET THE ANNOUNCEMENT OF THE NEXT CONTEST OVER THE RADIO

AMAZONS, ATTENTION! THE NEXT COMPETITION WILL BE A GIRL-ROPING CONTEST! GIRLS, GET YOUR LASSOS AND MOUNT YOUR KANGAS!

WONDER WOMAN HASTILY SADDLES HER FAVORITE KANGA.

YOU'RE GLAD TO SEE ME AGAIN AREN'T YOU, JUMPA? WE'LL SHOW THEM.

THIS CONTEST IS A FREE-FOR-ALL! YOU WILL LASSO AN OPPONENT, PULL HER TO THE GROUND, AND TIE HER UP. ATTENDANTS WILL FURNISH FRESH LARIATS AND CARRY DEFEATED CONTESTANTS OFF THE FIELD!

THE CONTEST IS ON! FURIOUSLY THE AMAZON GIRLS SWING THEIR LASSOS WHILE THEIR MIGHTY KANGAS LEAP FIFTY FEET INTO THE AIR.

GOT HER! THAT MAKES ELEVEN GIRLS I'VE CAPTURED!

AT LAST, ONLY WONDER WOMAN AND MALA, THE AMAZON CHAMPION, REMAIN IN THE CONTEST.

I'LL GET YOU THIS TIME, MYSTERY MAIDEN! AND I'LL PULL THAT MASK OFF YOUR FACE!

THAT'S WHAT YOU THINK!

MALA'S SKILL WITH THE LASSO IS UNCANNY AND—

HOW DO YOU LIKE THAT? NOW I'LL PULL YOU OFF YOUR KANGA AND TIE YOU UP!

WONDER WOMAN IS CAUGHT BUT NO ROPE CAN HOLD HER!

WHY DON'T YOU USE A STRONGER LASSO, MALA? LIKE MINE, FOR INSTANCE!

IT'S NOT FAIR! IF MY LASSO HADN'T BROKEN—

WHY DON'T YOU BREAK MY ROPE, IF YOU CAN?

WONDER WOMAN TIES HER OPPONENT IN WORKMANLIKE FASHION.

LET'S SEE YOU WIGGLE OUT OF THIS TIE-UP, GIRL-FRIEND!

I CAN'T— I SURRENDER!

⑤

THE GIRLS WONDER WOMAN HAS DEFEATED CARRY HER ENTHUSIASTICALLY TO THE JUDGE'S STAND—

HOLA! HOORAH FOR OUR ROPING CHAMP! SHE'S WONDERFUL!

I DECLARE YOU CHAMPION—ER—WHO ARE YOU? REMOVE YOUR MASK!

IT'S THE PRINCESS!

THE PRINCESS HAS RETURNED!

Panel 1: THE QUEEN, MEANWHILE, AT THE COMMAND OF APHRODITE AND ATHENA, DIRECTS HER CRAFTSWOMEN IN A STRANGE TASK.

DO YOU RECOGNIZE THIS BELT?

YES, YOUR MAJESTY! IT IS YOUR MAGIC GIRDLE, WHICH MAKES US INVINCIBLE!

Panel 2: THE MAGIC GIRDLE IS MADE OF MILLIONS OF FINE CHAIN LINKS. THESE ARE UNBREAKABLE! YOU WILL TAKE LINKS FROM THE GIRDLE AND MAKE A MAGIC LASSO, FLEXIBLE AS ROPE BUT STRONG ENOUGH TO HOLD HERCULES!

Panel 3: THE MAGIC LASSO IS DELIVERED TO THE QUEEN—

THIS IS THE SLENDEREST CHAIN EVER MADE, YOUR MAJESTY!

YET IT CANNOT BE BROKEN. YOU HAVE DONE WELL, METALA!

Panel 4: DAUGHTER! HOW GLAD I AM TO SEE YOU!

MOTHER!

Panel 5: I THOUGHT I'D NEVER BE PERMITTED TO COME BACK TO PARADISE ISLAND!

ALAS! YOU CANNOT STAY, DARLING! THE GODDESSES HAVE SUMMONED YOU TO REWARD YOU FOR YOUR SPLENDID WORK IN THE WORLD OF MEN!

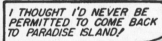

Panel 6: THIS MAGIC LASSO WAS MADE FOR YOU AT OUR GODDESSES' COMMAND!

WHY—IT'S MADE OF CHAIN! HOW MARVELOUS!

Panel 7: THIS CHAIN-ROPE IS PERFECTLY BALANCED! IT THROWS BEAUTIFULLY!

CAREFUL, DAUGHTER! YOU'LL HURT METALA!

AWK! THE PRINCESS DOESN'T KNOW HER OWN STRENGTH!

Panel 8: ALL NIGHT WONDER WOMAN PRAYS TO APHRODITE AND ATHENA, AND AT DAWN—

HAVING PROVED THYSELF BOUND BY LOVE AND WISDOM, WE GIVE THEE POWER TO CONTROL OTHERS! WHOMSOEVER THY MAGIC LASSO BINDS MUST OBEY THEE!

WONDER WOMAN TRIES OUT HER NEW POWER—

GOOD MORNING, MALA! YOU'RE UP EARLY!

I HEARD YOU WERE GOING BACK TO THE WORLD OF MEN. I WANT TO GO WITH YOU!

NO, MALA! I MUST GO ALONE! NO OTHER AMAZON MAIDEN MUST GIVE UP HER HERITAGE!

I DON'T CARE— I'M GOING ANYWAY!

MALA! YOU MUST NOT TRY TO FOLLOW ME—

I'M GOING TO FOLLOW YOU IN MY SPEED PLANE— TRY TO STOP ME!

SO YOU WANT ME TO STOP YOU, EH?

E-E-E-K! LET ME GO!

YOU ARE BOUND BY MY MAGIC LASSO— YOU MUST OBEY ME! PROMISE THAT YOU WILL NOT FOLLOW ME TODAY IN YOUR PLANE.

I PROMISE!

AFTER LOCATING THE MURDEROUS BARONESS ON THE MAGIC SPHERE, WONDER WOMAN BIDS HER MOTHER FAREWELL.

LET LOVE AND WISDOM GUIDE YOU, DAUGHTER, IN THE WORLD OF MEN!

OF COURSE! GOODBYE, MOTHER DARLING!

AND SO WONDER WOMAN'S SILENT, INVISIBLE PLANE GLIDES SWIFTLY BACK ACROSS FAR SEAS TO AMERICA—

BUT WONDER WOMAN'S HAPPY MEMORIES OF PARADISE ISLAND ARE SHATTERED ABRUPTLY AS SHE TURNS ON THE RADIO—

A BOMB EXPLODED TODAY IN MAJOR STEPHEN TREVOR'S OFFICE! FORTUNATELY TREVOR HAD CHANGED OFFICES.

SO THAT WARNING NOTE WAS NO FAKE. THE BARONESS'S AGENTS PLANTED THAT BOMB!

HIDING HER PLANE, **WONDER WOMAN** RACES AT A TERRIFIC RATE OF SPEED TO TREVOR'S OFFICE—

I MUST TELL STEVE WHAT I LEARNED IN THE MAGIC SPHERE ABOUT THE BARONESS—

HONK!!

WONDER WOMAN, MY ANGEL! YOU ALWAYS COME WHEN I NEED HELP!

THAT'S AN ANGEL'S JOB. TELL ME YOUR TROUBLES.

COLONEL DARNELL SAILED FOR ENGLAND ON A SECRET MISSION— HIS SHIP DISAPPEARED!

DISAPPEARED! WHAT DO YOU MEAN?

DARNELL'S SHIP WAS IN CONVOY. IT COULDN'T HAVE BEEN SUNK—NO SUBMARINES NEAR. WE LOST CONTACT! THE DESTROYERS SEARCHED BUT THE SHIP WAS GONE!

WHAT SHIP IS IT?

THE COLONEL IS ON THE GIGANTIC!

THE **GIGANTIC**! GREAT TEARS OF APHRODITE!

TO SOLVE THE MYSTERY OF THE DISAPPEARING SHIP, LET US GO BACK AND FOLLOW THE BARONESS PAULA, GESTAPO AGENT AND MURDERESS, ON HER WAY TO PRISON.

YOU ARE SO KIND, OFFICER— AND HANDSOME!

SORRY TO DO THIS BUT I MUST HAVE THE KEY TO THESE HANDCUFFS— AND SINCE YOU'D NEVER GIVE IT UP ALIVE— WELL—

RELEASING HERSELF FROM HER HANDCUFFS, THE BARONESS ESCAPES AND ISSUES ORDERS TO HER AGENTS.

WE HAF PLANTED THE TIME-BOMB, EXCELLENCY!

VERY GOOD. PREPARE THE TEST OF MY INVISIBLE RAY.

3

LIE ON THAT BED, SLAVE!

OH, NO! PLEASE DON'T KILL ME!

WHEN I TURN ON THE CURRENT, BOTH BED AND GIRL BECOME INVISIBLE. I MUST FIND OUT IF MY RAY INJURES ONE WHO DISAPPEARS.

AS THE METAL BED BECOMES ELECTRIFIED, IT GLOWS WITH A STRANGE RAY WHICH BAFFLES HUMAN EYESIGHT.

ACH! VONDERBAR! THE BED ISS GONE!

BUT I CAN HIT IT-

E-EEK! THAT'S ME YOU'RE HITTING!

MY RAY IS A SUCCESS. THE GLOWING METAL DOES NOT HURT HUMANS!

PACK MY INVISIBLE RAY IN THAT TRUNK. CARRY IT TO LADY CHUMPLEY'S CABIN ON THE GIGANTIC. I SHALL BE LADY CHUMPLEY.

IT'S SWEET OF YOU, MY DEAH LADY CHUMPLEY, TO LEND ME YOUR PASSPORT- HOW FORTUNATE THAT WE LOOK ALIKE!

I NEVER DISLIKED MY LOOKS UNTIL NOW! YOU'LL BE SHOT FOR THIS!

BUT THE BARONESS SAILS UNSUSPECTED. AT THE CAPTAIN'S TABLE SHE MEETS AN OLD FRIEND—

LADY CHUMPLEY, COLONEL DARNELL!

I SEEM TO REMEMBER MEETING YOU BEFORE-

OH, RAWTHER NOT, COLONEL! I'M QUITE FRIGHTFULLY SURE WE'VE NEVER MET BEFORE - BUT AFTER ALL WE'VE MET NOW, AND THAT'S WHAT COUNTS, ISN'T IT?

AS THE GIGANTIC NEARS EUROPE THE STRANGE GRIMY FIGURE OF A STOKER SLIPS INTO "LADY CHUMPLEY'S" CABIN—

AH, HANS! HAVE YOU ARRANGED TO DISABLE THE SHIP'S ENGINES?

JA, EXCELLENCY! WHEN-EVER YOU COMMAND!

LET THE ENGINES STOP IN HALF AN HOUR! I WILL MAKE THE VESSEL INVISIBLE!

HO! HO! THAT WILL FOOL THEM! COUNT ON ME, EXCELLENCY!

THROUGH THE PORTHOLE OF HER CABIN THE BARONESS PASSES THE ELECTRIC CABLE OF THE INVISIBLE RAY.

THE POWERFUL MAGNET ON THE END OF THIS CABLE WILL CLAMP IT TO THE SHIP'S METAL HULL.

I'LL TURN THE RAY ON NOW. IN FIFTEEN MINUTES THIS VESSEL WILL BE INVISIBLE! NOW TO WRECK THE SHIP'S RADIO—

CLICK!

GOOD EVENING, LADY CHUMPLEY! MAY I SEND A RADIOGRAM FOR YOU? AW-ULP-AH--

YES! GIVE PAULA VON GUNTHER'S REGARDS TO THE AMERICANS I HAVE KILLED— AND DELIVER THE MESSAGE YOURSELF!

BANG!

THIS SMALL BOMB OUGHT TO RUIN THE RADIO BEYOND REPAIR!

BOOM!

WHAT BLEW UP?

THE RADIO ROOM SIR, COMPLETELY WRECKED-SPARKS WAS SHOT-MUST BE SABOTEURS ON BOARD!

WE'RE LOSING SPEED—WHAT'S THE MATTER?

ENGINES HAVE STOPPED, SIR! WE CAN'T LOCATE THE TROUBLE!

THEY'RE LEAVING US BEHIND! RUN UP DISTRESS FLAGS AND SIGNAL THAT DESTROYER!

AYE, AYE, SIR!

THEY PAY NO ATTENTION, SIR! IT SEEMS THEY DON'T SEE US!

IMPOSSIBLE! THEY MUST SEE THIS SHIP DRIFTING HERE—THE GIGANTIC IS NO ROWBOAT!

THE BARONESS, MEANWHILE, DOES A LITTLE SIGNALING OF HER OWN WITH A PRIVATE RADIO TRANSMITTER.

AH!—THAT'S THE RADIO CODE SIGNAL OF VON LOCHNER'S U-BOAT! I'LL GIVE HIM OUR POSITION—

DIT-DIT DA-DIT

A NAZI SUB! SHALL WE TAKE A SHOT AT HIM, SIR?

NO—HE'S TOO CLOSE. HE'D SINK US BEFORE WE COULD LAUNCH THE BOATS!

BUT THE SUBMARINE COMMANDER CANNOT SEE THE GIGANTIC.

THIS IS THE POSITION THE BARONESS GAVE—BUT THERE'S NO SHIP HERE.

SOME MISTAKE, MEIN HERR! I'LL RADIO THE BARONESS AGAIN!

THE BARONESS, LEARNING THAT THE U-BOAT HAS ARRIVED, TURNS OFF THE INVISIBLE RAY.

NOW VON LOCHNER CAN SEE THE GIGANTIC AND BLOW IT UP! I'LL SAVE COLONEL DARNELL AND MAKE HIM TALK!

GRACIOUS LADY, YOU HAVE DONE BRILLIANTLY! DER FUEHRER HIMSELF COMMENDS YOU!

I HAVE AN UNEXPECTED PRIZE FOR YOU. COLONEL DARNELL, CHIEF OF AMERICAN INTELLIGENCE, IS ON THIS SHIP!

WE WILL TAKE HERR INTELLIGENCE COLONEL WITH US. TO THE REST OF YOU GOOD AMERICANS WE WILL BID FAREWELL.

OF COURSE, YOU'LL GIVE US TIME TO LAUNCH OUR BOATS, COMMANDER?

IT WILL DO LITTLE GOOD TO LAUNCH BOATS, CAPTAIN! I HAVE ORDERS TO SINK THIS SHIP WITH ALL ON BOARD WITHOUT TRACE!

YOU BUTCHERS! YOU MURDERERS! YOU—

WE TRY TO SINK HER WITH ONE TORPEDO. THAT'S GOOD SPORT!

YOU SHOULD HAVE LET THEM LAUNCH THE BOATS. IT WOULD BE FUN TO PICK THEM OFF WITH RIFLES!

MEANWHILE, IN WASHINGTON, TREVOR DESPAIRS OF SAVING THE GIGANTIC.

IT'S NO USE! THE GIGANTIC, WHEN LAST HEARD FROM, WAS TWO THOUSAND MILES AWAY—EVEN THE FASTEST PLANE WOULD TAKE FIVE HOURS TO REACH HER!

I'LL GET YOU THERE IN AN HOUR. COME ON!

LET'S JUMP—I'LL CARRY YOU, STEVE!

NO YOU WON'T! I'M NO PAPOOSE! I'LL GO DOWN THIS ROPE!

SPEEDING FASTER THAN HUMANS HAVE EVER FLOWN BEFORE, WONDER WOMAN HURLS HER SUPER PLANE ACROSS THE ATLANTIC!

THERE'S THE GIGANTIC, STEVE.

YES—AND LOOK! THERE'S A U-BOAT ABOUT TO SINK HER!

THERE GOES THE TORPEDO—WE'RE TOO LATE!

TOO LATE FOR REGRETS! I'M GOING TO POWER DIVE, BACK LOOP AND JUMP! I'LL STOP THE TORPEDO —YOU BOARD THE SUB!

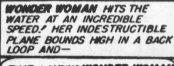

WONDER WOMAN HITS THE WATER AT AN INCREDIBLE SPEED! HER INDESTRUCTIBLE PLANE BOUNDS HIGH IN A BACK LOOP AND—

THAT LANDING WONDER WOMAN MADE WAS A MIRACLE. NOW TO GET THESE NASTIES.

WONDER WOMAN RACES AFTER THE TORPEDO!

THIS MAY BE A RACE WITH A BANG-UP FINISH!

JUST IN TIME SHE CLIMBS ABOARD THE DEADLY MISSILE AND TWISTS ITS STEERING MECHANISM.

BEFORE VON LOCHNER CAN LAUNCH ANOTHER TORPEDO, WONDER WOMAN THROWS HER MAGIC LASSO!

I'VE GOT YOU! ORDER YOUR MEN TO SURRENDER.

NEVER! YOU— ACH! BUT SOMETHING MAKES ME! MEN, LAY DOWN YOUR ARMS!

YOU BOYS MAY FEEL A BIT CHILLY SWIMMING OVER TO THE GIGANTIC. BUT YOU'LL GET A RECEPTION THAT'LL WARM YOU UP!

I THINK I'LL PUT THESE TWO IN A PRISON OF MY OWN CHOOSING AND SEE IF I CAN REFORM THEM! GOODBYE, STEVE. GIVE MY LOVE TO DIANA PRINCE!

YOU SAVED ME AND EVERYONE ON THE GIGANTIC! I DON'T KNOW HOW TO THANK YOU, TREVOR— KEEP 'EM FLYING!

FORGIVE THE USUAL REFRAIN, COLONEL, BUT THANK WONDER WOMAN! MY BEAUTIFUL ANGEL— SHE DID IT ALL!

WITH THIS GREAT GIFT I CAN CHANGE HUMAN CHARACTER! I CAN MAKE BAD MEN GOOD, AND WEAK WOMEN STRONG! BUT I CAN'T USE IT ON DIANA PRINCE. SHE WILL HAVE TO GO ON MOONING OVER STEVE TREVOR, WHILE HE GOES ON MOONING OVER WONDER WOMAN!

A NEW AND STARTLING ADVENTURE OF WONDER WOMAN IN SENSATION COMICS, EVERY MONTH!

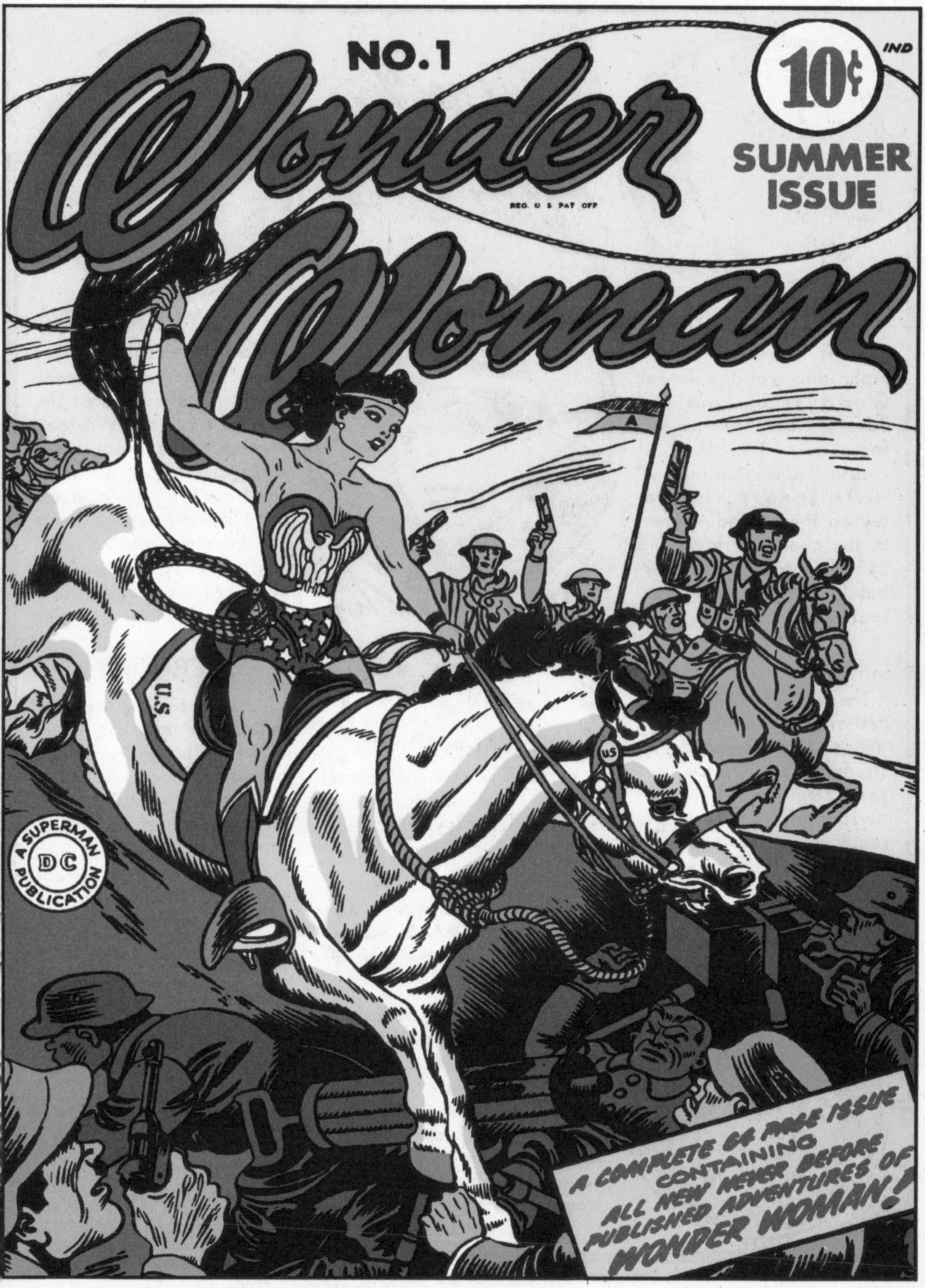
NO. 1
Wonder Woman
REG. U.S. PAT. OFF.
10¢
IND
SUMMER ISSUE
A SUPERMAN DC PUBLICATION
A COMPLETE 64 PAGE ISSUE CONTAINING ALL NEW NEVER BEFORE PUBLISHED ADVENTURES OF WONDER WOMAN!

BEAUTY

Wonder Woman

WISDOM

APHRODITE:-

Most beautiful of all, Aphrodite was the Greek Goddess of Love and Beauty. Born of the sea foam near the Island of Cyprus, she inspired all mortal lovers and protected them, binding men in the chains of love and beauty, forged by her husband, Vulcan, the blacksmith God!

ATHENA:-

Born from the head of Zeus, Father of all Greek Gods, Athena became the Goddess of Wisdom. Though she carried sword and spear to protect mortals from the evils of ignorance, she offered peace as her greatest gift to mankind. Her symbol was the olive branch, representing peace and plenty.

HERCULES:-

The God of Strength was half-mortal and half-God! When a mere child, he strangled two fierce serpents sent to slay him. He performed twelve labors requiring prodigious strength and upon his earthly death, was taken to Mount Olympus to dwell among the Gods ever after.

Who is she?

MERCURY:-

Known to the ancient Greeks as Hermes, God of speed, this gay mischievous young blade who could make himself invisible with his winged cap and transport himself in a flash with his winged sandals, always carried with him his sceptre of speed, two serpents entwined about a winged shaft.

WHERE does she come from? How did she obtain her human, yet invincible abilities?

These are the questions everyone is asking — for WONDER WOMAN has become the talk of the hour all over America!

With the beauty of Aphrodite, the wisdom of Athena, the strength of Hercules and the speed of Mercury, this glamorous Amazon Princess flashes vividly across America's horizon from that mysterious Paradise Isle, where women rule supreme

STRENGTH

SPEED

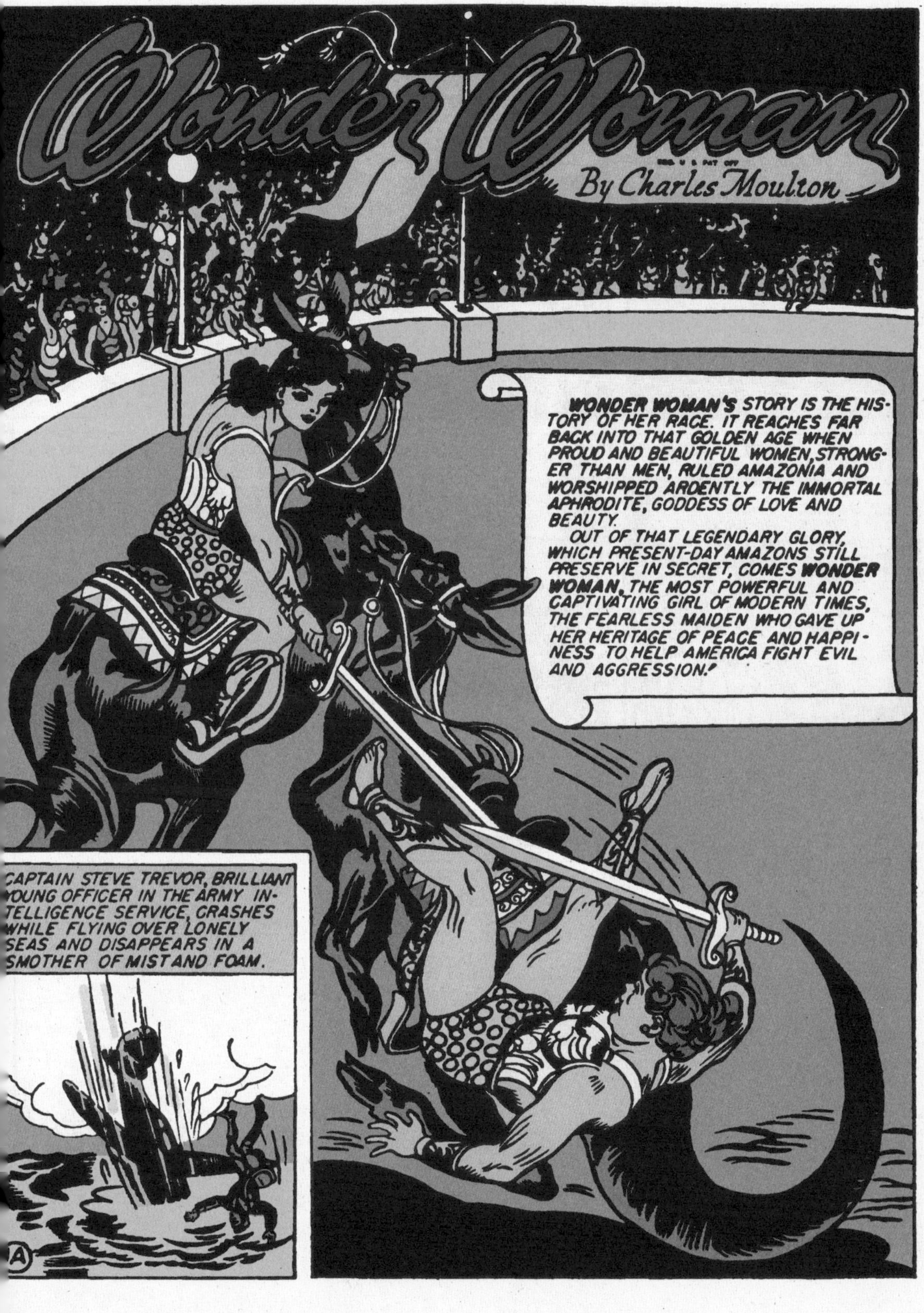
Wonder Woman
By Charles Moulton
WONDER WOMAN'S STORY IS THE HISTORY OF HER RACE. IT REACHES FAR BACK INTO THAT GOLDEN AGE WHEN PROUD AND BEAUTIFUL WOMEN, STRONGER THAN MEN, RULED AMAZONIA AND WORSHIPPED ARDENTLY THE IMMORTAL APHRODITE, GODDESS OF LOVE AND BEAUTY.
OUT OF THAT LEGENDARY GLORY, WHICH PRESENT-DAY AMAZONS STILL PRESERVE IN SECRET, COMES WONDER WOMAN, THE MOST POWERFUL AND CAPTIVATING GIRL OF MODERN TIMES, THE FEARLESS MAIDEN WHO GAVE UP HER HERITAGE OF PEACE AND HAPPINESS TO HELP AMERICA FIGHT EVIL AND AGGRESSION!
CAPTAIN STEVE TREVOR, BRILLIANT YOUNG OFFICER IN THE ARMY INTELLIGENCE SERVICE, CRASHES WHILE FLYING OVER LONELY SEAS AND DISAPPEARS IN A SMOTHER OF MIST AND FOAM.
A

COLONEL DARNELL, INTELLIGENCE CHIEF, REGRETFULLY ORDERS TREVOR OFFICIALLY LISTED AS "KILLED IN PURSUIT OF DUTY."

ISN'T THERE ANY HOPE HE MAY BE SAVED?

NONE WHAT-EVER. THERE'S NO LAND CHART-ED WITHIN A THOU-SAND MILES OF WHERE STEVE WENT DOWN!

BUT WEEKS LATER, TO THE UTTER ASTONISHMENT OF EVERYBODY, A BEAUTIFUL GIRL APPEARS FROM NOWHERE WITH CAPTAIN TREVOR IN HER ARMS!

WHY—UH—IT'S CAPTAIN TREVOR! BUT—BUT TREVOR'S DEAD!

NO! HE'S BAD-LY HURT BUT HE'LL RE-COVER!

AS MYSTERIOUSLY AS SHE APPEARED, THIS STRANGE GIRL VANISHES AGAIN!

WAIT! WHO ARE YOU? EXPLAIN!

YOU WOULDN'T UNDERSTAND! I'M JUST— A WOMAN!

MY WONDER WOMAN!

THE NURSE DISCOVERS A STRANGE CLEW TO WONDER WOMAN'S IDENTITY.

SEE, DOCTOR! THAT MYSTERIOUS GIRL DROPPED THIS PARCHMENT!

AN OLD PARCHMENT MANU-SCRIPT—THE LANGUAGE LOOKS LIKE ANCIENT GREEK! I'LL SHOW IT TO DR. HELLAS AT THE SMITH-SONIAN INSTITUTE.

DR. HELLAS, FAMOUS ARCHEOLO-GIST, IS ASTOUNDED!

THIS IS AMAZING—THE GREATEST FIND OF MODERN TIMES! IT'S AN ANCIENT DOCUMENT SOUGHT FOR CENTURIES —"THE HISTORY OF THE UNCONQUER-ABLE AMAZONS!"

"THE PLANET EARTH," BEGINS THE ANCIENT SCRIPT, "IS RULED BY RIVAL GODS—ARES, GOD OF WAR, AND APHRODITE, GODDESS OF LOVE AND BEAUTY."

MY MEN SHALL RULE WITH THE SWORD!

MY WOMEN SHALL CON-QUER MEN WITH LOVE!

2A

THE SWORDSMEN OF ARES (NOW CALLED MARS) SLEW THEIR WEAKER BROTHERS AND PLUN-DERED THEM.

WOMEN WERE SOLD AS SLAVES— THEY WERE CHEAPER THAN CATTLE.

WHAT SAY, HERO.' I'LL TRADE THESE FIVE BEAUTIFUL SLAVE GIRLS FOR THY GOAT.

BAH.' 'TWOULD TAKE A **DOZEN** WOMEN TO GET **MY** GOAT.'

BUT APHRODITE SHAPED WITH HER OWN HANDS A RACE OF SUPER WOMEN, STRONGER THAN MEN.

I WILL BREATHE LIFE INTO THESE WOMEN, AND ALSO THE POWER OF LOVE.' THEY SHALL BE CALL-ED "AMAZONS."

APHRODITE GAVE HER OWN MAGIC GIRDLE TO THE AMAZON QUEEN.

SO LONG AS YOUR LEADER WEARS THIS MAGIC GIRDLE YOU AMA-ZONS SHALL BE UNCONQUER-ABLE.'

THE AMAZONS BUILT A MAGNIFI-CENT CITY, AMAZONIA, AND EASILY DEFEATED ALL ARMIES WHICH ATTACKED THEM.

STUPID MEN.' YOU HAVE NO CHANCE AGAINST US WHILE I WEAR APHRODITE'S MAGIC GIRDLE.'

MARS WAS FURIOUSLY ANGRY AT APHRODITE.' BUT SHE LAUGHED IN HIS FACE.'

YOU CHEATED ME.' YOU MADE AMAZON WOMEN STRONGER THAN MEN.' BUT I WILL CONQUER YOUR AMA-ZONS AND PUNISH THEM.'

THAT FOR YOUR THREATS.'

SNAP! SNAP!

MARS INSPIRED HERCULES, STRONGEST MAN IN THE WORLD, TO MAKE WAR ON THE AMAZONS.'

I'LL TAKE THIS MAGIC GIRDLE FROM HIPPOLYTE, THE AMAZON QUEEN, AND BRING HER WOMEN BACK IN CHAINS.'

HERCULES, LEADING A MIGHTY ARMY TO AMAZONIA, CHALLENGED THE QUEEN TO PERSONAL COMBAT.'

COME FORTH, HIPPOLYTE, IF THOU DARE TO FIGHT THE STRONGEST MAN IN THE WORLD.'

I DARE FIGHT ANY MAN.'

3A

HERCULES'S CLUB SNAPPED THE QUEEN'S PUNY SWORD LIKE A DRY STICK, LEAVING HER UNARMED!

SURRENDER OR DIE!

OH.'

BUT THE MAGIC GIRDLE GAVE HER STRENGTH.

NO MERE MAN CAN CONQUER AN AMAZON!

AWWK— UGGH!

HERCULES, DEFEATED, RESORTED TO TREACHERY.

PROMISE TO RETURN HOME AND LEAVE US IN PEACE AND I WILL SPARE THY LIFE!

I PROMISE! I WILL MAKE LOVE TO HER AND STEAL THE MAGIC GIRDLE!

HERCULES PLANNED TO CAPTURE THE AMAZONS BY TREACHERY

I INVITE YOU BEAUTIFUL AMAZONS TO A BANQUET TONIGHT IN OUR TENTS TO SEAL OUR PACT OF ETERNAL FRIENDSHIP!

WE WILL COME.

HERCULES USED WOMAN'S OWN WEAPON AGAINST QUEEN HIPPO-LYTE. HE MADE LOVE TO HER!

THOU ART AS BEAUTI-FUL AS APHRODITE!

AND THOU ART STRONG AS ARES—WITH-OUT THIS MAGIC GIRDLE I COULD NEVER HAVE CON-QUERED THEE!

LET ME HOLD THY GIRDLE, O QUEEN— JUST TO TOUCH IT WILL SEND MY SPIRITS SOARING SINCE THOU HAST WORN IT!

I OUGHT NOT—BUT I CANNOT RESIST THEE!

I HAVE THE MAGIC GIRDLE—THE AMA-ZONS ARE HELP-LESS! SEIZE THEM, MEN!

HERCULES HAS BETRAYED ME! TO ARMS, AMAZONS!

FIGHT, SISTERS! APHRODITE, AID US!

THE AMAZONS FOUGHT FURIOUSLY BUT WITHOUT THE MAGIC GIRDLE THEY WERE DEFEATED.

BIND THE PRISONERS; WE WILL LOOT THE CITY!

HOLA! AMAZONIA IS OURS!

4A

THE GREEKS, FEARING THE STRENGTH OF THEIR CAPTIVES, PUT THE AMA-ZONS IN HEAVY CHAINS.

LOADED WITH FETTERS, BEATEN AND TORMENTED BY THEIR CAPTORS, THE AMAZONS WERE IN DESPAIR

THE CAPTIVE QUEEN PRAYED TO APHRODITE FOR HELP.

O DIVINE GODDESS, FORGIVE MY SIN! GIVE US STRENGTH TO BREAK OUR CHAINS AND RECOVER THE MAGIC GIRDLE!

THE GODDESS APHRODITE ANSWERED HIPPOLYTE'S PRAYER—

YOU MAY BREAK YOUR CHAINS. BUT YOU MUST WEAR THESE WRIST BANDS ALWAYS TO TEACH YOU THE FOLLY OF SUBMITTING TO MEN'S DOMINATION!

WE WILL OBEY, GODDESS!

THE AMAZONS CONQUERED THEIR CAPTORS.

APHRODITE IS WITH US! HOLA!

AWK! UNH! HAVE MERCY!

KONK!

QUEEN HIPPOLYTE RECOVERED THE MAGIC GIRDLE.

BONG!

QUICKLY ARMING THEMSELVES, THE AMAZONS BOARDED THE GREEK SHIPS.

5A

GUIDED BY APHRODITE, THE AMAZONS SAILED FAR SEAS TO THEIR PROMISED HAVEN OF PEACE AND PROTECTION

ON PARADISE ISLE THEY BUILT A SPLENDID CITY WHICH NO MAN MAY ENTER — A PARADISE FOR WOMEN ONLY!

HERE ENDS THE ANCIENT "HISTORY OF THE AMAZONS" AS TOLD IN THE PARCHMENT **WONDER WOMAN** LEFT! RELYING ON LATER SOURCES OF INFORMATION, WE SHALL CONTINUE THE STORY OF THE BEGINNINGS OF WONDER WOMAN!

THE QUEEN, UNDER DIRECTION OF ATHENA, GODDESS OF WISDOM, LEARNS THE SECRET ART OF MOULDING A HUMAN FORM!

HIPPOLYTE ADORES THE TINY STATUE SHE HAS MADE AS PYGMALION WORSHIPED GALATEA. APHRODITE, GRANTING THE QUEEN HER PRAYER, BESTOWS UPON IT THE DIVINE GIFT OF LIFE!

I NAME THEE DIANA, AFTER THE MOON GODDESS, MISTRESS OF THE CHASE!

BABY DIANA, TO HER MOTHER'S ASTONISHMENT, LEAPS HIGH INTO THE QUEEN'S ARMS!

HOW MARVELOUS—SHE IS MY LITTLE WONDER CHILD!

AT THREE, THE WONDER CHILD PULLS UP A FRUIT TREE BY ITS ROOTS.

GREAT THUNDERBOLTS OF ZEUS! SHE PULLS THAT TREE UP LIKE A WEED!

ALREADY OUR LITTLE PRINCESS HAS THE STRENGTH OF HERCULES!

AT FIVE, DIANA, LIKE HER NAMESAKE THE GODDESS OF THE CHASE, RACES DEER THROUGH THE FOREST.

THE QUEEN'S CHILD IS SWIFTER THAN MERCURY!

AT 15, THE YOUNG AMAZON GIRL RECEIVES HER BRACELETS OF SUBMISSION AT APHRODITE'S ALTAR.

I PLEDGE MYSELF FOREVER TO THY SERVICE, O GODDESS OF LOVE AND BEAUTY!

6A

DRINK, DIANA, FROM THE FOUNTAIN OF ETERNAL YOUTH! BEAUTY AND HAPPINESS ARE YOUR AMAZON BIRTHRIGHT SO LONG AS YOU REMAIN ON PARADISE ISLAND!

IT IS A WONDERFUL BIRTHRIGHT. I'LL NEVER GIVE IT UP!

BUT WHO CAN FORETELL THE FUTURE? YEARS LATER, AS THE PRINCESS AND HER FRIEND MALA STAND TOGETHER ON A CLIFF, OVERLOOKING THE SEA---

LOOK, MALA! A BROKEN AEROPLANE WING.

AND SOMEBODY'S ON IT!

COME ON--WE'LL SEE WHO IT IS!

OH! I HOPE IT'S A MAN-- I'D LIKE TO SEE ONE!

RACING SWIFTLY THROUGH THE WATER, DIANA REACHES THE WRECKAGE FIRST.

IT IS A MAN! HIS HEART STILL BEATS, I THINK!

WITH LONG, POWERFUL, STROKES THE AMAZON GIRLS TOW THE FALLEN FLYER TO PARADISE ISLAND.

THESE IDENTIFICATION PAPERS SHOW THAT HE IS CAPTAIN STEVE TREVOR, OF THE AMERICAN ARMY INTELLIGENCE SERVICE!

HOW STRANGE THAT HE DRIFTED TO OUR SHORES-- IT SEEMS LIKE FATE!

A MAN ON PARADISE ISLAND! YOU CAN'T TAKE HIM INTO THE CITY - IT'S AGAINST THE LAW OF THE AMAZONS!

I WILL TAKE HIM TO MY LABORATORY - THAT'S OUTSIDE THE CITY, AND DON'T TELL MOTHER!

7A

THE ROYAL PHYSICIAN GIVES LITTLE HOPE FOR THE STRANGER'S RECOVERY.

HE HAS BRAIN CONCUSSION, SHOCK, AND EXHAUSTION-- HIS CHANCES ARE SLIGHT!

WE MUST SAVE HIM!

IN THE LABORATORY DIANA WORKS DAY AND NIGHT TO PERFECT A HEALING RAY WHICH WILL SAVE TREVOR'S LIFE.

YOU MUST STOP WORKING, DIANA! YOU'VE HAD NO SLEEP FOR THREE DAYS AND NIGHTS!

LET ME ALONE--I'VE ALMOST GOT IT!

Panel 1: ON THE FIFTH DAY DIANA, NEARLY DEAD WITH FATIGUE, COMPLETES HER WORK — TOO LATE!

DOCTOR! COME QUICK — I'VE FOUND THE PURPLE HEALING FREQUENCY!

MY POOR DIANA! IT'S TOO LATE — THE PATIENT IS DEAD!

Panel 2: BUT DIANA FIERCELY INSISTS UPON TRYING TO REVIVE THE STRICKEN MAN.

PUT HIM THERE — UNDER THE RAY TUBES. I *WILL* *NOT* BELIEVE IT IS TOO LATE!

Panel 3: A WEIRD, PURPLE LIGHT BATHES THE PATIENT'S BATTERED BODY — FINALLY HIS PULSES STIR ONCE MORE TO LIFE!

A MIRACLE IS HAPPENING! YOUR HEALING RAY IS BRINGING HIM BACK TO LIFE.

THANK APHRODITE!

Panel 4: DOCTOR ALTHEA REPORTS TO THE QUEEN.

DIANA WORKED DAY AND NIGHT TO SAVE HIM. SHE SEEMS — ER — STRANGELY INTERESTED —

OH, WOE THE DAY THAT BROUGHT A *MAN* TO PARADISE ISLAND! SEND DIANA TO ME IMMEDIATELY.

Panel 5: THIS STRANGER MUST RETURN AT ONCE TO THE WARRING WORLD OF MEN!

BUT HE CANNOT TRAVEL ALONE UNTIL HE GETS WELL!

Panel 6: I CAN FLY CAPTAIN TREVOR TO AMERICA, MOTHER, IN MY NEW INVISIBLE PLANE! OH, *PLEASE* LET ME!

NO! IF YOU LEAVE PARADISE ISLAND, YOU LOSE YOUR BIRTHRIGHT!

DIANA HAS FALLEN IN LOVE WITH THIS MAN! APHRODITE, HELP ME!

Panel 7: MEANTIME, UNSEEN BY HUMAN EYES, MARS, THE GOD OF WAR, TAUNTS APHRODITE.

HO! HO! THE WHOLE WORLD'S AT WAR — I RULE THE EARTH!

YOUR RULE WILL END WHEN AMERICA WINS! AND AMERICA *WILL* WIN! I'LL SEND AN AMAZON TO HELP HER!

8A

Panel 8: APHRODITE APPEARS TO THE QUEEN.

A YOUNG AMAZON MUST TAKE THE CAPTAIN BACK TO AMERICA — SHE MUST REMAIN THERE TO FIGHT WAR AND EVIL! SELECT YOUR STRONGEST MAIDEN FOR SHE WILL NEED ALL HER STRENGTH!

I OBEY, O GODDESS!

NEXT MORNING, ON THE MENTAL RADIO-TELEVISION OF THE AMAZONS, DIANA HEARS THE QUEEN'S DECREE.

--- AND SO, TO SELECT OUR STRONGEST MAIDEN, AN ATHLETIC TOURNAMENT WILL BE HELD AT AMAZON STADIUM! ENTRIES TO BE FILED ---

DIANA HURRIES TO THE PALACE.

OH, MOTHER! I JUST HEARD YOUR BROADCAST- HOW EXCITING! I WANT TO ENROLL FOR THIS TOURNAMENT!

NO, MY DAUGHTER, I FORBID IT! YOU CANNOT COMPETE!

DON'T ARGUE, MY CHILD! THE WINNER OF THIS CONTEST MUST LEAVE PARADISE ISLAND AND LIVE IN THE WORLD OF MEN! YOU CANNOT GIVE UP YOUR BIRTHRIGHT.

BUT MOTHER! SOME GIRL MUST DO IT!

I'LL WEAR THIS MASK. ALL CONTESTANTS DRESS ALIKE AND MOTHER WON'T KNOW ME!

THE GREAT DAY ARRIVES AND AMAZON ATHLETES PARADE BEFORE THEIR QUEEN.

DIANA PRETENDS TO STUMBLE AS SHE PASSES THE QUEEN'S BOX.

I'D BETTER NOT LET MOTHER SEE ME SO CLOSE, EVEN WITH A MASK ON!

THE FIRST CONTEST IS FENCING FROM THE BACKS OF AMAZON HORSES --- KANGAS! A GAME WHICH REQUIRES GREAT SKILL AND SURE HORSEMANSHIP.

9A   H G PETERO

IN THE FINAL ROUND, A BATTLE ROYAL RAGES BETWEEN NUMBER 21, A HUGE AMAZON, AND NUMBER 7, THE MASKED MAIDEN.

I'LL WEAR YOU DOWN, LITTLE TULIP. YOU NEED WEIGHT FOR THIS SPORT!

BACKBONE'S BETTER THAN BEEF!

BUT THE MASKED FIGHTER CATCHES HER POWERFUL OPPONENT OFF BALANCE AND—

LIGHT LANDINGS, BIG GIRL!

OOMF! YOU'VE GOT ME!

MALA, DIANA'S BEST FRIEND, FEELS DEPRESSED DURING HER WRESTLING BOUT WITH FATSIS.

WHEW! HOT WORK—I BETTER REST AWHILE!

WHOOSH! IF I DON'T GET THIS TWO-TON GREASE HEAP OFF ME QUICKLY I'LL SUFFOCATE!

BUT WITH A DEFT STRANGLEHOLD, MALA THROWS FATSIS FOR THE TITLE.

THAT CERTAINLY IS A WEIGHT OFF MY CHEST!

OOF!

THE HIGH-JUMP ROPING CONTEST IS A UNIQUE AMAZON EVENT. THE JUMPER MUST LEAP OVER HER OPPONENT'S LASSO WITHOUT BEING CAUGHT.

HA! HA! YOU COULDN'T CLEAR A TEN FOOT ROPE!

AS THE LASSO ROPE IS LENGTHENED, THE CONTESTANT MUST JUMP HIGHER AND HIGHER TO CLEAR IT.

HUH! I JUMPED THAT HIGH MYSELF. BUT LET'S SEE YOU CLEAR THE 40-FOOT LASSO, MYSTERY GIRL!

HIGHER AND EVEN HIGHER SWINGS THE WHIRLING LOOP, BUT LIKE A BIRD THE MASKED JUMPER SOARS OVER IT!

HOLA! HOLA! SHE MADE A RECORD. HOORAH FOR OUR NEW CHAMPION!

FROM SUNRISE TO SUNSET THE GRUELING TESTS OF STRENGTH AND ENDURANCE CONTINUE. ONE BY ONE, THE AMAZON GIRLS ARE ELIMINATED, UNTIL ONLY NUMBER 7, THE MASKED MAIDEN, AND HER RIVAL MALA, REMAIN IN THE CONTEST. A DEEP, HUSH FALLS OVER THE HUGE AMPHITHEATRE AS THE QUEEN RISES.

ONLY TWO GIRLS SURVIVE THIS TOURNAMENT—NUMBERS 7 AND 12. BOTH HAVE WON 11 CONTESTS! THE FINAL TEST FOR ENTRANCE INTO THE WORLD OF MEN WILL BE—BULLETS AND BRACELETS!

BULLETS AND BRACELETS!

EACH OF YOU WILL SHOOT FIVE TIMES. YOUR OPPONENT MUST CATCH THE BULLETS ON HER BRACELETS—OR ELSE EXPECT TO BE WOUNDED! NOW TAKE YOUR PLACES! NUMBER 12 WILL SHOOT FIRST.

THE COMMAND... AND THE GIRL FIRES POINT-BLANK AT NUMBER 7, THE MASKED MAIDEN!

THE ULTIMATE TEST OF SPEED OF EYE AND MOVEMENT! NO.7'S BRACELETS BECOME SILVER FLASHES OF STREAKING LIGHT AS THEY PARRY THE DEATH-THRUSTS OF THE HURTLING BULLETS!

NO.7 PASSES THE TEST UNSCATHED! NOW IT IS HER TURN TO FIRE. HER OPPONENT'S FAST—BUT NOT FAST ENOUGH!

UGH! MY SHOULDER!

THE WINNER—--- CONTESTANT NO.7—THE MASKED MAIDEN!

YOU MAY REMOVE YOUR MASK, NUMBER 7! I WANT TO SEE THE FACE OF THE STRONGEST AND MOST AGILE OF ALL THE AMAZONS! DAUGHTER! YOU!

I—I WISH YOU HAD NOT WON, DIANA! BUT—BUT I AM VERY PROUD OF YOU! I AWARD YOU, AS WINNER, THIS COSTUME AND MAGIC LASSO, PREPARED UNDER APHRODITE'S PERSONAL DIRECTION TO WEAR IN AMERICA!

OH, MOTHER— HOW WONDERFUL!

DIANA, LIKE ANY OTHER GIRL WITH NEW CLOTHES, CANNOT WAIT TO TRY THEM ON!

11A

THE AMAZON ATHLETES, CHEERING DIANA, CARRY HER AROUND THE ARENA!

HOLA! HOLA! HAIL THE PRINCESS DIANA, OUR NEW CHAMPION!

THE QUEEN EXPLAINS THE MAGIC LASSO TO DIANA.

IT IS MADE OF TINY GOLDEN LINKS WHICH ARE UNBREAKABLE. THEY WERE TAKEN, AT APHRODITE'S COMMAND, FROM THE MAGIC GIRDLE ITSELF!

THIS CHAIN IS SO FINE — IT IS LIKE SILK!

THE MAGIC LASSO CARRIES APHRODITE'S POWER TO MAKE MEN AND WOMEN SUBMIT TO YOUR WILL! WHOMEVER YOU BIND WITH THAT LASSO MUST OBEY YOU!

OBEY ME — BUT MOTHER — WHAT—

DOCTOR ALTHEA INTERRUPTS THE CONFERENCE.

SORRY, DOCTOR, I'M BUSY!

I'LL TRY THIS MAGIC LASSO ON THE DOC!

DOCTOR! STAND ON YOUR HEAD!

S-STAND ON MY HEAD! CERTAINLY NOT! NOT EVEN FOR YOU, PRINCESS!

I THOUGHT YOU WOULD REFUSE TO STAND ON YOUR HEAD BUT WE'LL SEE—

EE-EK! ARE YOU CRAZY, DIANA?

NOW STAND ON YOUR HEAD!

N-N-YES, PRINCESS! I WOULDN'T DO IT BUT SOMETHING COMPELS ME!

STOP YOUR SILLY TRICKS, DIANA! THINK OF THE DOCTOR'S DIGNITY!

I CAME TO REPORT THAT CAPTAIN TREVOR IS BETTER. I REMOVED HIS EYE BANDAGES AND—

BIND HIS EYES AGAIN IMMEDIATELY! HE MUST SEE NOTHING ON PARADISE ISLAND!

NOTHING EXCEPT ME! I'LL BIND HIM AGAIN — MYSELF!

MY EYES MUST BE BAD AGAIN! YOU'RE THE SCIENTIST WHO SAVED MY LIFE BUT YOU LOOK TO ME LIKE THE MOST BEAUTIFUL GIRL IN THE WORLD!

HM — IF YOUR EYES ARE BAD, I HOPE THEY STAY THIS WAY!

12A

TELL ME YOUR STORY.

MY JOB IN AMERICA IS CATCHING SPIES. I FOLLOWED AN IMPORTANT ENEMY AGENT TO AN ISLAND — SEE? THERE ON THE MAP. MACHINE GUNS OPENED UP ON ME AND I CRASHED — MUST HAVE DRIFTED, UNCONSCIOUS, FOR DAYS — UNTIL YOU FOUND ME!

TOO SOON THE DAY ARRIVES WHEN PRINCESS DIANA MUST LEAVE PARADISE ISLAND — PERHAPS FOREVER!

FAREWELL, MY CHILD! BE GUIDED ALWAYS BY OUR TWIN GODDESSES OF LOVE AND WISDOM!

I PROMISE, MOTHER — GOODBYE!

AMID THE CHEERS AND TEARS OF AMAZON WOMEN, DIANA'S SILENT INVISIBLE PLANE SWEEPS UPWARD INTO THE BLUE, BEARING THE PRINCESS AND THE MAN SHE LOVES TOWARD THE DISTANT SHORES OF AMERICA!

FAREWELL, PRINCESS! HOLA! UNTIL WE MEET AGAIN!

SAYING NOTHING TO STEVE TREVOR OF HER INTENTIONS, DIANA FLIES HER TRANSPARENT PLANE AT TERRIFIC SPEED TO THE SPY ISLAND WHERE HE CRASHED.

HOLD EVERYTHING, STEVE — I'M GOING DOWN AFTER THAT SPY!

JUMPING JEHOSOPHAT! DON'T — YOU'LL BE KILLED —

SPOTTING STEVE'S SPY RUNNING FRANTICALLY TOWARD HIS PLANE, DIANA SWOOPS LOW AND CLEVERLY LASSOES HIM.

BOUND BY THE MAGIC LASSO, THE JAPANESE AGENT IS FORCED TO TELL TREVOR EVERYTHING HE KNOWS — AND THAT IS PLENTY!

WHO IS HITLER'S CHIEF AGENT IN SAN FRANCISCO?

HEINRICH FRITZ UBER!

COLONEL DARNELL, TREVOR'S CHIEF, VISITS HIM AT THE HOSPITAL.

YOU DID A SPLENDID JOB, MY BOY, CATCHING THAT SPY! YOU'VE BEEN PROMOTED TO MAJOR!

BUT I DON'T DESERVE IT — WONDER WOMAN DID EVERYTHING!!

13A

WHEN STEVE, NEXT MORNING, MEETS HIS NEW NURSE, DIANA PRINCE, HE LITTLE REALIZES THAT BENEATH THAT DEMURE DISGUISE HIDES THE GLAMOROUS BEAUTY OF THE AMAZON PRINCESS!

IF ONLY WONDER WOMAN WOULD STAY NEAR ME!

PERHAPS SHE'S NEARER THAN YOU THINK! I'M SURE SHE'LL ALWAYS COME QUICKLY WHEN YOU NEED HER!

--- AND SO BEGAN THE CAREER OF WONDER WOMAN!

Wonder Woman
by CHARLES MOULTON

THE CIRCUS! THE SPANGLES AND BRIGHT COSTUMES OF GRACEFUL TRAPEZE ARTISTS, AND THE WEIRD COMICAL HYSTERIA OF WHITE FACED CLOWNS, THE AMAZING AND CONSTANT ENTERTAINMENT GOING ON IN THREE RINGS AT ONCE... THE AWE-INSPIRING MAJESTY OF FEROCIOUS DENIZENS OF THE JUNGLE, PERFORMING OBEDIENTLY TO THE TUNE OF A GALA BRASS BAND!

INTO THIS MAZE OF REHEARSED FANTASY COMES WONDER WOMAN, TOPPING EVERY ATTRACTION ON THE BILL AND SOLVING A WEIRD MYSTERY AT THE SAME TIME!

WONDER WOMAN GOES TO THE CIRCUS!

DIANA PRINCE AND MAJOR TREVOR LEAVE THE OFFICE TOGETHER.

LOOK, STEVE! KING'S CIRCUS IS COMING TO TOWN!

UH-HUH—IT OUGHT TO MAKE A LOT OF MONEY FOR THE ARMY WELFARE FUND.

KING'S COLOSSAL CIRCUS!

ARMY BENEFIT PERFORMANCE SAT, JUNE 27TH TICKETS ON SALE HERE

1B

DRUGS

COME ON-- I'M GOING TO BUY TICKETS AND TAKE THOSE SETTLEMENT KIDS TO THE CIRCUS. YOU'RE GOING TO HELP ME!

HUH? WHY PICK ON ME? WELL-- ALL RIGHT. YOU'D BETTER BRING ETTA CANDY-- KIDS CAN BE TOUGH TO HANDLE SOMETIMES.

AT THE CIRCUS ON SATURDAY THE CHILDREN VISIT THE ANIMAL CAGES.

CHILDREN, WHAT ANIMALS DO YOU WANT TO SEE FIRST?

THE ELEPHANTS! WE LIKE THE ELEPHANTS BEST!

DIANA TALKS WITH ELVA KING, THE CIRCUS OWNER'S NIECE, WHO TRAINS THE ELEPHANTS.

WHAT WONDERFUL ELEPHANTS!

YES, THESE ANIMALS COME FROM BURMA WHERE ELEPHANTS ARE WORSHIPPED. THEY ARE VERY VALUABLE.

THIS IS SAN YAN, OUR HEAD ELEPHANT MAN. THESE BURMESE CAME OVER WITH THE ELEPHANTS-- DIDN'T YOU, SAN?

OH, SURE! ELEPHANT OUR FATHER - MOTHER! HONORABLE ANCESTORS SOULS IN ELEPHANTS-- WE GUARD WITH OUR LIVES.

DAMLEE, MOTHER OF A BABY ELEPHANT, SUDDENLY COLLAPSES, TRUMPETING THE DEATH CRY!

EE-YEA-EEH!

待用了檸檬

POOR DAMLEE! SHE IS THE SEVENTH ELEPHANT THAT DIED THIS WEEK. IT WILL RUIN UNCLE ED'S CIRCUS. WHAT CAN BE KILLING THEM?

IT LOOKS LIKE POISON-- SOMEONE SHOULD INVESTIGATE!

DARING DOM CARNEY, FLYING TRAPEZE PERFORMER, IS IN LOVE WITH ELVA--

OH DOM, ANOTHER ELEPHANT GONE! THIS WILL RUIN UNCLE ED--

SERVES HIM RIGHT! HE THREATENED TO FIRE ME FOR ASKING TO MARRY YOU. I'M AFRAID I CAN'T SYMPATHIZE WITH HIM--

DON'T FEED PAM. HER ACT GOES ON FIRST AND FEEDING NOW IS BAD FOR HER!

DO NOT FEED THE ANIMALS

WHAT DO I CARE IF ALL KING'S ELEPHANTS DIE. YOU'LL HAVE NO JOB. THEN YOU'LL MARRY ME!

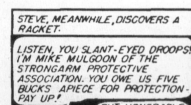

STEVE, MEANWHILE, DISCOVERS A RACKET.

LISTEN, YOU SLANT-EYED DROOPS! I'M MIKE MULGOON OF THE STRONGARM PROTECTIVE ASSOCIATION. YOU OWE US FIVE BUCKS APIECE FOR PROTECTION—PAY UP!

BUT HONORABLE SIR! WE NEED NO PROTECTION—

SO YOU DON'T NEED PROTECTION! SMART GUYS, HEH? WE'LL SHOW YER!

STEVE LENDS A HAND.

COUNT ME IN ON THIS, BOYS—I'M IN THE "PROTECTION" BUSINESS MYSELF.

UG!—BLUB—LET GO MY COLLAR! WE'LL GET YOU FOR THIS!

YOU MONKEYS BETTER NOT COME BACK OR I MIGHT LOSE MY TEMPER!

WE'LL BE BACK AND IF THOSE PUNKS DON'T PAY, WE'LL FIX 'EM!

WHO'D BE MEAN ENOUGH TO POISON ELEPHANTS?

IT'S PROBABLY MIKE MULGOON AND HIS RACKETEERS—BUT WE HAVE NO PROOF.

NO, NO! ITS THE HANDSOME MAN ON THE FLYING TRAPEZE—I HEARD HIM SAY HE'D LIKE TO SEE THEM DEAD!

IN THE BIG TOP—ELVA PUTS THE HUGE PAM THROUGH HIS PACES.

THE CHILDREN ARE DELIGHTED!

WHAT A BIG ELEPHANT!

THAT GIRL IS BRAVE—I WOULDN'T DARE STAND UNDER HIM!

OOH—SUPPOSIN' HE FELL ON HER!

38

DIANA WITH HER SUPER-KEEN EYESIGHT, SEES THE ELEPHANT SUDDENLY QUIVER!

GREAT LABORS OF HERCULES! THAT ELEPHANT IS SICK—HE'S FALLING!

ELVA—LOOK OUT!!

BUT DIANA'S WARNING COMES TOO LATE! THE GREAT PACHYDERM CRASHES TO THE GROUND, PINNING ELVA HELPLESSLY BENEATH HIM!

EE-YEA EEH!

HELP!

THE ELEPHANT IS DEAD--POISONED!

ELVA'S KILLED TOO!

STAND BACK, EVERY-BODY! THE GIRL MAY BE ALIVE-- GIVE HER AIR!

LUCKILY AN ELEPHANT STAND SUPPORTS PART OF THE ANIMAL'S WEIGHT-ELVA IS UNCONSCIOUS BUT STILL BREATHING!

SHE'S ALIVE-WE'VE GOT TO LIFT THE ELEPHANT OFF HER LEGS!

OKAY-I'LL GET OUR STRONGMAN AND ROUSTABOUTS!

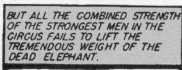

BUT ALL THE COMBINED STRENGTH OF THE STRONGEST MEN IN THE CIRCUS FAILS TO LIFT THE TREMENDOUS WEIGHT OF THE DEAD ELEPHANT.

NO USE--PUFF--CAN'T BUDGE IT!

WHEW! THIS CONSARNED ELEPHANT WEIGHS FORTY TONS!

SUDDENLY, FROM APPARENTLY NOWHERE, A BIZARRE AND BEAUTIFUL FIGURE LEAPS LIGHTLY INTO THE MIDST OF THE GROUP.

HOLY HANNAH! IT'S WONDER WOMAN!

BOY! OH BOY! SHE MUSTA DROPPED FROM HEAVEN!

GIVE ME ROOM, BOYS-THERE'S NOT A MINUTE TO LOSE! WHEN I LIFT THE ELEPHANT, YOU PULL THE GIRL CLEAR!

HO! HO! YOU LIFT THAT ELEPHANT? WHAT A LAUGH!

YEAH, YOU AND HOW MANY DERRICKS?

AW, LET HER DO IT-- C'MON WONDER WOMAN!

48

GRASPING THE ELEPHANT'S HARNESS, WONDER WOMAN QUICKLY RAISES ITS VAST WEIGHT FROM THE GROUND.

THIS IS EASY-WHAT MADE YOU FELLOWS THINK THIS ELEPHANT IS HEAVY?

GEE WHILLIKERS! WHAT A WOMAN!

SHE'S SUPERB! MAGNIFICENT!

THE CROWD SHOUTS FOR WONDER WOMAN.

YIPEE! WONDER WOMAN! GIVE US WONDER! WOMAN!

WE WANT WONDER WOMAN!

THE CROWD IS CRAZY FOR YOU, WONDER WOMAN! THEY THINK YOU'RE PART OF THE SHOW! WON'T YOU PUT ON AN ACT FOR THEM WHILE WE TAKE CARE OF ELVA?

I WILL IF THEY'LL GIVE A SPECIAL COLLECTION FOR THE SOLDIERS!

WONDER WOMAN JUMPS ON A CIRCUS HORSE AND GOES INTO HER ACT.

YEAH! WONDER WOMAN!

THEN SHE GIVES THE HORSE A RIDE!

YEA! WONDER WOMAN!

?

WONDER WOMAN DASHES TO A CAGE AND WRESTLES WITH A FEROCIOUS LION—

WHEE!

BRAVO WONDER WOMAN!

THEN TOSSES THE KING OF BEASTS INTO HIS CAGE AGAIN!

I HOPE I WASN'T TOO ROUGH WITH PUSSY— I DON'T WANT TO HURT HIM!

LAD-EES AND GENTLEMEN! WONDAH WOMAN WILL NOW ATTEMPT THE LONGEST DIVE EVER MADE BY MAN OR WOMAN! SHE WILL HURL HERSELF THE ENTIRE LENGTH OF THE BIG TOP, LANDING SAFELY—WE PRAY— ON YONDER TRAPEZE!

58

A TENSE SILENCE GRIPS THE SPECTATORS—THE CROWD HOLDS ITS BREATH AS WONDER WOMAN HURTLES THROUGH THE AIR IN HER DEATH-DEFYING LEAP--

I CAN MAKE IT IF THE TRAPEZE HOLDS STEADY!

SUDDENLY A STONE IS THROWN BY AN UNKNOWN HAND, HITS THE TRAPEZE AND STARTS IT SWINGING!

JUST AS **WONDER WOMAN** REACHES THE TRAPEZE, IT SWINGS BEYOND THE REACH OF HER FINGERS.

BLACK HOUNDS OF HADES! SOMEBODY SWUNG THAT TRAPEZE— THEY WANT TO KILL ME!

QUICKER THAN THOUGHT, **WONDER WOMAN** BENDS HER KNEES AND CATCHES THE BAR WITH HER LEGS!

WITH WILD ENTHUSIASM THE SPECTATORS RUSH DOWN INTO THE ARENA AND RAISE **WONDER WOMAN** ON THEIR SHOULDERS.

YEA! WONDER WOMAN!

SHE'S WONDERFUL— QUEEN OF THEM ALL!

I THANK YOU FOR YOUR GENEROUS APPLAUSE! PLEASE BE AS GENEROUS WITH YOUR CONTRIBUTIONS TO THE ARMY FUND. HOLLIDAY GIRLS WILL PASS THE BUCKETS!

GEE, YOU'RE HANDSOME AND STRONG! COME OVER AND EAT CANDY WITH ME SOMETIME!

OH, I'D LOVE TO— I BET WE'RE SOUL-MATES!

NOW, TORRENCE! I NEED YOUR MONEY MORE THAN THE SOLDIERS! YOU PROMISED ME A FUR COAT!

YOU'LL GET IT, BABY— I'M TOO TOUGH TO FALL FOR THAT SLUSH!

OH, I THINK YOU CAN BE MADE TO FALL, TORRENCE!

HEY!---YOU SURE GOT YOUR NERVE! ANY DAME WHO KIN KNOCK DOWN SLUGGER McGEE DESOIVES A HUNNERT BUCKS!

68

ED KING, CIRCUS OWNER, THANKS **WONDER WOMAN** FOR ALL SHE HAS DONE.

I CAN'T THANK YOU ENOUGH, **WONDER WOMAN!** BUT MY CIRCUS WILL BE RUINED UNLESS I CAN STOP THESE ELEPHANT KILLINGS!

KING'S COLOSSAL STUPENDOUS SHOWS

IT'S CLEAR WHO THE KILLERS ARE—MULGOON AND HIS RACKETEERS!

YOU'RE WRONG, MAJOR—IT'S THAT SCOUNDREL DOM CARNEY!

THE ELEPHANT MURDERER TRIED TO KILL ME, TOO, ON THE TRAPEZE! I HAVE A PLAN—

WONDER WOMAN BORROWS A STUFFED BABY ELEPHANT FROM THE CIRCUS MUSEUM.

I'VE NEVER DISGUISED MYSELF AS AN ELEPHANT BEFORE—I HOPE THIS IDEA WORKS!

MUSEUM

WONDER WOMAN AND ETTA CANDY TAKE THE PLACE OF THE ELEPHANT'S STUFFING AND THE HOLLIDAY GIRLS SEW THEM UP.

I DON'T MIND BEING A BABY ELEPHANT, BUT I'D RATHER BE THE MOUTH THAN THE HIND LEGS!

DOWN ETTA! STEADY **WONDER WOMAN!** I'LL HAVE TO GIVE THIS ELEPHANT LOTS OF TRAINING.

WITH KING'S HELP, THE HUMAN ELEPHANT SECRETLY REPLACES THE CIRCUS BABY PACHYDERM.

ISN'T THAT BABY ELEPHANT CUTE! IT LOVES CANDY!

THROW THE PEANUTS BACK! MAKE 'EM FEED US MORE CANDY.

WHEN THE LAST VISITOR LEAVES, AND DARKNESS ENVELOPS THE ANIMAL TENT, MYSTERIOUS LIGHTS MOVE SLOWLY TOWARD THE ELEPHANTS.

HEY, LET'S LIE DOWN— MY FEET ACHE!

SHH! SOMEBODY'S COMING!

WONDER WOMAN WATCHES A WEIRD CEREMONY—

小人未曾瞧見

THROUGH THE GLASS EYES OF THE BABY ELEPHANT, **WONDER WOMAN** RECOGNIZES SAN YAN, WHO ACTS AS HIGH PRIEST.

WONDER WOMAN, WHO HAD TO LEARN ALL HUMAN LANGUAGES ON PARADISE ISLAND, TRANSLATES FOR ETTA CANDY.

HE IS PROMISING THE ELEPHANTS THAT TONIGHT THEY SHALL TRAMPLE THE FOREIGN DEVILS!

ETTA, EXCITED, FORGETS TO LOWER HER VOICE —

WOO WOO! WE'RE GOING TO SQUASH THE ELEPHANT KILLER!

THE SOUL OF OUR ANCESTOR SPEAKS!

THE LITTLE GOD SAYS KILLER OF ELEPHANTS SHALL BE CRUSHED!

AA—AH!

OH OH-H-OOM!

AT THIS MOMENT A BIG ELEPHANT, SUSPICIOUS, PRODS THE BABY ELEPHANT WITH HIS TUSKS.

HEY! STOP TICKLING ME!

ANGRY, THE BIG ELEPHANT SEIZES THE BABY IN HIS TRUNK AND HURLS IT HIGH IN THE AIR.

WOO WOO! WHAT'S HAPPENING TO US?

WE'RE TAKING A LITTLE AIR TRIP— DON'T GET NERVOUS!

THE BABY ELEPHANT SKIN BREAKS AND TWO "SPIRITS" BURST FORTH!

AH-OOM! THE SPIRITS OF OUR ANCESTORS APPEAR TO US!

BUT SAN YAN THINKS OTHERWISE!

THOSE ARE NOT OUR ANCESTORS— THEY ARE FOREIGN DEVILS! THEY CAME TO BETRAY US!

FOREIGN DEVILS! THEY PROFANED OUR SACRED ELEPHANTS! SLAY THEM! CUT THEM IN PIECES!

SAN YAN HAS A BETTER IDEA — LET THESE FOREIGNERS DIE THE DEATH OF THE UNBELIEVER! WE WILL TAKE THEM TO THE SECRET TEMPLE AND SACRIFICE THEM TO THE SACRED ELEPHANTS!

A STRONG SAFETY NET IS SUDDENLY THROWN OVER WONDER WOMAN —

SAY! THIS SACRIFICE IDEA DOESN'T SOUND SO GOOD TO ME!

SACRIFICE IS GOOD FOR THE SOUL, ETTA! I HAVE A YEARNING TO VISIT THIS SECRET TEMPLE OF THE SACRED ELEPHANTS!

THE PRISONERS ARE CARRIED AWAY, LEAVING THREE BURMESE WITH THE ELEPHANTS.

STEVE TREVOR, MEANWHILE, IS TRAILING MIKE MULGOON AND HIS RACKETEERS.

WE GRAB THESE SLANT-EYED MUGS, SEE? AND TAKE 'EM FOR A RIDE!

NIX, MIKE! YOU WAS SEEN TALKIN' TO THESE GUYS TODAY. IF THEY'RE FADED, WE'LL FRY FOR IT!

OKAY— WE'LL MAKE 'EM TAKE US WHERE THEY LIVE AND BUMP THEM OFF THERE! THEN THEIR OWN PALS'LL BE BLAMED!

STEVE, MOVING FORWARD TO CAPTURE THE GANGSTERS, IS KNOCKED UNCONSCIOUS BY A MIGHTY PAW OF THE TIGER IN THE CAGE!

UGH!

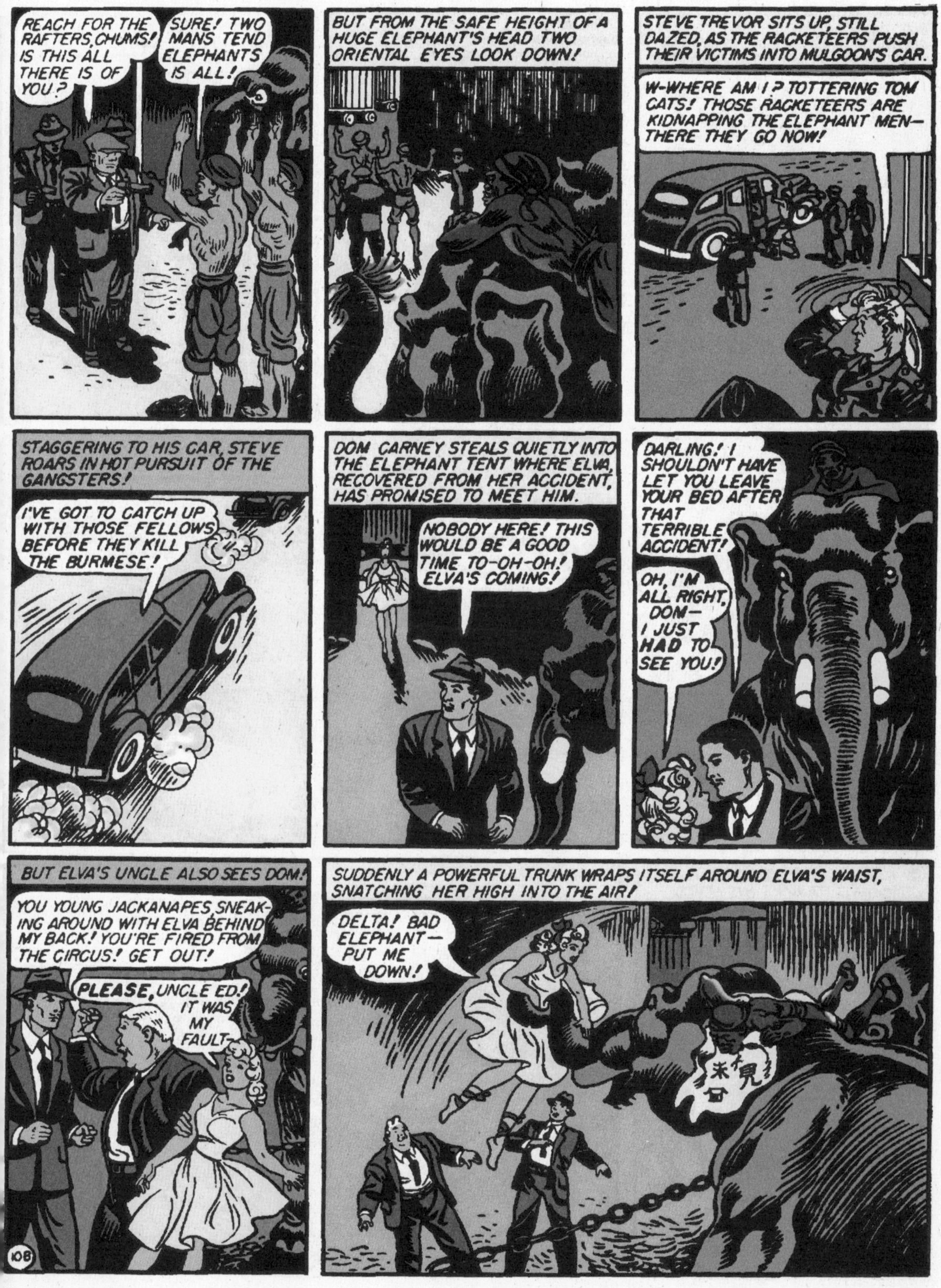
REACH FOR THE RAFTERS, CHUMS! IS THIS ALL THERE IS OF YOU?
SURE! TWO MANS TEND ELEPHANTS IS ALL!
BUT FROM THE SAFE HEIGHT OF A HUGE ELEPHANT'S HEAD TWO ORIENTAL EYES LOOK DOWN!
STEVE TREVOR SITS UP, STILL DAZED, AS THE RACKETEERS PUSH THEIR VICTIMS INTO MULGOON'S CAR.
W-WHERE AM I? TOTTERING TOM CATS! THOSE RACKETEERS ARE KIDNAPPING THE ELEPHANT MEN-THERE THEY GO NOW!
STAGGERING TO HIS CAR, STEVE ROARS IN HOT PURSUIT OF THE GANGSTERS!
I'VE GOT TO CATCH UP WITH THOSE FELLOWS BEFORE THEY KILL THE BURMESE!
DOM CARNEY STEALS QUIETLY INTO THE ELEPHANT TENT WHERE ELVA, RECOVERED FROM HER ACCIDENT, HAS PROMISED TO MEET HIM.
NOBODY HERE! THIS WOULD BE A GOOD TIME TO-OH-OH! ELVA'S COMING!
DARLING! I SHOULDN'T HAVE LET YOU LEAVE YOUR BED AFTER THAT TERRIBLE ACCIDENT!
OH, I'M ALL RIGHT, DOM-I JUST **HAD** TO SEE YOU!
BUT ELVA'S UNCLE ALSO SEES DOM!
YOU YOUNG JACKANAPES SNEAKING AROUND WITH ELVA BEHIND MY BACK! YOU'RE FIRED FROM THE CIRCUS! GET OUT!
PLEASE, UNCLE ED! IT WAS MY FAULT-
108
SUDDENLY A POWERFUL TRUNK WRAPS ITSELF AROUND ELVA'S WAIST, SNATCHING HER HIGH INTO THE AIR!
DELTA! BAD ELEPHANT-PUT ME DOWN!

BUT THE ELEPHANT OBEYS ANOTHER VOICE SPEAKING IN HIS EAR. WITH A POWERFUL LUNGE HE BREAKS HIS LEG CHAIN!

TRIUMPHANTLY TRUMPETING, THE MAMMOTH ANIMAL CRASHES THROUGH THE TENT TO FREEDOM!

EE-EK! SAVE ME, DOM!

COME ON — THESE HORSES CAN OUTRUN AN ELEPHANT! WE'VE GOT TO SAVE ELVA!

CROSSING AN OPEN FIELD THE RESCUERS BEGIN TO GAIN—

FASTER! FASTER!

BUT UNFORTUNATELY THE CIRCUS HORSES ARE TRICK ANIMALS—AT THE COMMAND "FASTER", THEY ARE TRAINED TO LIE DOWN!

FASTER, YOU GOAT! FASTER!

DOM'S HORSE HAS LEARNED TO IMITATE HIS RING LEADER—

UP-UP! STAND UP YOU FOOL!

GIDDAP! ON YOUR FEET!

BY CHANCE, DOM GIVES THE RIGHT COMMAND TO MAKE HIS HORSE GET UP.

WELL, LIE DOWN THEN, YOU MULE! WHY DIDN'T I THINK! THESE HORSES ARE TRAINED TO WORK WITH CLOWNS!

THE ELEPHANT HAS A BIG START ON US NOW!

BUT WE MUST CATCH HIM — ELVA'S LIFE DEPENDS ON IT!

MEANWHILE **WONDER WOMAN** AND ETTA ARE CARRIED TO A DESERTED HILLSIDE.

A HUGE ROCK ROLLS ASIDE EASILY, REVEALING THE ENTRANCE TO A NATURAL CAVERN STUDDED WITH GLITTERING STALACTITES AND STALAGMITES—

FOREIGN DEVILS WALK NOW INTO CAVE.

ISN'T THIS CAVE BEAUTIFUL! IT'S WORTH THE PRICE OF ADMISSION!

IF THOSE ICICLES WERE ONLY CANDY!

IN THE BURMESE SECRET TEMPLE, GREAT STALAGMITES HAVE BEEN HEWN INTO THE SHAPE OF ELEPHANTS

AIEE—AH—OOM! LEAD THE DEFILERS OF THE SACRED ELEPHANTS TO THEIR DOOM!

SAN YAN, HIGH PRIEST, DIRECTS THE PREPARATION OF THE SACRIFICE!

LET THE FOREIGN DEVILS BE CHAINED WITH THE SAME SHACKLES WHICH HUMBLED THE PROUD SPIRITS OF OUR ANCESTORS!

CRIES OF TRIUMPH FILL THE TEMPLE AS THE ELEPHANT, DELTA, ENTERS BEARING ELVA IN HIS TRUNK—

AH—OOM! OUR GODS HAVE CONQUERED THEIR ENEMIES! ANOTHER SACRIFICE FOR OUR GODS!

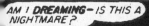

AM I **DREAMING**—IS THIS A NIGHTMARE?

NO, MY DEAR, YOU'RE WIDE AWAKE! SAN YAN AND THE BURMESE ARE THE REAL ELEPHANT KILLERS, AS HE WILL TELL US SHORTLY—

CAPTIVES, HEAR YOUR DOOM! YOUR BODIES SHALL BE TRAMPLED ON BY A SACRED ELEPHANT WHOSE SPIRIT YOU HAVE KEPT IN BONDAGE! THEN WE SHALL FREE THE REMAINING SOULS OF OUR ANCESTORS!

YOU MEAN KILL MORE ELEPHANTS?

28

YES—TO FREE OUR ANCESTORS' SPIRITS WE MUST KILL THESE ELEPHANTS WHOM YOU HOLD CAPTIVE, FAR FROM THEIR NATIVE COUNTRY! FOR THIS PURPOSE WE CAME FROM FAR BURMA ACROSS THE PACIFIC OCEAN!

バビツト末日

OH! OH! THAT FELLOW IS TALKING BURMESE WITH A STRONG JAPANESE ACCENT! THAT'S ALL I WANTED TO KNOW—NOW WE'LL STOP THIS SILLY SACRIFICE BUSINESS—

BUT BEFORE WONDER WOMAN CAN BREAK HER FETTERS, SAN YAN PULLS A LEVER HURLING THE AMAZON MAIDEN UNDER THE FEET OF THE ELEPHANT.

NOT EVEN WONDER WOMAN CAN ESCAPE THE VENGEANCE OF OUR GODS!

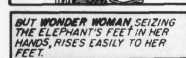

BUT WONDER WOMAN SEIZING THE ELEPHANT'S FEET IN HER HANDS, RISES EASILY TO HER FEET.

ELEPHANT WRESTLING WOULD BE FUN IF THE ANIMAL HAD MORE PEP!

YOU'RE NO BURMESE, SAN YAN, YOU'RE A JAP SPY! YOU PLANNED THESE ELEPHANT MURDERS TO STOP KING'S CIRCUS FROM MAKING MONEY FOR AMERICAN SOLDIERS! CONFESS OR I'LL DROP THE ELEPHANT!

IS TRUE! LET ME GO— I TELL ALL!

INTO THE TEMPLE RUSH STEVE, THE RACKETEERS, KING AND DOM CARNEY—THEY ALL JOIN BATTLE AGAINST THE COMMON ENEMY.

I'M AFRAID I HIT THE LITTLE JAP TOO HARD!

I HOPE SO!

DOM, FREED FROM SUSPICION, WINS THE AVUNCULAR BLESSING.

YOU CAN BOTH KEEP YOUR JOBS! NOW THAT WONDER WOMAN HAS CAUGHT THE ELEPHANT KILLERS, MY SHOW CAN CARRY ON!

WONDER WOMAN—MY BEAUTIFUL ANGEL! DON'T LEAVE ME. STAY WITH ME ALWAYS!

STEVE DARLING—I CANNOT! THE AMAZON LAW FORBIDS IT. BUT I SHALL ALWAYS BE NEAR YOU—NEAREST SOMETIMES WHEN YOU LEAST SUSPECT IT!

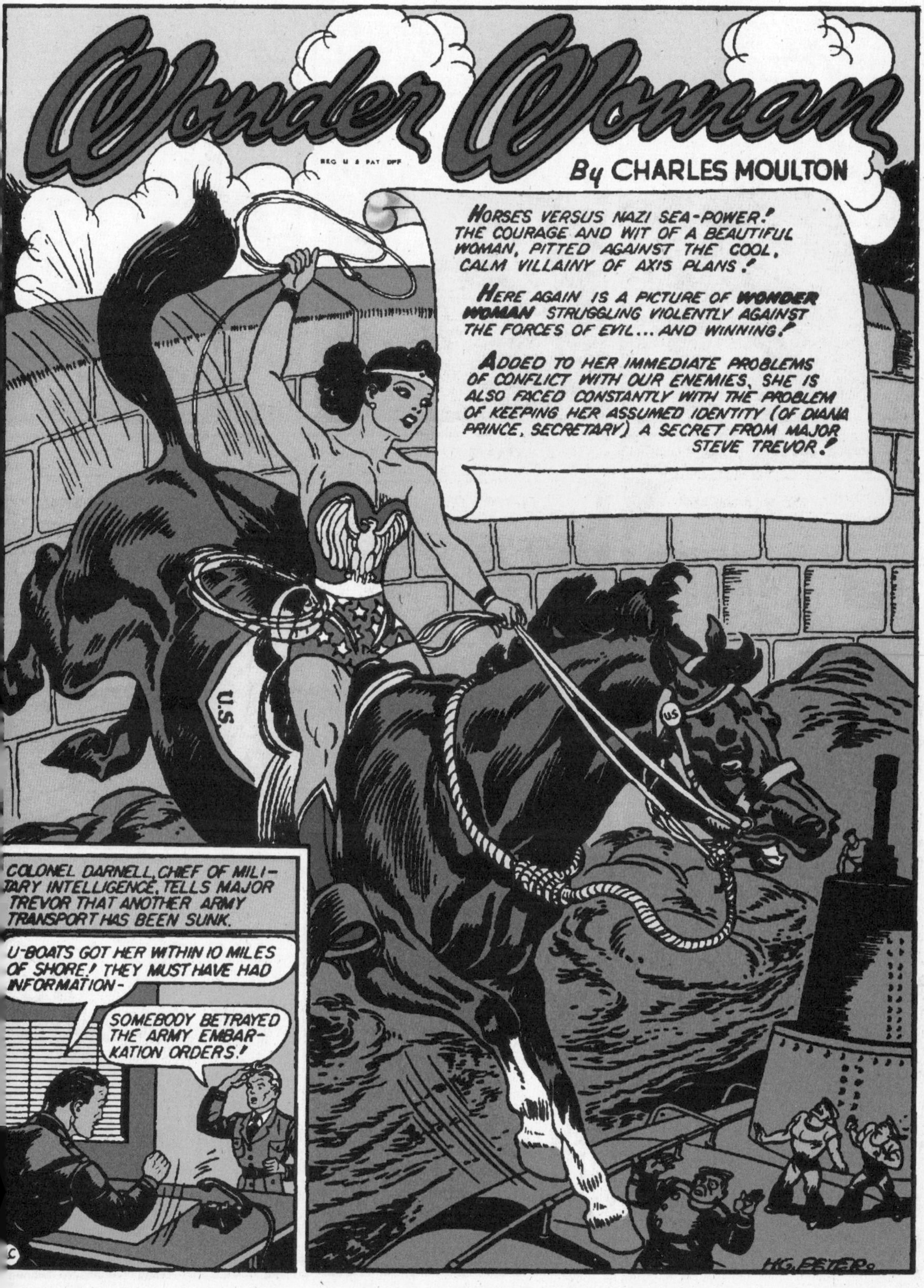
Wonder Woman
By CHARLES MOULTON
HORSES VERSUS NAZI SEA-POWER! THE COURAGE AND WIT OF A BEAUTIFUL WOMAN, PITTED AGAINST THE COOL, CALM VILLAINY OF AXIS PLANS!
HERE AGAIN IS A PICTURE OF WONDER WOMAN STRUGGLING VIOLENTLY AGAINST THE FORCES OF EVIL... AND WINNING!
ADDED TO HER IMMEDIATE PROBLEMS OF CONFLICT WITH OUR ENEMIES, SHE IS ALSO FACED CONSTANTLY WITH THE PROBLEM OF KEEPING HER ASSUMED IDENTITY (OF DIANA PRINCE, SECRETARY) A SECRET FROM MAJOR STEVE TREVOR!
U.S.
US
H.G. PETER
COLONEL DARNELL, CHIEF OF MILITARY INTELLIGENCE, TELLS MAJOR TREVOR THAT ANOTHER ARMY TRANSPORT HAS BEEN SUNK.
U-BOATS GOT HER WITHIN 10 MILES OF SHORE! THEY MUST HAVE HAD INFORMATION-
SOMEBODY BETRAYED THE ARMY EMBARKATION ORDERS!

HOW COULD THAT BE? ONLY THE GENERAL HIMSELF KNEW THOSE ORDERS!

THE NAZI AGENTS ARE CLEVER! THEY'VE BEEN BUILDING THEIR SPY SYSTEM FOR YEARS!

THE BARONESS PAULA VON GUNTHER HEADED THE GESTAPO SYSTEM IN AMERICA. I'LL BET SHE KNOWS HOW THEY'RE GETTING THIS INFORMATION!

BUT THE BARONESS IS IN PRISON— WONDER WOMAN CAPTURED HER!

I WANT YOU TO GO UP TO THE FEDERAL PRISON, AND QUESTION HER JUST THE SAME!

ALL RIGHT, COLONEL, I'LL TAKE DIANA PRINCE ALONG. SHE'S A SWELL STENOGRAPHER AND A GOOD DETECTIVE, TOO.

MEANWHILE, DIANA, AT HOME, IS PACKING HER BAG FOR A WEEK-END VISIT.

I'D BETTER TAKE MY WONDER WOMAN CLOTHES AND THE MAGIC LASSO—NEVER CAN TELL WHEN I'LL NEED THEM!

STEVE, ANXIOUS TO FIND DIANA, BURSTS INTO HER ROOM UNCEREMONIOUSLY.

HEY, DIANA! OH, I BEG YOUR PARDON! DID I STARTLE YOU, BARGING IN LIKE THIS?

WELL—NATURALLY!

I HOPE TO APHRODITE HE DIDN'T SEE MY WONDER WOMAN COSTUME!

WE'RE GOING UP TO THE PENITENTIARY TO QUESTION THE BARONESS AGAIN—WHEN WE'RE THROUGH I'LL DRIVE YOU TO THE TRAIN AND YOU CAN STILL HAVE TIME FOR YOUR WEEK-END!

2C

STEVE AND DIANA ARE ADMITTED TO THE PRISON GROUNDS.

I'LL TAKE YOU TO THE WARDEN'S HOUSE—HE'S EXPECTING YOU!

THANKS!

HOW D'YOU DO, MAJOR! IF THE YOUNG LADY WILL LEAVE HER BAG HERE WE'LL GO OVER TO THE WOMEN'S CELL HOUSE.

OKAY, WARDEN!

BARONESS PAULA VON GUNTHER IS SPECIALLY PREPARED FOR THE INTERVIEW.

THIS PRISONER IS INCORRIGIBLE. IF SHE GIVES YOU ANY TROUBLE—LET ME KNOW!

THAT SHOULDN'T BE NECESSARY—I'M AN OLD FRIEND OF HERS!

KINDNESS FROM YOU TWO OVERWHELMS ME! WHAT DO YOU WANT?

WE WANT INFORMATION, BARONESS—ABOUT THE NAZI SPY ORGANIZATION IN AMERICA!

BUT I KNOW NOTHING! THEY KEEP ME IN A DARK SOLITARY CELL UNDER-GROUND. HOW COULD I CONTACT ANYONE?

I DON'T KNOW BUT YOU ARE PRETTY CLEVER, PAULA!

IF YOU WILL TELL ME HOW NAZI AGENTS LEARN ABOUT OUR TROOPS SAILING, I'LL GET YOU OUT OF SOLI-TARY, AND SEE THAT YOU HAVE SPECIAL PRIVILEGES.

POOF FOR YOUR SPECIAL PRIVILEGES! I KNOW NOTHING, I TELL YOU!

WELL PERHAPS YOU'RE TELLING THE TRUTH—WILL YOU TAKE THE LIE DETECTOR TEST?

NO-NO! YOU CANNOT MAKE ME—THE AMERICAN LAW FORBIDS!

YOU CUR—YOU SWINE—TAKE THOSE TUBES OFF!

AMERICAN LAW DOES NOT PRO-TECT ENEMY SPIES IN WAR-TIME—YOU'LL TAKE THIS TEST AND LIKE IT!

IN A MAD RAGE THE BARONESS BREAKS LOOSE AND SMASHES THE LIE DETECTOR---

IT IS I WHO PUT THE LIE DETECTOR ON YOU—HOW DO YOU LIKE IT?

UGH!

GUARDS OVERPOWER THE BARONESS, BUT THE LIE DETECTOR IS BEYOND REPAIR

THERE'S NO DOUBT OUR GENTLE PAULA HAS GUMMED THE WORKS! I'LL HAVE TO GET A NEW MACHINE!

THIS PRISONER IS A DEVIL!

MEANWHILE, THE WARDEN'S YOUNG SON, FREDDY, IS PLAYING COWBOY, HIS FAVORITE GAME

GEE WHIZ! I GOTTA FIND SOMEBODY TO LASSO. WHERE'S SIS, I WONDER?

THERE'S SIS. BETCHA I GET HER FIRST THROW—

WHOA, THAR, MEHITABEL! TAKE IT EASY—I GOTTA BRAND YA!

EEEE-EK! YOU LET ME GO OR I'LL TELL DAD. AND DON'T CALL ME MEHITABEL— MY NAME'S MABEL AND YOU KNOW IT!

YOU LITTLE FIEND! WAIT TILL I CATCH YOU!

YA-AAH! WAIT TILL YOU DO! YOU COULDN'T EVEN CATCH A COLD!

FREDDY, STILL LOOKING FOR SOMETHING TO LASSO, SEES DIANA'S BAG.

YAH! WATCH ME LASSO THAT BAG!

YIPPEE! GOT IT THE FIRST TIME! I'M BETTER'N GENE AUTRY!

WHEN THE BAG HITS THE FLOOR ITS LOCK SPRINGS OPEN AND THE MAGIC LASSO FALLS OUT.

OH BOY! WHAT'S THIS? A LASSO ROPE MADE OF GOLD CHAIN!

FREDDY PUTS THE BAG BACK—BUT FORGETS TO RETURN THE MAGIC LASSO!

WOW! WHAT A BEAUTY! IT WON'T HURT IF I THROW IT A COUPLA TIMES!

DIANA TAKES HER BAG. NEVER SUSPECTING THAT IT HAS BEEN OPENED.

I'LL TAKE YOUR BAG, DIANA.

NO, THANKS. I'D RATHER CARRY IT MYSELF! PLEASE DRIVE ME HOME. I'VE MISSED THE TRAIN FOR MY WEEK-END PARTY!

THE BARONESS IS SENT BACK TO THE PRISON DUNGEON.

GET ALONG, MY GIRL, IT'S THE DARK HOLE FOR YOU AGAIN!

ALL RIGHT, ALL RIGHT- YOU NEEDN'T BE SO ROUGH!

I HADDA BE ROUGH OR SOME STOOLIE'D GET WISE! I'M SUPPOSED TO KEEP BRACELETS AND LEG IRONS ON YOU BUT I AIN'T DOIN' IT!

HOW CONSIDERATE OF YOU!

DIS DOUGH IS OKAY, SAY, BARONESS, WHYN'T YER BREAK OUTA DIS JOINT? FER A COUPLA GRAND IT COULD BE ARRANGED!

NO THANKS, I LOVE MY BRIGHT COZY CELL TOO WELL TO LEAVE IT!

WHEN THE GUARD HAS GONE, PAULA SIGNALS AND A TRAP DOOR OPENS.

TAP TAP

PAULA DESCENDS INTO AN OLD TIER OF TORTURE CELLS, LONG SEALED BENEATH THE PRISON AND FORGOTTEN. HERE THE CLEVER SPY QUEEN MEETS HER AGENTS AND SLAVES WHO ENTER BY A SECRET PASSAGE.

LET US HELP YOU, MISTRESS.

YOUR EXCELLENCY, VE HAF CAPTURED CAPTAIN LOYAL WHO CARRIES SECRET ORDERS FOR TROOPS TO EMBARK! DERE VAS NO PAPERS ON HIM!

HE MUST CARRY THE ORDERS IN HIS MEMORY. BRING HIM IN. I'LL MAKE HIM TALK!

GOOD EVENING, CAPTAIN! I WANT THE SAILING ORDERS YOU WERE CARRYING TO GENERAL HALCOMB. YOU'D BETTER GIVE THEM TO ME NOW AND SPARE US BOTH UNPLEASANTNESS!

I WON'T TALK--YOU CAN DO WHAT YOU LIKE- I WON'T TALK!

PAULA TRIES A HYPNOTIC EXPERIMENT WITH A FLICKER WHEEL.

QUIET-QUIET-LET YOUR MIND SLEEP! OBEY ME-YOU MUST OBEY ME!

I—WILL OBEY!

I COMMAND YOU—REPEAT THE ORDERS FOR GENERAL HALCOMB!

YOU WILL EMBARK YOUR MEN ON THE U.S. TRANSPORT—

WITH A TERRIFIC EFFORT OF WILL, CAPTAIN LOYAL THROWS OFF THE BARONESS'S HYPNOTIC INFLUENCE!

ON THE TRANSPORT-TRANSPORT NO! I WILL NOT TELL-I WILL NOT OBEY YOU!

ZUT! HIS WILL IS TOO STRONG!

GO TO WORK ON HIM, HEINRICH-SOFTEN HIM UP!

BUT I DOUBT THAT WE CAN BREAK HIM-THESE AMERICANS ARE TOO TOUGH! THAT'S THE WEAK POINT IN OUR SYSTEM--I NEED SOMETHING TO MAKE OUR PRISONERS TALK!

LATER, PAULA, UNDER SPECIAL GUARD, IS PERMITTED TO EXERCISE WITH THE OTHER WOMAN PRISONERS.

THESE CONVICTS ANNOY ME! TAKE ME TO THAT PRIVATE WALK BY THE WARDEN'S GROUNDS.

OKAY-THAT'LL COST YA ANOTHER FIVER!

THROUGH A WIRE FENCE PAULA SEES FREDDY PLAYING WITH THE MAGIC LASSO.

FREDDY'S SISTER, AS USUAL, PROVES AN IRRESISTIBLE TARGET.

OH FOOEY-THAT PEST AGAIN! STOP IT, FREDDY!

YAY-BO! I GOTCHA, MEHITABEL!

YOU WAIT TILL I GET LOOSE! I'LL FIX YOU—

NO FAIR-YOU'RE BIGGER THAN ME-STOP PULLIN'!

THIS IS AWFUL! SOMETHING'S **MAKING** ME OBEY FREDDY!

WHAT'S HAPPENED TO SIS? SHE STOPPED PULLIN'! SHE NEVER DID ANYTHING I TOLD HER BEFORE!

DOWN ON YOUR KNEES, WOMAN, AND BEG FOR MERCY!

SHE'S DOIN' IT! SHE MUST LIKE THIS GAME.

HAVE MERCY, COWBOY! MY FATHER WILL PAY THE RANSOM!

THE BARONESS, WHO HAS FELT THE STRANGE POWER OF THE MAGIC LASSO, RECOGNIZES IT INSTANTLY!

I CAN'T IMAGINE HOW HE GOT IT, BUT THAT'S **WONDER WOMAN'S** LASSO—JUST WHAT I NEED TO MAKE PRISONERS TALK.

GET ME THAT BOY'S METAL ROPE—QUICKLY!

OKAY—BUT IT'LL COST YOU PLENTY, SISTER!

WHERE'D YER GIT THAT ROPE FREDDY? YA STOLE IT, DIDN'TCHA?

I—I JUST BORROWED IT FROM MAJOR TREVOR'S SUITCASE! OH, PLEASE DON'T TELL DAD!

GIMME THE ROPE—I'LL TAKE CARE OF IT! AN' NOT A YAP TO YER OLD MAN, REMEMBER!

I WON'T TELL DAD—HE'D WALLOP ME! THANKS FOR FIXIN' IT!

TREVOR MUST HAVE BORROWED **WONDER WOMAN'S** LASSO TO MAKE ME TALK. LUCKY THE CHILD TOOK IT!

IF ANYONE LEARNS I HAVE THIS LASSO, YOU WILL REGRET IT!

DON'T THREATEN ME, SISTER—YOU'RE STILL A PRISONER!—AND IT'S GONNA COST YOU PLENTY FROM TIME TO TIME TO KEEP ME QUIET—

FREED FROM THE MAGIC LASSO, MABEL TURNS ON HER TORMENTOR!

YOU LITTLE SNIPE! MAKE ME DO TRICKS LIKE A TRAINED MONKEY, WILL YOU! I'LL TEACH YOU!

AW GEE, MABEL, IT WAS A GOOD GAME—AW GEE!

INTENSE EXCITEMENT PREVAILS IN TREVOR'S OFFICE NEXT DAY AS U-BOATS ATTACK GENERAL HAL-COMB'S TRANSPORTS!

RADIO THE 10TH SQUADRON PATROL PLANES! CONTACT DESTROYER X59—OUR REPORTS SHOW SHE'S NEAR THE SPOT!

SWOOPING LIKE AVENGING EAGLES FROM THE SKY, AMERICAN PATROL PLANES ATTACK AND SINK THE U-BOATS.

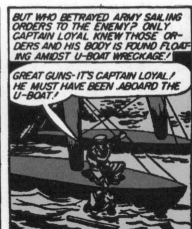

BUT WHO BETRAYED ARMY SAILING ORDERS TO THE ENEMY? ONLY CAPTAIN LOYAL KNEW THOSE ORDERS AND HIS BODY IS FOUND FLOATING AMIDST U-BOAT WRECKAGE!

GREAT GUNS-IT'S CAPTAIN LOYAL! HE MUST HAVE BEEN ABOARD THE U-BOAT!

COLONEL DARNELL MAKES HIS OFFICIAL REPORT.

I'M SORRY TO REPORT, GENERAL, THAT CAPTAIN LOYAL BETRAYED US!

I DON'T BELIEVE IT-CAPTAIN LOYAL WAS NO TRAITOR! THIS IS A JOB FOR WONDER WOMAN!

WONDER WOMAN, DONNING HER COSTUME, SEARCHES HER BAG IN VAIN FOR THE MAGIC LASSO.

THUNDERS OF ZEUS! THE MAGIC LASSO IS GONE!

SOMEONE AT THE PRISON TOOK MY LASSO. IF I ASK ABOUT IT AS DIANA PRINCE THEY'LL KNOW I'M WONDER WOMAN. IF I ASK ABOUT IT AS WONDER WOMAN, THEY'LL KNOW I AM DIANA PRINCE. WHAT A DILEMMA!

WONDER WOMAN VISITS THE PRISON UNANNOUNCED.

I HAVEN'T DONE ANY POLE VAULTING SINCE I LEFT PARADISE ISLAND - WISH I HAD MORE TIME FOR SPORTS!

8C

WONDER WOMAN FINDS FREDDY AT HIS FAVORITE GAME.

MAYBE THIS YOUNG COWBOY KNOWS SOMETHING ABOUT MY MISSING LASSO!

HI-YAH, COWBOY! LET'S SEE YOU LASSO ME!

WOW! YOU'RE WONDER WOMAN! D'YOU REALLY WANT TO PLAY COWBOY AND INDIAN?

AFTER SEVERAL ATTEMPTS, FREDDY ROPES **WONDER WOMAN.**

YOU'RE MY PRISONER NOW—YOU HAVE TO BE TIED UP!

I SURRENDER! YOU CAN TIE ME TO THAT POST.

NOW I BET YOU CAN'T GET AWAY!

YOU WANT ME TO TRY?

SURE—LET'S SEE YOU GET AWAY WOW! GEE! YOU'RE STRONGER THAN ANYBODY IN THE WORLD!

WONDER WOMAN TEACHES FREDDY TO THROW THE LASSO.

GOOD WORK, FREDDY! A PERFECT THROW!

YEAH, BUT YOU SHOWED ME—YOU MUSTA BEEN A COWBOY --ER, COWGIRL, ONCE.

I'LL SEND YOU A REAL LASSO, FREDDY. YOU NEED A HEAVIER ROPE.

BOY! YOU OUGHTA SEEN THE ONE I HAD. IT WAS MADE OF CHAIN, BUT GUARD SWIPE TOOK IT AWAY FROM ME.

WONDER WOMAN WAITS BEHIND A GUARD TOWER FOR SWIPE WHEN SUDDENLY THE PRISON SIREN SOUNDS.

SO GUARD SWIPE HAS THE LASSO, EH? WHERE IS THAT GUARD? HUH? WHAT'S THAT—SOUNDS LIKE AN ALARM!

WHEEEOOOOO

WHEEE OOOOOOO!

STEPPING FROM BEHIND THE TOWER, **WONDER WOMAN** IS SURROUNDED INSTANTLY BY ARMED GUARDS.

WONDER WOMAN! WHAT ARE YOU DOING HERE? WHY DID YOU KILL GUARD SWIPE?

I DIDN'T KILL HIM. I WAS WAITING FOR HIM--- BUT---

9C

ARREST HER FOR MURDER! —HEY!

SORRY, BOYS, I HAVEN'T TIME TO BE ARRESTED TODAY— SEE YOU LATER!

VAULTING HIGH OVER THE GUARDS' HEADS, **WONDER WOMAN** MAKES A DIFFICULT TARGET.

THIS'LL GIVE YOU PRACTICE FOR SHOOTING AT PARACHUTE TROOPS!

WONDER WOMAN TELEPHONES STEVE AND TELLS HIM OF HER PREDICAMENT.

THEY'RE ACCUSING YOU OF **MURDER**? WHAT DAD-GASTED STUPIDITY! I'LL FIND OUT WHO MURDERED SWIPE AND CLEAR YOU!

HOURS LATER—

I BROKE THAT CASE QUICK! THE AUTOPSY ON SWIPE SHOWED HE WAS POISONED. A PRISON GUARD SAW HIM TAKE A DRINK FROM A BOTTLE THE BARONESS GAVE HIM. A MINUTE LATER, HE TUMBLED OFF THE TOWER, DEAD!

GOOD WORK, STEVE!

HOW WILL YOU GET WORD TO **WONDER WOMAN**?

SHE PROMISED TO CALL ME. I'LL WAIT HERE UNTIL SHE CALLS. SHE'LL HAVE TO GO TO THE PRISON TO CLEAR HERSELF OF CHARGES.

I'D BETTER HURRY HOME SO **WONDER WOMAN** CAN CALL STEVE.

WELL—I'LL BE GOING—

OH NO, YOU WON'T. YOU'LL STAY HERE— **WONDER WOMAN** MAY WISH TO DICTATE A STATEMENT AND I'LL WANT YOU TO TYPE IT—

LONG HOURS PASS BUT STILL **WONDER WOMAN** DOESN'T CALL.

PLEASE LET ME GO HOME, STEVE!

POSITIVELY NOT! **WONDER WOMAN** IS MORE IMPORTANT THAN YOUR PRIVATE AFFAIRS!

AT LAST DIANA TAKES A CHANCE AND CALLS STEVE ON AN OFFICE EXTENSION.

STEVE? THIS IS **WONDER WOMAN**.

MY BEAUTIFUL ANGEL! I'VE FOUND THE MURDERER -BUT YOU'LL HAVE TO MAKE A STATEMENT— WAIT-OH, DIANA!

DIANA DOES SOME QUICK THINKING.

OH DIANA! COME HERE, **WONDER WOMAN** IS ON THE WIRE! HEY WHO ARE YOU CALLING?

OH-ER-NOBODY! THAT IS, I'M LISTENING IN! YOU SAID **WONDER WOMAN** MIGHT WANT ME TO TAKE DICTATION!

FINALLY FREE, DIANA LEAVES THE OFFICE AND HURRIES TO THE PRISON—WHERE SHE IS ARRESTED.

BUT THE BARONESS POISONED SWIPE!

THE ONLY WITNESS AGAINST THE BARONESS HAS DISAPPEAR-ED. HE WENT TO HER CELL TO MAKE HER TALK—SO HE SAID—AND VAN-ISHED!

PAULA KILLED THE WITNESS—SHE HAS THE MAGIC LASSO. I MUST SEE HER.

WILL YOU PUT ME IN A CELL NEXT TO THE BARONESS?

CERTAINLY NOT! ONLY INSUB-ORDINATE PRISONERS ARE KEPT IN SOLI-TARY.

WONDER WOMAN IMMEDIATELY BECOMES INSUBOR-DINATE!

DANCE DAINTILY, NOW, FOR MAMA!

HELP! STOP HER, SOMEBODY!

UGH-OW! LEMME AT HER!

HOW ABOUT IT, WARDEN? DO I RATE THE DARK HOLE?

YOU DO! GRAB HER, BOYS! PUT HER IN SOLITARY!

WEARING DOUBLE HANDCUFFS AND LEG IRONS WONDER WOMAN IS PUT IN A CELL NEXT TO PAULA'S.

GREAT SAMSON'S GHOST! I'LL BE GLAD WHEN SHE'S LOCKED UP!

EASILY BREAKING HER SHACKLES, WONDER WOMAN PRESSES HER EAR TO THE FLOOR OF HER CELL.

I'M SURE I HEARD VOICES DOWN BELOW!

THE BARONESS, OPENING THE CELL DOOR STEALTHILY WITH A SKELETON KEY, THROWS THE MAGIC LASSO OVER WONDER WOMAN.

AT LAST I'VE GOT YOU! COME WITH ME!

I—I MUST OBEY YOU! THE MAGIC LASSO COMPELS ME!

IN THE BARONESS'S SECRET DUN-GEON, WONDER WOMAN MEETS A FELLOW PRISONER, CONDEMNED LIKE HERSELF TO DEATH.

FREDDY! WHAT ARE YOU DOING HERE?

SAME AS YOU, WONDER WOMAN— THEY'RE GOING TO KILL BOTH OF US!

PAULA LEAVES, TO MAKE FINAL PREPARATIONS.

GEE, **WONDER WOMAN**, I'M AWFUL SORRY I SWIPED YOUR MAGIC LASSO! I'M TO BLAME—

CHIN UP, FREDDY NOBODY CAN BREAK THIS LASSO, BUT I CAN PULL THE POST DOWN!

I'LL FREE YOU IN A MINUTE, FREDDY, THEN YOU CAN UNTIE ME.

HOPPING TO FREDDY'S CAGE ON BOUND FEET, **WONDER WOMAN** SMASHES THE BARS WITH HER SHOULDER.

YIPPEE! YOU'RE TOUGHER THAN A TANK!

BUT JUST AS FREDDY UNTIES **WONDER WOMAN'S** HANDS, THE BARONESS RETURNS AND SEIZES THE MAGIC LASSO.

JUST IN TIME! HANDS UP, **WONDER WOMAN**!

FREDDY, UNNOTICED BY PAULA, THROWS HIS OWN LASSO AS **WONDER WOMAN** TAUGHT HIM.

GREAT WORK, FREDDY! YOU SAVED OUR LIVES!

THE BARONESS FLEES THROUGH THE SECRET PASSAGE.

I'LL LET PAULA KEEP AHEAD OF ME—I MUST FOLLOW HER TO THE SECRET NAZI HEAD-QUARTERS.

STEVE, MEANWHILE, LEARNS OF A FORTIFIED U-BOAT BASE ON A HID-DEN INLET NEAR THE PRISON.

COMMANDING OFFICER, 103RD CAVALRY? THE GENERAL'S COM-PLIMENTS. YOU WILL ATTACK THE SUBMARINE BASE WITH YOUR REGIMENT IMMEDIATELY!

THE CAVALRY CHARGES BRAVELY BUT FUTILELY INTO A WITHERING FIRE!

MANY OFFICERS ARE KILLED OR WOUNDED—THE REGIMENT IS TEMPORARILY LEADERLESS.

RECKON IT'S UP TO YOU, LIEUTENANT, TO LEAD THE REGIMENT!

THERE MUST BE OFFICERS WHO RANK HIGHER THAN ME—I DON'T KNOW OUR ORDERS!

AT THIS MOMENT WONDER WOMAN ARRIVES. FOLLOWING PAULA, WHO HAS SLIPPED INTO THE NAZI RANKS.

COME ON BOYS—LET'S GO GET 'EM!

YEA! WONDER WOMAN! COME ON! LET'S GO!

CHEERING MADLY, THE CAVALRY FOLLOWS WONDER WOMAN INTO THE ENEMY FORTRESS.

YA-A-A! WONDER WOMAN!

WE'LL FOLLOW! WONDER WOMAN!

RACING TO THE NAZI DOCK WONDER WOMAN JUMPS HER HORSE TO THE DECK OF AN ESCAPING U-BOAT.

SURRENDER YOUR SHIP, COMMANDER!

ACH—DONNERWETTER! I HAF TO DO IT—I DON'T KNOW VY—BUT SOMEDING MAKES ME!

A STRAY BULLET PUTS THE BARONESS BEYOND THE REACH OF JUSTICE!

HEIL HIT—OHH HH...

THE 103 RD CAVALRY PAYS HONOR TO WONDER WOMAN.

WONDER WOMAN, OUR REGIMENT HAS ELECTED YOU HONORARY COLONEL.

I COMMAND YOU ALL TO BE TRUE TO YOUR WIVES AND SWEETHEARTS!

YOU ARE MY HERO, FREDDY!

AW GEE—ER—THANKS FOR THIS KEEN LASSO, WONDER WOMAN!

AW SAY—WHY DON'T I RATE A KISS AS MUCH AS FREDDY?

WONDER WOMAN SAYS—

"WHEN YOU SEE THESE MINUTE MAN POSTERS, BOYS AND GIRLS, REMEMBER HE'S TALKING TO YOU!

FOR VICTORY BUY UNITED STATES SAVINGS BONDS AND STAMPS

Wonder Woman

by Charles Moulton

LITTLE DO AMERICANS REALIZE THAT THE FATE OF A NEIGHBOR NATION AND OUR OWN DESTINY IN THE PACIFIC REST UPON THE CARMINED LIPS OF A LOVELY, DARK AND DANGEROUS SPANISH GIRL, THE ONLY WOMAN MATADOR WHO EVER SLEW FIFTY BULLS WITH THE LIGHTNING DOWN-THRUST OF HER HEAVY *ESTOQUE*, THE TRADITIONAL SWORD OF THE BULL-FIGHTER.

BUT ETTA CANDY KNOWS HER SOLDIER BROTHER'S SKULL WAS NOT FRACTURED FOR FUN AND ETTA CALLS ON *WONDER WOMAN* TO UNRAVEL THE MYSTERY. APPEARING SUDDENLY AT THE POINT OF DANGER, THAT MARVELOUS MAIDEN FROM PARADISE ISLAND, SECRET HOME OF THE AMAZONS, ELECTRIFIES THE WORLD BY PERFORMING WHAT NEWSPAPERS CALL "THE GREATEST FEAT OF DARING IN HUMAN HISTORY!"

DIANA PRINCE, ALONE IN HER ROOM, TURNS ON HER MENTAL RADIO, THAT AMAZING AMAZON INVENTION WHICH PICKS UP BRAIN WAVES.....

I HAVE A FEELING THAT SOMEONE IS TRYING TO SEND ME A MENTAL MESSAGE!

PUFF – PUFF – EAT PUFF – CHOCOLATE –

WHY, IT'S ETTA CANDY! HA! HA! I NEVER THOUGHT ETTA WOULD GET BRAIN-WAVE AMBITIONS! WHAT IN THE WORLD IS SHE TRYING TO SAY?

CAW-CALLING WONDER WOMAN! I NEED YOUR HELP! MY BROTHER–IN THE ARMY–SPIES ATTACKED HIM–LISTEN.

WITH THE AID OF HER OWN TELEPATHIC POWER, DIANA PIECES ETTA'S STORY TOGETHER.

ETTA'S BROTHER, PRIVATE MINT CANDY, IS A DISPATCH RIDER IN A TEXAS ARMY CAMP.

GEE! THIS IS A TOUGH LIFE. NOT ENOUGH EXCITEMENT TO KEEP A GUY AWAKE.

MINT CANDY'S DROWSY EYES FAIL TO OBSERVE A ROPE STRETCHED ACROSS THE ROAD WITH SINISTER INTENT.

OH-BOY–WOULD I LIKE TO TAKE A NAP!

MINT GETS HIS WISH. HIS MOTORCYCLE HITS THE ROPE AND THE RESULTING CRASH SENDS HIM TO DREAMLAND!

CRACK!!

TWO DAYS LATER, MINT CANDY WAKES UP IN THE HOSPITAL.

SHUT UP, BIRDS! I NEVER DID LIKE CANARIES.

QUIET, SON! YOU'VE GOT A SKULL FRACTURE!

TWEET TWEET

THE GENERAL QUESTIONS MINT.

ENEMY AGENTS GOT YOU, CANDY! WERE YOU CARRYING ANY PAPERS?

NO SIR! I CARRIED THE SECRET ORDERS IN MY HEAD. GEE! I HOPE THEY DIDN'T SPILL OUT WHEN MY SKULL CRACKED!

PLEASE, WONDER WOMAN, CAPTURE THE SPIES WHO ATTACKED MY BROTHER!

POOR ETTA! I'D LIKE TO HELP HER BUT IT ISN'T MY JOB! I'LL REPORT THE MATTER TO COLONEL DARNELL TOMORROW.

2D

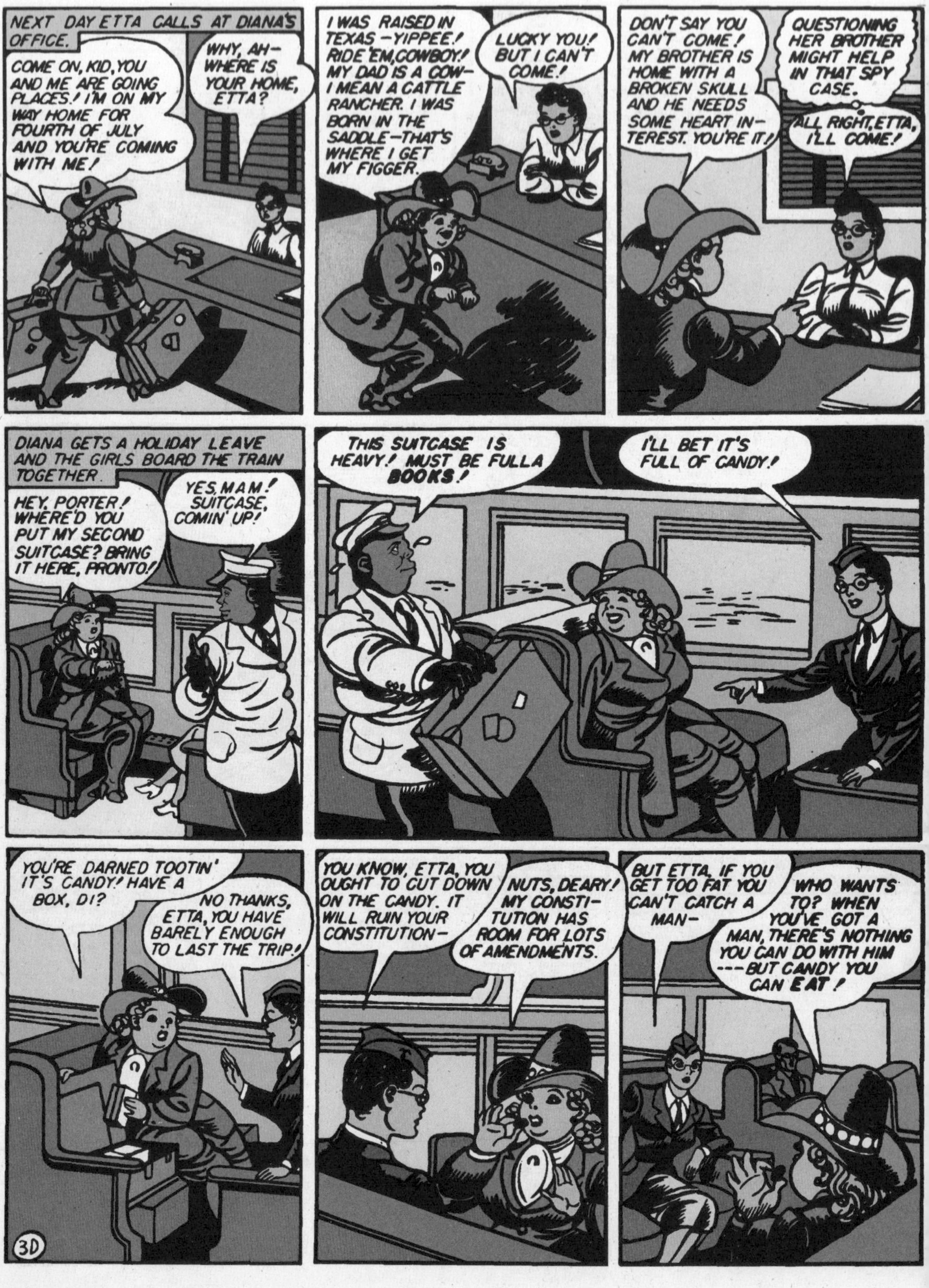
NEXT DAY ETTA CALLS AT DIANA'S OFFICE.
COME ON, KID, YOU AND ME ARE GOING PLACES! I'M ON MY WAY HOME FOR FOURTH OF JULY AND YOU'RE COMING WITH ME!
WHY, AH- WHERE IS YOUR HOME, ETTA?
I WAS RAISED IN TEXAS -YIPPEE! RIDE 'EM, COWBOY! MY DAD IS A COW- I MEAN A CATTLE RANCHER. I WAS BORN IN THE SADDLE-THAT'S WHERE I GET MY FIGGER.
LUCKY YOU! BUT I CAN'T COME!
DON'T SAY YOU CAN'T COME! MY BROTHER IS HOME WITH A BROKEN SKULL AND HE NEEDS SOME HEART INTEREST. YOU'RE IT!
QUESTIONING HER BROTHER MIGHT HELP IN THAT SPY CASE.
ALL RIGHT, ETTA, I'LL COME!
DIANA GETS A HOLIDAY LEAVE AND THE GIRLS BOARD THE TRAIN TOGETHER.
HEY, PORTER! WHERE'D YOU PUT MY SECOND SUITCASE? BRING IT HERE, PRONTO!
YES, MAM! SUITCASE, COMIN' UP!
THIS SUITCASE IS HEAVY! MUST BE FULLA BOOKS!
I'LL BET IT'S FULL OF CANDY!
YOU'RE DARNED TOOTIN' IT'S CANDY! HAVE A BOX, DI?
NO THANKS, ETTA, YOU HAVE BARELY ENOUGH TO LAST THE TRIP!
YOU KNOW, ETTA, YOU OUGHT TO CUT DOWN ON THE CANDY. IT WILL RUIN YOUR CONSTITUTION-
NUTS, DEARY! MY CONSTITUTION HAS ROOM FOR LOTS OF AMENDMENTS.
BUT ETTA, IF YOU GET TOO FAT YOU CAN'T CATCH A MAN-
WHO WANTS TO? WHEN YOU'VE GOT A MAN, THERE'S NOTHING YOU CAN DO WITH HIM ---BUT CANDY YOU CAN EAT!
3D

BUT DON'T YOU LIKE TO BE ADMIRED?

SURE, MEN ALWAYS SAY I'M BEAUTIFUL—IF THEY DIDN'T, I'D KNOCK 'EM FOR A LOOP!

TAKING OFF WEIGHT WILL MAKE YOU FEEL BETTER AND BESIDES IT'S UNPATRIOTIC TO HOARD EVEN FAT!

OKAY. I'LL TAKE OFF TEN POUNDS. IF I LIKE IT, I'LL TAKE OFF 50 MORE. IF I DON'T, WELL—!

AT BRAZOS, TEXAS, THE GIRLS ARE MET BY MINT GANDY.

HI, SIS! BRING YER BAGS OVER, I KAINT LEAVE THE JALOPY-SHE MIGHT RUN AWAY ON ME!

MINT, SHAKE HANDS WITH MY PAL, DIANA PRINCE. ISN'T SHE PRETTY?

AW—ER—YEAH. PLEASE' TA MEET YER. LET'S GET GOIN'!

I CAN SEE I'M A FLOP AS MINT'S HEART INTEREST!

AT THE BAR "L" RANCH, THE CHIEF RECREATION IS HORSEBACK RIDING.

PANCHO, SADDLE UP THREE HOSSES. I'M GOING TO SHOW THE LADIES THE OLD RADIUM MINE, YONDER.

I DO HIM, BOSS.

BUT BEFORE GOING TO THE CORRAL, PANCHO MAKES A PECULIAR TELEPHONE CALL.

SI, SI! OLD MINE, — MUY PRONTO!

I FORGOT TO ASK YOU, MA'AM — CAN YOU RIDE?

WHY, YES, I CAN RIDE A LITTLE, IF YOU DON'T GO TOO FAST.

ETTA, RIDING AHEAD, DROPS HER HANDKERCHIEF——-

HEY ETTA! YA DROPPED SOMETHING!

I'LL GET IT FOR HER!

WOO-WOO!

4D

WOW! CAN THAT BABY RIDE! WHAT A KIDDIN' SHE GAVE ME ABOUT NOT RIDIN' FAST.

HEY, KID, WHO YOU TRYING TO IMITATE, LIGHT-HORSE HARRY LEE? YOU MUSTA BEEN A TRICK RIDER ONCE IN A CIRCUS!

AT THE ABANDONED MINE, DIANA'S KEEN EARS PICK UP THE FAINT SOUND OF A HUMAN VOICE.

LISTEN! I HEAR SOMEONE CALLING FROM THAT OLD SHAFT HOUSE!

HELP HELP

PEERING DOWN THE DARK, ABANDONED MINE SHAFT, DIANA SEES THE WHITE BLUR OF A FACE, FAR BELOW.

I CAN'T SEE A THING.

THERE'S A GIRL DOWN THERE! SOMEBODY'LL HAVE TO GO DOWN AFTER HER!

MINT CANDY, DESPITE HIS INJURY, INSISTS ON DESCENDING THE SHAFT.

I'VE GOT THE ROPE AROUND HER— PULL HER UP! I'LL CLIMB MY ROPE AND HELP CARRY HER WEIGHT!

DIANA PRETENDS THAT THE GIRL'S WEIGHT IS ALMOST TOO MUCH FOR HER STRENGTH.

OH— PUFF! UGH! THIS STRAW IS BREAKING MY BACK.

HOLD TIGHT, MISS DIANA! I'LL BE RIGHT UP THERE TO HELP YOU!

5D

BOY, IS SHE A BEAUTY! WHY WOULD ANYBODY WANT TO THROW A GIRL LIKE THIS DOWN A MINE SHAFT?

PROBABLY SOMEBODY HAD A GOOD REASON.

REVIVED AT LAST, THE GIRL TELLS HER STORY.

MY NAME IS PEPITA VALDEZ. I DANCE AT ZEE CASA D'ORO, MEXICO CITY. SEÑOR GOMAS HE MAK' LOVE TO ME — I NO LIKE HEEM!

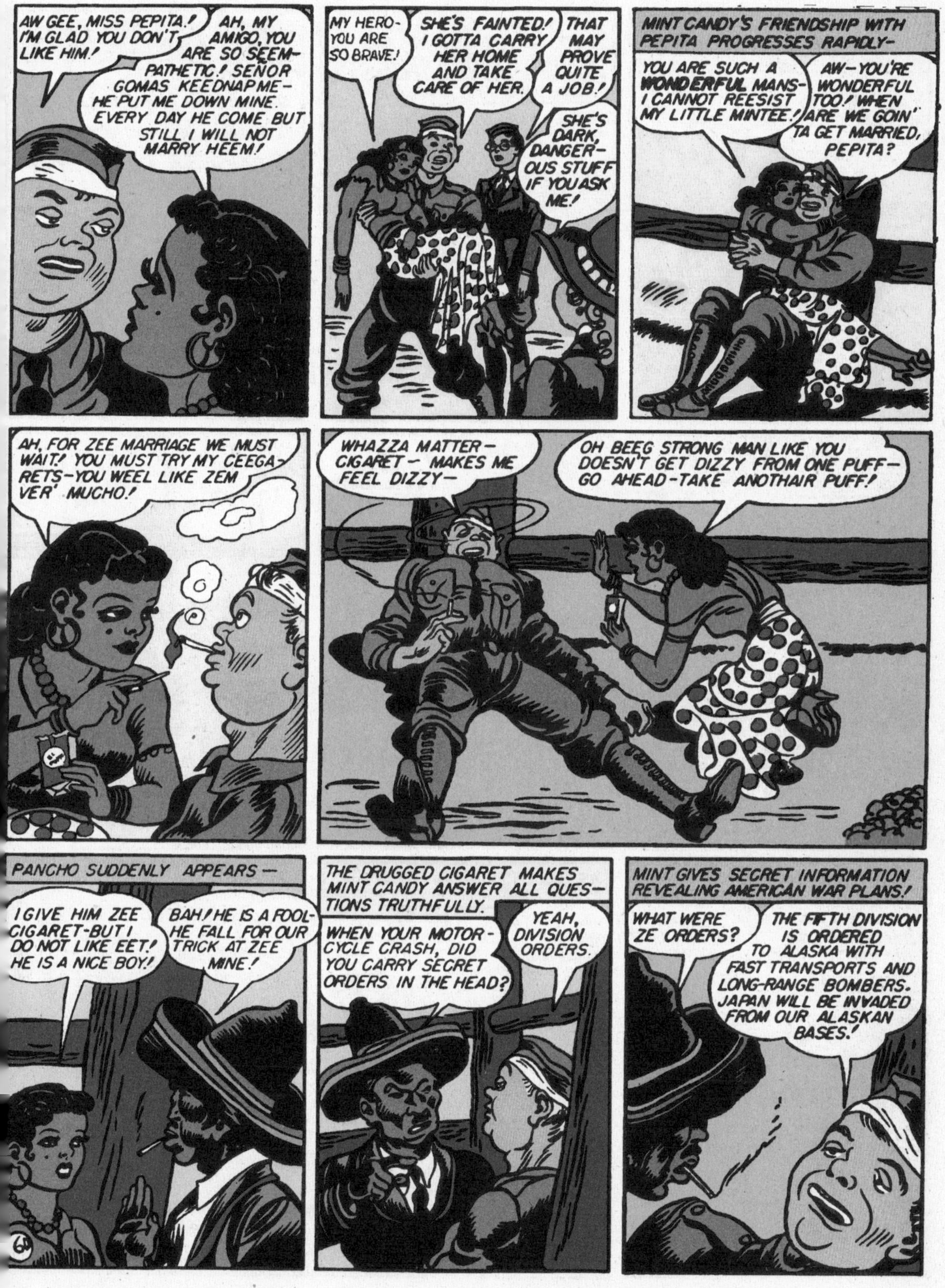
AW GEE, MISS PEPITA! I'M GLAD YOU DON'T LIKE HIM!
AH, MY AMIGO, YOU ARE SO SEEMPATHETIC! SEÑOR GOMAS KEEDNAP ME— HE PUT ME DOWN MINE. EVERY DAY HE COME BUT STILL I WILL NOT MARRY HEEM!
MY HERO— YOU ARE SO BRAVE!
SHE'S FAINTED! I GOTTA CARRY HER HOME AND TAKE CARE OF HER.
THAT MAY PROVE QUITE A JOB!
SHE'S DARK, DANGEROUS STUFF IF YOU ASK ME!
MINT CANDY'S FRIENDSHIP WITH PEPITA PROGRESSES RAPIDLY—
YOU ARE SUCH A WONDERFUL MANS— I CANNOT REESIST MY LITTLE MINTEE!
AW—YOU'RE WONDERFUL TOO! WHEN ARE WE GOIN' TA GET MARRIED, PEPITA?
AH, FOR ZEE MARRIAGE WE MUST WAIT! YOU MUST TRY MY CEEGARETS—YOU WEEL LIKE ZEM VER' MUCHO!
WHAZZA MATTER— CIGARET— MAKES ME FEEL DIZZY—
OH BEEG STRONG MAN LIKE YOU DOESN'T GET DIZZY FROM ONE PUFF— GO AHEAD—TAKE ANOTHAIR PUFF!
PANCHO SUDDENLY APPEARS—
I GIVE HIM ZEE CIGARET—BUT I DO NOT LIKE EET! HE IS A NICE BOY!
BAH! HE IS A FOOL— HE FALL FOR OUR TRICK AT ZEE MINE!
THE DRUGGED CIGARET MAKES MINT CANDY ANSWER ALL QUESTIONS TRUTHFULLY.
WHEN YOUR MOTORCYCLE CRASH, DID YOU CARRY SECRET ORDERS IN THE HEAD?
YEAH, DIVISION ORDERS.
MINT GIVES SECRET INFORMATION REVEALING AMERICAN WAR PLANS!
WHAT WERE ZE ORDERS?
THE FIFTH DIVISION IS ORDERED TO ALASKA WITH FAST TRANSPORTS AND LONG-RANGE BOMBERS. JAPAN WILL BE INVADED FROM OUR ALASKAN BASES!

THAT INFORMATION IS DYNAMITE! PANCHO SPURS HIS HORSE MADLY TO CONTACT HIS SUPERIORS.

AT LAST ZEE PAY-OFF! I MAK' ZEM PAY ME ONE MILLION DOLLAR MEX!

BUT THERE'S MANY A DIP TWIXT A MEX AND A NIP, AS, INSTANCE, A GOPHER HOLE! CAN PANCHO CRAWL TO A TELEPHONE, OR DOES THE FALL FINISH HIM?

I WILL DELIVER MY INFORMATION OR DIE!

ETTA, MEANWHILE, RESTLESS FOR CANDY, RELIEVES HER YEARNING IN SONG.

OH FOR THE "CHAPS" OF A COWBOY AND HIS FROLICKING, ROLLICKING STEED
HIS KNOWLEDGE WAS NOT LEARNED IN COLLEGE
SALOON SIGNS ARE ALL HE CAN READ!

THE TWO GIRLS FIND PEPITA LEANING OVER MINT'S UNCON-SCIOUS BODY.

YOU BLACK WEASEL! YOU'VE KILLED MY BROTHER—NOW YOU'RE ROBBING HIM!

NO, NO! I FEEL MINT'S HEART—

I'LL CHOKE THE PHONEY BREATH OUT OF YOU—

FAT FROUSE! I PULL YOUR HAIR OUT!

I CUT YOUR HEART OUT!

AT LEAST I GOT ONE—'AT'S MORE'N I CAN SAY FOR YOU!

PEPITA, BREAKING LOOSE FROM ETTA, DRAWS AN AUTOMATIC AND—

STOP OR I SHOOT! IT EES MY LIFE OR YOURS!

SHOOT, YOU HUSSY— I DARE YOU!

7

AS BULLETS STREAK FROM THE AUTOMATIC, DIANA KNOCKS PEPITA'S PISTOL HAND ASIDE---

TAKE IT EASY, GIRLY--- THAT TEMPER'LL GET YOU INTO TROUBLE!

ESCAPING SWIFTLY TO A HORSE, PEPITA ESCAPES—

ADIOS—I HAVE NOT TIME TO FIGHT YOU BUT I WEEL RETURN—

TAKING QUICK ADVANTAGE OF ETTA'S ABSENCE, DIANA TRANSFORMS HERSELF INTO WONDER WOMAN.

THINGS ARE GETTING SERIOUS—IT IS TIME FOR ME TO ACT—I'LL HIDE THESE CLOTHES HERE IN THE MESQUITE!

WONDER WOMAN HYPNOTIZES MINT CANDY AND LEARNS WHAT HE HAS TOLD PANCHO.

OBEY ME, SOLDIER! SPEAK!

I—I TOLD THEM OUR DIVISION WAS GOING TO ALASKA TO ATTACK JAPAN—

WONDER WOMAN! YOU MUSTA GOT MY MENTAL MESSAGE, BUT WHERE'S DIANA?

I HEARD YOU, ETTA, ON MY MENTAL RADIO I JUST SENT DIANA TO—ER—TO PREPARE FOR A TRIP. BUT WE CAN'T WAIT—HOP ON MY SHOULDERS!

CARRYING THE PLUMP ETTA WITHOUT EFFORT, WONDER WOMAN RACES AFTER PEPITA'S FLEEING HORSE WITH THE SPEED OF A BULLET.

WOO WOO! RIDE 'EM, COWGIRL!

PEPITA, OVERTAKEN, FIRES AT HER PURSUER BUT THE BULLETS GLANCE HARMLESSLY FROM WONDER WOMAN'S BRACELETS.

CARAMBA! WHAT A WOMAN! I CANNOT SHOOT HER—I WILL LEAD HER INTO AMBUSH!

WHEELING HER HORSE INTO A CANYON, PEPITA SIGNALS HER HIDDEN COMPANIONS.

BANG! BANG! BANG!

8D

MASKED MEN LEAP SUDDENLY FROM BEHIND ROCKS AND SURROUND WONDER WOMAN AND ETTA CANDY.

COME ON, WONDER WOMAN, LET'S FIGHT THESE FATHEADS!

NO, IF WE SURRENDER THEY'LL LEAD US TO THEIR HIDE OUT.

BOUND TO PEPITA'S STIRRUPS, WONDER WOMAN AND ETTA ARE MARCHED ACROSS THE MESA.

WALK FASTER, MY CAPTIVES, OR YOU WEEL CHOKE!

MEANWHILE, IN WASHINGTON CAPTAIN DÍAZ OF MEXICO REPORTS A STARTLING DISCOVERY.

WE HAVE DISCOVERED THAT THE JAPANESE HAVE A BASE ON THE MEXICAN COAST!

WAIT! MAJOR TREVOR MUST HEAR THIS!

YOU SAY THE JAPS PLAN TO CONQUER MEXICO?

YES, MAJOR! WE ARE INFORMED THAT THEY ALREADY HAVE 3500 PLANES AND 100,000 TROOPS IN AN UNDERGROUND FORTRESS! BUT WE CANNOT LOCATE IT EXACTLY.

MAJOR TREVOR, YOU WILL FLY TO MEXICO CITY IMMEDIATELY WITH CAPTAIN DIAZ. FIND THIS JAP BASE AT ANY COST. CALL ON ME FOR MEN OR ANYTHING YOU NEED.

YES, SIR!

WONDER WOMAN AND ETTA CANDY ALSO START FOR MEXICO CITY BOUND HAND AND FOOT, THEY ARE PLACED IN SEPARATE CARS FILLED WITH JAPANESE AGENTS.

ETTA'S CAPTORS DISCUSS HER FATE.

THIS FAT ENCUMBRANCE PROFITS US NOTHING—LET US KILL HER.

IS NICE IDEA! LET US DROP HER IN ROAD FOR SECOND CAR TO RUN OVER!

HEY! YOU COLD BLOODED COYOTES! WONDER WOMAN'LL GET YOU FOR THIS!

90

THE JAPS CARRY OUT THEIR PLAN.

HELP! WONDER WOMAN—HELP!

VERY SAD— WONDER WOMAN CANNOT HELP YOU. SHE WEARS MANY BONDS—SO SUITABLE FOR FEMALE!

AS THE SECOND CAR RUSHES TOWARD HER, ETTA SHUTS HER EYES AND PREPARES TO MEET HER MAKER!

BUT **WONDER WOMAN**, AT ETTA'S CALL, BURSTS HER HEAVY ROPES LIKE COTTON THREADS TO THE UNHAPPY SURPRISE OF HER GUARDS.

SORRY I CAN'T PLAY PRISONER WITH YOU ANY LONGER — YOUR BOYS UP FRONT ARE CHEATING!

SEIZING THE STEERING WHEEL, **WONDER WOMAN** SWERVES THE CAR OFF THE ROAD.

THE JAPS' CAR, MISSING ETTA BY INCHES, CRASHES INTO A TREE AS **WONDER WOMAN** JUMPS CLEAR.

ETTA, FREED BY **WONDER WOMAN**, THINKS SHE IS IN HEAVEN.

THAT WASN'T A BAD WAY TO DIE — BUT SAY, ANGEL, CAN YOU GET ME SOME CANDY?

WAKE UP, ETTA YOU'RE NOT DEAD AND I'M NOT AN ANGEL —

THE TWO GIRLS, FOLLOWING THE ENEMY, TRUDGE TOWARD MEXICO CITY

AS LONG AS I'M NOT DEAD, WE GOTTA FIND THOSE NIPS THAT TOSSED ME OUT! DID THE CRASH GET ALL THE REST?

YES, APPARENTLY THEY WERE TOO LAZY TO JUMP IN TIME!

IN THE MEXICAN CAPITAL, THEY DISCOVER THAT PEPITA IS A FAMOUS WOMAN BULL-FIGHTER!

WOO WOO! I HAD A FEELING PEPITA COULD THROW THE BULL!

WE MUST FIND PEPITA — WE'LL ATTEND TODAY'S BULL-FIGHT.

PLAZA DE TOROS
SEÑORITA PEPITA
WORLD'S GREATEST WOMAN MATADOR SHE HAS SLAIN 50 BULLS

SECURING FRONT SEATS AT THE PLAZA DE TOROS, THE GIRLS SEE PEPITA ENTER THE ARENA AMID CHEERS FROM THE AUDIENCE.

BRAVA! VIVA PEPITA! PEPITA THE UNCONQUERABLE!

UNCONQUERABLE — HUH! I GOT A HUNCH **THIS** BULL IS GONNA LIQUIDATE HER!

BUT ETTA PROVES A POOR PROPHET — PEPITA CLEVERLY SLAYS THE BULL WITH ONE STROKE OF HER ESTOQUE, OR MATADOR'S SWORD, WINNING THUNDEROUS APPLAUSE.

BRAVA! PEPITA! MAGNIFICO! HOORAH! PEPITA IS BEST OF ALL ESPADAS.

THE PRESIDENT OF THE CORRIDA (BULLFIGHT) THEN ANNOUNCES THE NEXT EVENT.

THERE NOW ARRIVES THAT TERRIBLE BLACK BULL, EL TERRIFICO, STRONGEST AND MOST SAVAGE BULL IN ALL MEXICO! THE BEAUTIFUL SEÑORITA PEPITA WILL FIGHT EL TERRIFICO!

PEPITA, RECEIVING A NEW OUTBURST OF APPLAUSE, FACES THE PRESIDENT, HER BACK TO THE PEN OF TERRIFICO.

PEPITA, KNOWING THE BULL WILL NOT BE RELEASED UNTIL THE *PICADORES* ENTER THE ARENA, PAYS NO ATTENTION AS THE RAGING ANIMAL CHARGES HIS GATE AT FULL SPEED.

HEARING THE TERRIFIC CRASH BEHIND HER, PEPITA TURNS SWIFTLY AND LEAPS NIMBLY ASIDE, AVOIDING THE BULL'S FIRST RUSH.

BUT PEPITA TRIPS ON THE **BANDERILLERO'S** CAPE, CARELESSLY DROPPED. SHE TWISTS HER ANKLE AND FALLS HEADLONG IN THE PATH OF EL TERRIFICO!

PEPITA, WITH UNCONQUERABLE COURAGE, RISES ON ONE KNEE TO MEET THE BULL'S CHARGE. BUT GROANS FILL THE ARENA AS SPECTATORS REALIZE THEIR HEROINE IS DOOMED.

AH-H-H! OH-H! OW-W-OAN!

SUDDENLY, LIKE A STREAK OF LIGHT, A BEAUTIFUL FIGURE FLASHES DOWNWARD INTO THE ARENA.

WONDER WOMAN, PLANTING HER FEET FIRMLY, SEIZES EL TERRIFICO BY THE HORNS AND STOPS THE FURIOUS BULL IN MIDSTRIDE!

NOT WISHING TO KILL THE ANIMAL, **WONDER WOMAN** FORCES HIM TO HIS KNEES, THEN THROWS THE MAGIC LASSO OVER HIS HORNS.

EL TERRIFICO, COMPELLED BY THE LASSO TO OBEY **WONDER WOMAN'S** ORDERS, BECOMES A VERITABLE FERDINAND.

I COMMAND YOU TO LICK MY HAND!

STAND ON YOUR HEAD, MY HANDSOME CREATURE!

STANDING ON THE BULL'S BACK, **WONDER WOMAN** RIDES HIM ACROSS THE ARENA AND THE AUDIENCE GOES WILD WITH ENTHUSIASM.

VIVA **WONDER WOMAN!** YEA-A! SHE IS STUPENDOUS! SUPERB! **WONDER WOMAN!**

WONDER WOMAN CARRIES PEPITA TO HER DRESSING ROOM.

I TRY TO KEEL YOU—AND YOU SAVE MY LIFE! YOU ARE MOS' WONDERFUL GIRL IN ZEE WORLD!

YOU ARE BRAVE, PEPITA—WHY NOT USE YOUR BRAVERY IN A GOOD CAUSE?

I DO NOT WANT TO BE BAD—ZOZE JAP DEVILS CAPTURE MY POOR OLD FATHER. ZEY SAY I MUS' BE SPY OR ZEY KEEL HIM BY TORTURE!

HMM! I SUSPECTED SOMETHING LIKE THAT.

I TELL YOU EVERYTHING! SEE—HERE IS ZEE SECRET JAPANESE BASE—

THAT'S ALL I WANT TO KNOW— I'LL FLY THERE AT ONCE!

AT THE AIRFIELD, **WONDER WOMAN** MEETS STEVE TREVOR AND CAPTAIN DIAZ JUST ARRIVING.

STEVE! I'VE FOUND THE JAP BASE—HERE'S A MAP, I'M FLYING AHEAD—YOU FOLLOW WITH A FLOCK OF FIGHTING PLANES!

BUT— MY ANGEL! —WAIT—

12

LANDING NEAR THE JAP BASE, **WONDER WOMAN** SURRENDERS TO A JAPANESE PATROL.

I HAVE INFORMATION OF THE UTMOST IMPORTANCE—TAKE ME TO YOUR COMMANDER-IN-CHIEF!

GIRLS NOT ARMED—WILL DO! GENERAL WILL DECIDE WHAT TO DO!

BUT THE JAPANESE GENERAL RECOGNIZES **WONDER WOMAN**.

FOOLS! THIS IS **WONDER WOMAN**! IF SHE TRIES FUNNY BUSINESS, RUN BAYONET INTO FAT GIRL'S STOMACH!

HEY, LISTEN, YOU GUYS, I MAY BE FAT BUT I'M NO PINCUSHION! ---OW!

WHIRLING SWIFTLY, **WONDER WOMAN** SEIZES THE BAYONET WITH ONE HAND AND WITH THE OTHER LASSOES THE GENERAL!

I'M THROUGH FOOLING WITH YOU JAP BOYS—NOW I'M GOING TO DO A PEARL HARBOR!

AT THIS MOMENT STEVE ARRIVES

WONDER WOMAN! I COULDN'T WAIT FOR THE PLANES—

HUSH, STEVE! GENERAL, I COMMAND YOU TO SURRENDER THIS BASE IMMEDIATELY TO MAJOR STEVE TREVOR, OF THE UNITED STATES ARMY!

I-I SURRENDER! SOMETHING COMPELS ME!

NEXT DAY AT HIS OFFICE, STEVE SENDS FOR ALL THE NEWSPAPER ACCOUNTS OF **WONDER WOMAN'S** EXPLOIT.

THE ONLY AID I GAVE HER WAS TO DISOBEY ORDERS—WHAT A WOMAN! WHAT A BEAUTIFUL ANGEL!

WASHINGTON DAILY
WONDER WOMAN SAVES MEXICO
FEAT OF DARING UNPARALLELED IN HISTORY! AIDED BY MAJOR TREVOR

WONDER WOMAN, RETURNING, FINDS PEPITA ENTERTAINING A VISITOR.

YES, FONNY BOY, I LOVE YOU! BUT I WOULD BREENG YOU DANGER.

AW GEE! WHAT'S DANGER? ANYHOW, YOUR DAD'S FREE, THE JAPS 'RE CAUGHT, PANCHO'S DEAD, SO-WHY DON'T YOU WAIT FER ME TILL AFTER THIS WAR'S OVER---HUH?

APHRODITE BLESS YOU, MY CHILDREN!

13o

WELL, DI, I KEPT MY PROMISE. I TOOK OFF TEN POUNDS, BUT I DON'T LIKE IT—GIMME MY CANDY!

THERE'S ONE COMFORT—MY RIVAL, **WONDER WOMAN**, MAY BE SMART BUT SHE CAN'T MAKE ETTA CANDY LIKE DIETING ANY BETTER THAN I CAN.

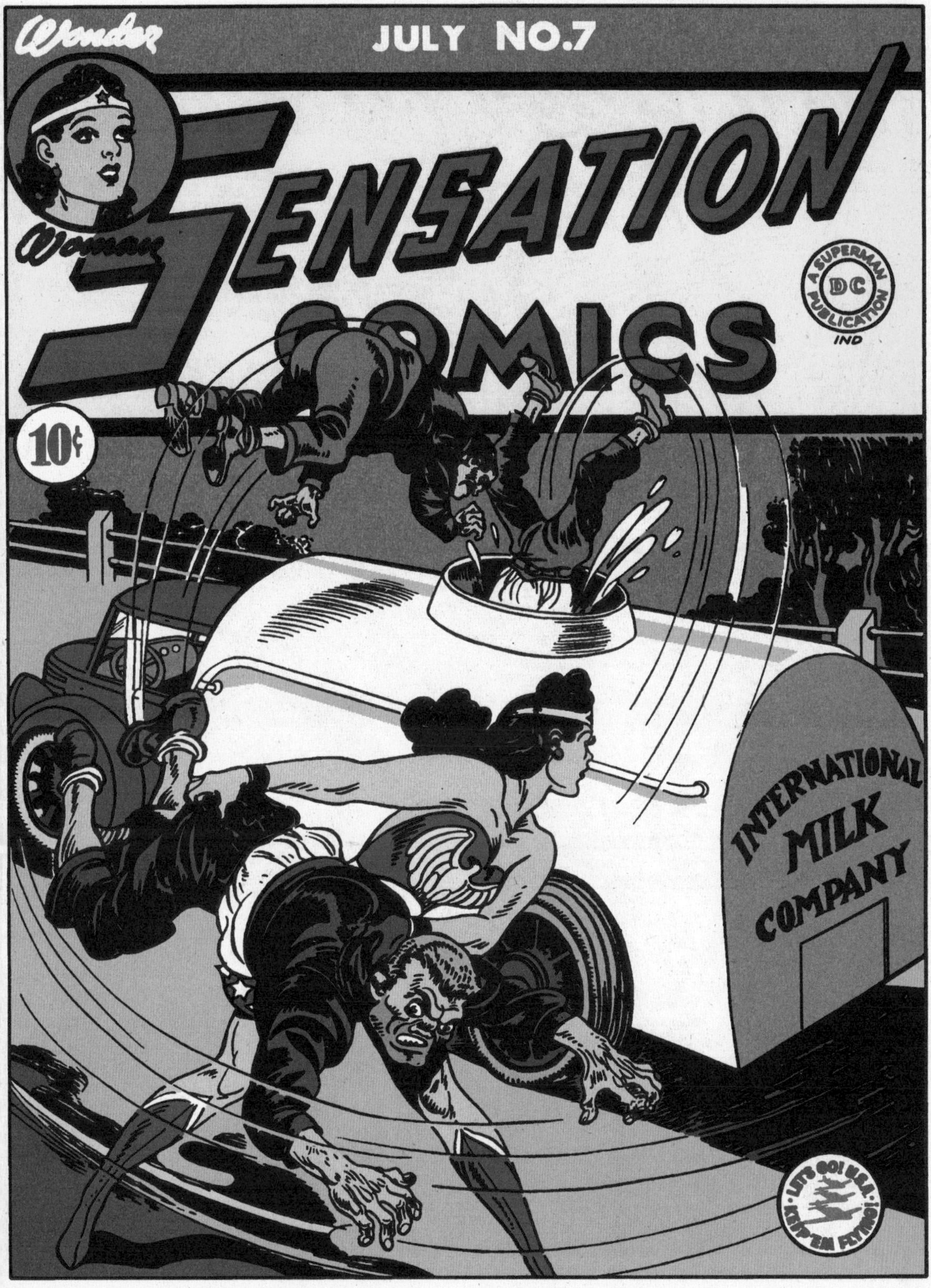
Wonder
JULY NO.7
Wonder Woman
SENSATION
COMICS
A SUPERMAN DC PUBLICATION
IND
10¢
INTERNATIONAL
MILK
COMPANY
LET'S GO! U.S.A.
KEEP 'EM FLYING!

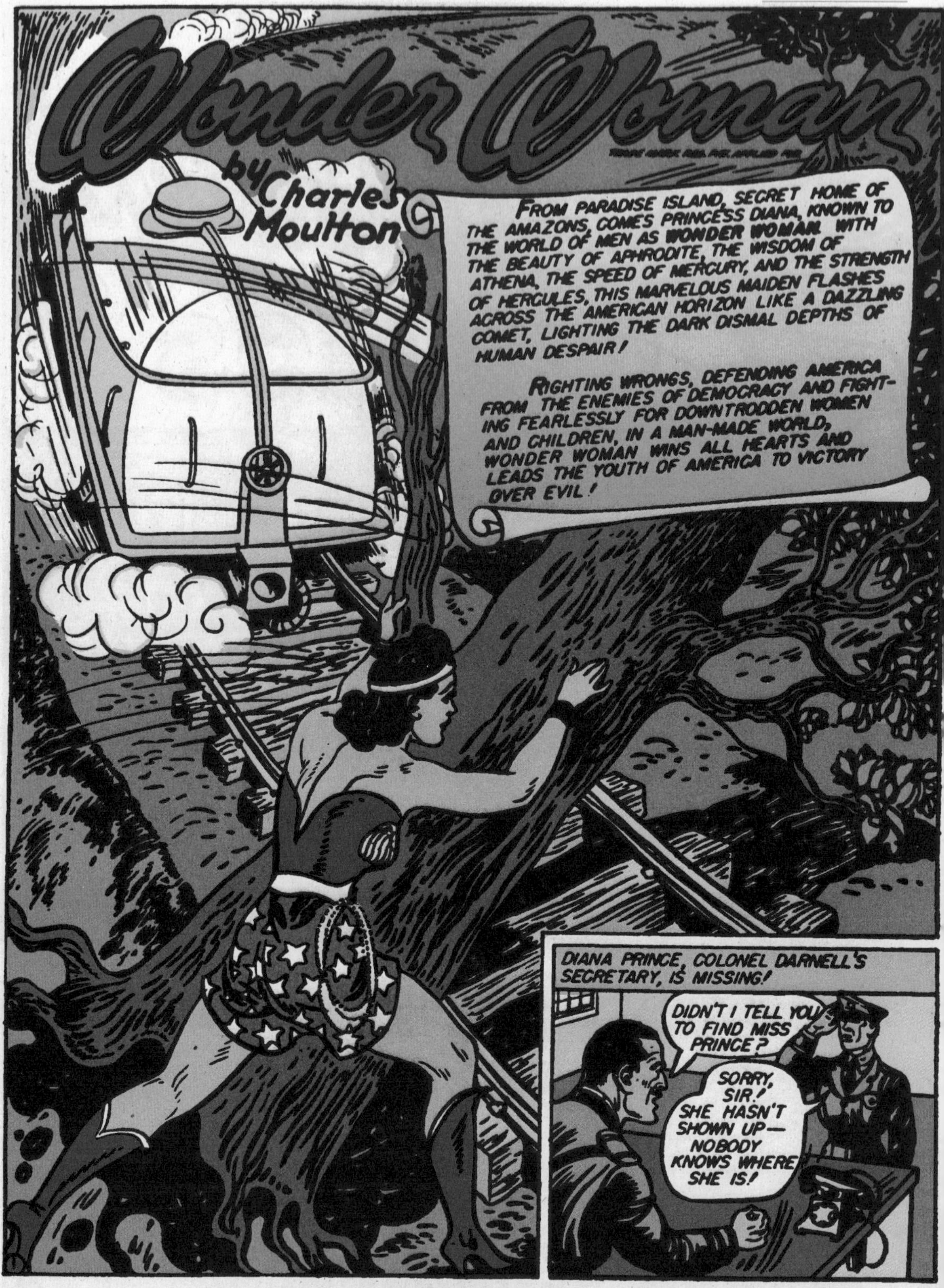
Wonder Woman
by Charles Moulton
FROM PARADISE ISLAND, SECRET HOME OF THE AMAZONS, COMES PRINCESS DIANA, KNOWN TO THE WORLD OF MEN AS WONDER WOMAN. WITH THE BEAUTY OF APHRODITE, THE WISDOM OF ATHENA, THE SPEED OF MERCURY, AND THE STRENGTH OF HERCULES, THIS MARVELOUS MAIDEN FLASHES ACROSS THE AMERICAN HORIZON LIKE A DAZZLING COMET, LIGHTING THE DARK DISMAL DEPTHS OF HUMAN DESPAIR!
RIGHTING WRONGS, DEFENDING AMERICA FROM THE ENEMIES OF DEMOCRACY AND FIGHTING FEARLESSLY FOR DOWNTRODDEN WOMEN AND CHILDREN, IN A MAN-MADE WORLD, WONDER WOMAN WINS ALL HEARTS AND LEADS THE YOUTH OF AMERICA TO VICTORY OVER EVIL!
DIANA PRINCE, COLONEL DARNELL'S SECRETARY, IS MISSING!
DIDN'T I TELL YOU TO FIND MISS PRINCE?
SORRY, SIR! SHE HASN'T SHOWN UP— NOBODY KNOWS WHERE SHE IS!

YOU SAY MISS PRINCE LEFT FOR WORK AS USUAL?

YES, COLONEL! SHE WAS GOING TO STOP AT THE HOSPITAL TO SEE NURSE BYRNES, A FRIEND OF HERS---

THIS IS NURSE BYRNES! YES, DIANA STOPPED HERE ON HER WAY TO WORK. HAD A SUITCASE- SAID SHE WAS GOING TO SPEND THE WEEKEND WITH MRS. LANSING IN BALTIMORE-

A FEW MINUTES LATER—

YES, I AM MRS. LANSING OF BALTIMORE—WHY, YES! I DID EXPECT DIANA, BUT SHE CALLED UP TO SAY SHE COULDN'T COME—

DIANA BROKE HER WEEK-END ENGAGEMENT BY PHONE! WHAT DO YOU MAKE OF THAT, TREVOR?

SEEMS PECULIAR! WHY DIDN'T SHE PHONE US, TOO?

WE'VE GOT TO FIND MISS PRINCE! PUT FIFTY MEN ON IT! NOTIFY THE POLICE! COMB THE DISTRICT-

YES, YES SIR! YESSIR—

BROADCAST HER DESCRIPTION! TRACE HER PHONE CALL—

YES, SIR! YESSIR!

LATER, WHEN NO TRACE OF DIANA IS FOUND, STEVE HAS A QUEER HUNCH—

IT'S NO USE! THAT GIRL HAS VANISHED INTO THIN AIR!

WAIT, COLONEL! I'VE GOT AN IDEA!

WARDEN GRIMLY OF STATE'S PRISON SPEAKING! YES, MAJOR TREVOR, THE MURDER-ESS, BARONESS PAULA VON GUNTHER WAS A PRISONER HERE. BUT SHE DIED IN THE ELECTRIC CHAIR LAST WEEK!

MY HUNCH WAS WRONG! I THOUGHT MAYBE THE BARONESS HAD ES-CAPED AGAIN AND KIDNAPPED DIANA FOR REVENGE. BUT THE FAIR PAULA SEEMS TO HAVE PAID THE FINAL PENALTY FOR HER CRIMES LAST WEEK.

IF ONLY STEVE HAD FOLLOWED HIS HUNCH A LITTLE FURTHER, DIANA MIGHT HAVE BEEN FOUND! LET US GO BACK A FEW HOURS AND FOLLOW HER AS SHE LEFT THE HOSPITAL—

POOR WOMAN— I WONDER WHAT SHE'S CRYING ABOUT.

WHAT'S THE MATTER— CAN I HELP YOU?

NOBODY CAN HELP ME— NOBODY CAN BRING BACK MY BOY DANNY! HE'S GONE FOREVER!

I AM SO SORRY! BUT SINCE DANNY COULDN'T BE SAVED---

BUT HE COULD HAVE BEEN SAVED! THE DOCTOR SAID DANNY WAS UNDERNOURISHED. I COULDN'T BUY MILK FOR HIM WHEN THE PRICE WENT UP.

I'LL BUY SOME MILK FOR YOUR LITTLE GIRL. SHE LOOKS THIN.

SHE HASN'T HAD ANY MILK FOR WEEKS AND SHE'S NOT THE ONLY CHILD WHO'S DONE WITHOUT IT— POOR PEOPLE JUST CAN'T AFFORD TO PAY FOR MILK NOW!

TWENTY-SIX CENTS A QUART! WHY, THAT'S OUTRAGEOUS!

WE CAN'T HELP IT, LADY! THE INTERNATIONAL MILK CO. CONTROLS THE ENTIRE SUPPLY. THEY PUSHED THE PRICE UP---

I'LL SEND YOU MILK EVERY DAY. AND I'M GOING TO INVESTIGATE THIS INTERNATIONAL MILK CO.!

THANK YOU--- OH, THANK YOU, MISS---

LATER----

INTERNATIONAL MILK

EXECUTIVE OFFICES

INTERN MILK CO

THIS MUST BE SOME SORT OF RACKET! I'VE GOT TO STOP IT, OR THOUSANDS OF OTHER AMERICAN CHILDREN WILL SUFFER.

3

I WANT TO SEE THE PRESIDENT OF THIS COMPANY!

ER— IF YOU DON'T HAVE AN APPOINTMENT, I'M AFRAID HE WON'T SEE YOU— MR. DE GYPPO ONLY SEES IMPORTANT PEOPLE!

PRESIDENT'S OFFICE

ALMONDO GYPPO

PRIVATE

WELL, I HAVE NO APPOINTMENT, BUT MY TIME IS VALUABLE, TOO-- I'M NOT GOING TO WASTE IT ON BUMPTIOUS BLONDES!

HEY, YOU! WHERE ARE YOU GOING?

SAY! YOU CAN'T GO IN THERE!

WHAT MAKES YOU THINK SO?

RESIDENT ALPHONSO DE GYPPO PRIVATE

YOU SHOULD KNOW BETTER THAN TO STAND IN A LADY'S WAY, BIG BOY!

WO-OOF! WHO LET THAT THUNDER STORM IN?

I AM DIANA PRINCE, SECRETARY TO COLONEL DARNELL OF U.S. INTELLI- GENCE SERVICE!

A PLEASURE TO MEET YOU, MISS PRINCE! AND WHAT DOES THE U.S. INTELLIGENCE WANT TO KNOW ABOUT MY BUSINESS?

THIS CALL IS UNOFFICIAL. I WANT TO KNOW HOW YOUR COMPANY DARES CHARGE THE POOR SUCH TERRIBLE PRICES FOR MILK!

"DARE" CHARGE? I RESENT THAT, MISS PRINCE! EVERYTHING WE DO IS ABSOLUTELY LEGAL!

IT CAN'T BE LEGAL TO DEPRIVE POOR CHILDREN OF MILK!

YOU'VE GOT THE WRONG SLANT— LET ME EXPLAIN OUR BUSINESS METHODS.

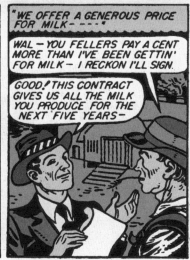

"WE OFFER A GENEROUS PRICE FOR MILK----"

WAL — YOU FELLERS PAY A CENT MORE THAN I'VE BEEN GETTIN' FOR MILK — I RECKON I'LL SIGN.

GOOD! THIS CONTRACT GIVES US ALL THE MILK YOU PRODUCE FOR THE NEXT FIVE YEARS-

"WE CHARGE HIGH PRICES — SO WHAT?"

SAY, LISTEN! MY CUSTOMERS CAN'T PAY THAT MUCH FOR MILK!

BREAD

OK, SAP! THEY'LL PAY OUR PRICE OR GO WITHOUT MILK!

4

"WHEN WE CAN'T SELL OUR MILK, WE HAVE TO DUMP IT--"

THIS IS GOOD MILK--IT'S A SHAME TO WASTE IT!

YEAH! IT WOULD FEED ABOUT FIVE HUNDRED KIDS!

"BUT IT COSTS US PLENTY TO CONTROL THE MILK SUPPLY--WE'VE LOST THIS MUCH ALREADY--"

FINANCIAL STATEMENT

DEFICIT 7,138,423.00

SO WE'VE GOT TO CHARGE HIGH MILK PRICES TO MAKE UP OUR LOSSES!

WHERE DID YOU GET SEVEN MILLION DOLLARS TO BUY UP THIS ENTIRE MILK SUPPLY?

MY DEAR YOUNG WOMAN -- THERE ARE SOME PHASES OF OUR BUSINESS DEAL-INGS THAT WE HAVE A RIGHT TO KEEP TO OURSELVES!

NOT THIS KIND OF BUSINESS DEALING! YOU'VE GOT TO STOP MILK-STARVING OUR AMERICAN CHILDREN!

ALL RIGHT-- WAIT JUST A MINUTE, MISS PRINCE! I'LL CALL MY CHIEF--

STEPPING INTO A SMALL PRIVATE PHONE BOOTH, DE GYPPO TAPS THE MOUTHPIECE SEVERAL TIMES WITH A PENCIL.

GET MY CODE SIGNAL, CHIEF?

YES! YES! WHAT'S ON YOUR MIND?

THERE'S A GIRL HERE-- A GOVERNMENT AGENT--SECRE-TARY TO COLONEL DARNELL OF ARMY INTELLIGENCE--SHE MAY MAKE TROUBLE!

I KNOW THAT WOMAN--SHE IS DANGEROUS! DON'T LET HER GO! FIND OUT WHO SENT HER AND THEN---! --UNDERSTAND?

5

DE GYPPO RETURNS TO HIS DESK--PRESSES AN ELECTRIC BUTTON, AND----

OOF! JUMPING SASSAFRAS!

CLICK

GOODBYE, MISS PRINCE, I'M SORRY YOU MUST LEAVE SO SUDDENLY!

DIANA SUBMITS TO BEING TIED TO A CHAIR.

COME ON, BABY! TELL US WHERE YOUSE WAS GOIN' WID DIS BAG—

OH! I'M SO FRIGHTENED! I WAS GOING TO A FRIEND OF MINE— MRS. LANSING IN BALTIMORE—

THE BUMPTIOUS BLONDE DOES SOME TELE-PHONING—

HELLO! MRS LANSING? THIS IS DIANA PRINCE. I'M SORRY, BUT I CAN'T COME FOR THE WEEK-END—

IT AIN'T LEGAL TO HIT ANYBODY WITH GLASSES. SO I'M GOING TO SHOOT YA INSTEAD, SEE?

HE'S TRYING TO SCARE ME, TO MAKE ME TALK. I'LL LET HIM THINK I'M FRIGHTENED!

OH, PLEASE DON'T K-KILL ME!

I WON'T SHOOT YA IF YA'LL TELL US WHO SENT YA TO SPY ON INTERNATIONAL MILK!

HE WON'T SHOOT ME UNTIL I TELL!

I—I CAN'T TELL YOU THAT!

WE'LL TAKE THIS DAME TO THE MILK PLANT AND MAKE HER SING!

BUT I C-CAN'T SING— I NEVER TOOK SINGING LESSONS!

DAT AIN'T FUNNY, SISTER—

AT THE INTERNATIONAL MILK COMPANY'S PLANT—

OH, WHAT A PRETTY WHITE TANK! IS IT FULL OF MILK?

NO, BUT IT WILL BE! DO YOU LIKE MILK BATHS, BABY?

TIE THAT HAMMER ON TIGHT, BOYS— WE DON'T WANT HER SWIMMING IN THE MILK!

THEY'RE GOING TO DROWN ME IN MILK— WHAT A WASTE OF GOOD BABY-FOOD!

MILK'S UP TO HER SHOULDERS, SLUG!

OKAY—HOLD IT! IF SHE WON'T TALK, WE'LL GO ON POURIN'— SLOW— UNTIL SHE DROWNS!

6

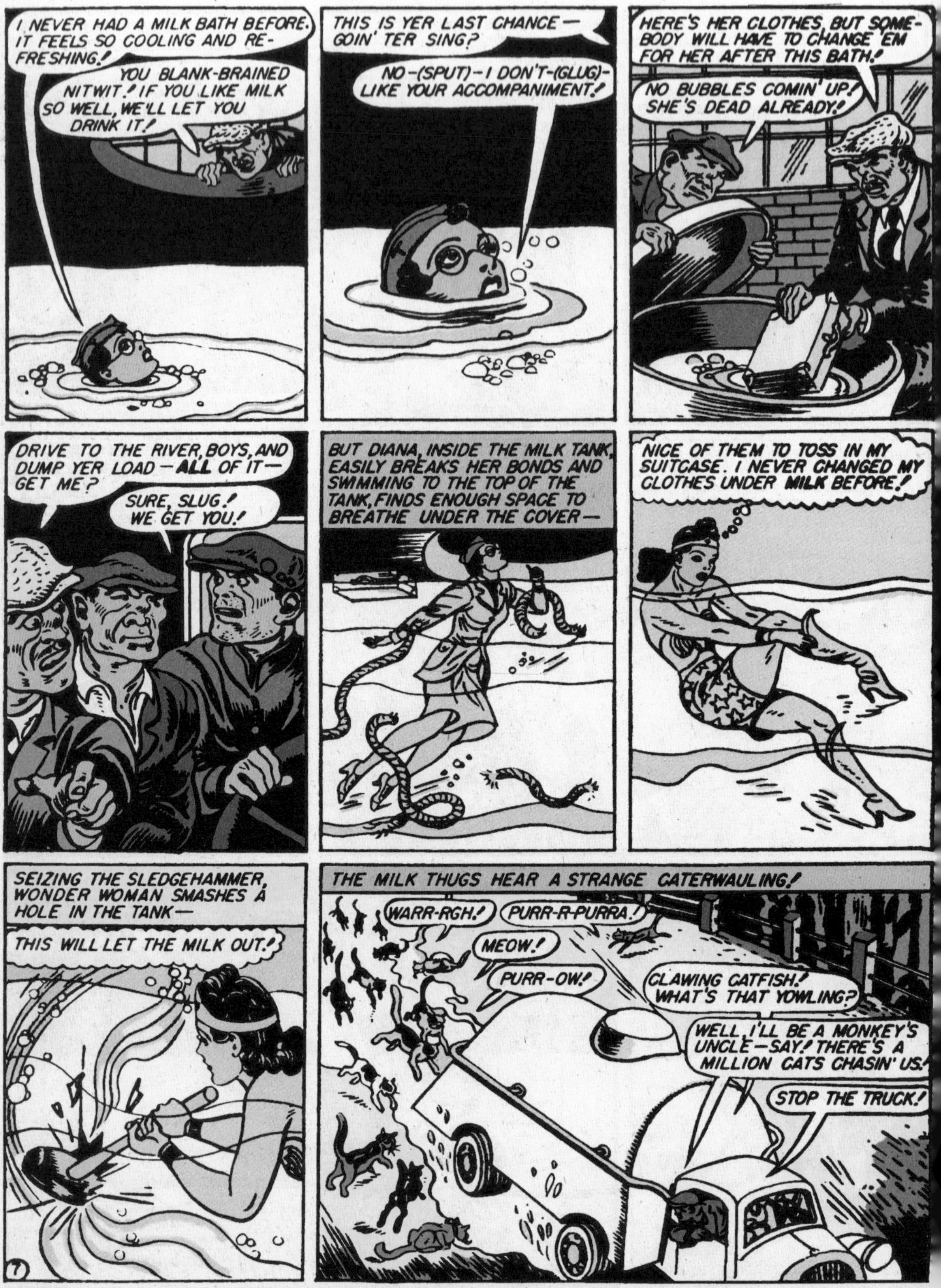
I NEVER HAD A MILK BATH BEFORE. IT FEELS SO COOLING AND REFRESHING!
YOU BLANK-BRAINED NITWIT! IF YOU LIKE MILK SO WELL, WE'LL LET YOU DRINK IT!
THIS IS YER LAST CHANCE— GOIN' TER SING?
NO—(SPUT)—I DON'T—(GLUG)— LIKE YOUR ACCOMPANIMENT!
HERE'S HER CLOTHES, BUT SOMEBODY WILL HAVE TO CHANGE 'EM FOR HER AFTER THIS BATH!
NO BUBBLES COMIN' UP! SHE'S DEAD ALREADY!
DRIVE TO THE RIVER, BOYS, AND DUMP YER LOAD—ALL OF IT— GET ME?
SURE, SLUG! WE GET YOU!
BUT DIANA, INSIDE THE MILK TANK, EASILY BREAKS HER BONDS AND SWIMMING TO THE TOP OF THE TANK, FINDS ENOUGH SPACE TO BREATHE UNDER THE COVER—
NICE OF THEM TO TOSS IN MY SUITCASE. I NEVER CHANGED MY CLOTHES UNDER MILK BEFORE!
SEIZING THE SLEDGEHAMMER, WONDER WOMAN SMASHES A HOLE IN THE TANK—
THIS WILL LET THE MILK OUT!
7
THE MILK THUGS HEAR A STRANGE CATERWAULING!
WARR-RGH!
PURR-R-PURRA!
MEOW!
PURR-OW!
CLAWING CATFISH! WHAT'S THAT YOWLING?
WELL, I'LL BE A MONKEY'S UNCLE—SAY! THERE'S A MILLION CATS CHASIN' US!
STOP THE TRUCK!

HOLY HANNAH! I NEVER SAW THE LIKES OF THAT.

PURR!

PURR!

PURR-R

WHO COULD'A PLUGGED THAT HOLE IN THE TANK?

HOW ARE YOU, BOYS? TOO BAD TO SMASH YOUR TANK, BUT THERE WAS A BODY IN THERE THAT I HAD TO GET OUT!

YEEOW! LOOKS LIKE WONDER WOMAN!

HOW'D SHE CATCH UP WID US?

HOW IS IT WE KEEP MISSIN' HER?

SHE'S A SUPER WOMAN! I'M EMPTYING MY GUN ON HER --- AND SHE'S STILL THERE!

HER BRACELETS MOVE FASTER THAN THE BULLETS!

WHEN THE THUGS STOP TO RE-LOAD—

I'M TIRED OF THAT GAME, PLAYMATES! LET'S TRY ANOTHER!

WHILE BOUND WITH MY MAGIC LASSO, YOU ARE COMPELLED BY APHRODITE TO OBEY ME! WHO RUNS THIS MILK RACKET?

WE DUNNO!

I HEARD DE GYPPO SAY- A DEAD WOMAN!

FASTER THAN THE FASTEST RACING CAR, WONDER WOMAN SPEEDS TO A TELEPHONE.

THEY WERE TELLING THE TRUTH- THAT'S ALL THEY KNOW— BUT A DEAD WOMAN! WHO COULD THAT BE? I MUST PHONE STEVE TO INVESTIGATE!

HONK!

WONDER WOMAN!!--- WHO WHERE— WHAT—?

NEVER MIND ME! DIANA PRINCE WAS KIDNAPPED BY INTERNATIONAL MILK COMPANY GANGSTERS. THE HEAD OF THE RACKET IS A "DEAD WOMAN"! YOU MUST FIND HER— GOODBYE!

"A DEAD WOMAN." THAT MUST MEAN THE BARONESS! BUT PAULA WAS ELECTROCUTED— GREAT CALAMITY KITTENS! I'M GOING MAD!

SUSPECTING THAT THE PRISON DOCTOR MIGHT HAVE FALSELY CERTIFIED THE BARONESS'S DEATH, STEVE GIVES HIM A LIE DETECTOR TEST.

THE BARONESS WAS DEAD WHEN TAKEN FROM THE CHAIR!

HUH! HE'S TELLING THE TRUTH! CAN I BE ON THE WRONG TRACK?

I PERFORMED AN AUTOPSY AND SAW THE BODY BURIED!

OH! OH! THAT'S A LIE, DOCTOR! YOUR BLOOD PRESSURE HIT THE CEILING *THAT* TIME!

COME CLEAN, NOW—THE LIE DETECTOR SHOWS YOU'RE NOT TELLING THE TRUTH!

ALL RIGHT—I'LL CONFESS! I GAVE HER BODY TO FRIENDS AFTER THE EXECUTION, BUT WHAT HARM WAS THAT? THEY COULDN'T BRING HER BACK TO LIFE!

WONDER WOMAN AGAIN CALLS STEVE—

HELLO? THAT YOU, WONDER WOMAN? THE BARONESS MAY HAVE INVENTED SOME WAY OF BRINGING HERSELF BACK TO LIFE, BUT SHE'S DISAPPEARED!

WE'LL DRAW HER OUT OF HIDING! I WILL ARRANGE A MILK PARADE. YOU CALL THE NEWSPAPERS AND NEWSREELS

WONDER WOMAN LEADS A GIGANTIC DEMONSTRATION AGAINST THE MILK RACKET.

The INTERNATIONAL MILK COMPANY IS STARVING AMERICA'S CHILDREN!!

ETTA CANDY AND HER HOLLIDAY COLLEGE BAND PLAY MARTIAL MUSIC

THE STREETS ARE PACKED FOR MILES WITH POOR MOTHERS AND CHILDREN WHO FOLLOW WONDER WOMAN WHILE CAMERAS CLICK AND NEWSREELS GRIND!

WE'LL DROWN INTERNATIONAL IN A CAN OF SOUR MILK! AMERICA MUST MARCH ON!

The INTERNATIONAL MILK COMPANY IS STARVING AMERICA'S CHILDREN!!

AT LAST THE PARADE IS OVER AND---

WONDER WOMAN, I HAVE A MESSAGE FOR YOU!

WHEW! HOT WORK-ER-WHAT'S THIS?

COME TO THIS ADDRESS QUICKLY! A WOMAN WILL GIVE YOU IMPORTANT INFORMATION ABOUT THE MILK RACKET!

THOSE MARKS ON HER WRISTS! THIS GIRL HAS BEEN WEARING CHAIN BANDS! SHE MUST BE ONE OF THE SLAVES OF THE BARONESS!

I WILL COME!

THE ADDRESS IS IN A TOUGH DISTRICT AND---

PUT 'EM UP, WONDER WOMAN!

I EXPECTED THIS!

GO AHEAD AND SHOOT! I DARE YOU!

BUT WHILE GUNMEN HOLD WONDER WOMAN'S ATTENTION, ROPES DROP OVER HER FROM ABOVE.

WE GOT HER THIS TIME!

I'D BETTER PRETEND I'M HELPLESS - THEY'LL TAKE ME TO THE BARONESS!

YAHOO! WE CAPTURED WONDER WOMAN! SHE'S JUST A DUMB DAME, AFTER ALL!

SURE, IT JUST GOES TA SHOW YA-REAL MEN CAN OUTSMART ANY WOMAN ANY TIME! HA! HA!

NOW THAT YOU'VE GOT ME, BOYS, WHAT COMES NEXT?

FIRST WE'RE GOING TO CHAIN YOU UP!

YEAH-TH' CHIEF SAYS CHAINS MAKE YOU WEAK!

HAVE A HEART, BOYS! ONLY THE BARONESS KNOWS MY SECRET WEAKNESS OR THINKS SHE DOES!

WONDER WOMAN IS TAKEN TO THE INTERNATIONAL MILK PLANT-

OH! THESE CHAINS ARE TOO HEAVY FOR A POOR WEAK WOMAN!

HA! HA! THESE CHAINS DID THE TRICK, BOYS! WE'LL HELP HER CARRY THEM!

PRESIDENT DE GYPPO WELCOMES A DISTINGUISHED GUEST.

I GREET THE WORLD-FAMOUS WONDER WOMAN-WHAT A PLEASURE! SIT DOWN, PROUD BEAUTY.

THANKS, I PREFER, TO STAND! WHERE'S MY HOSTESS, BARONESS VON GUNTHER?

10

YOU SENT THE BARONESS TO THE ELECTRIC CHAIR! DO YOU EXPECT TO SEE A DEAD WOMAN?

NO. I EXPECT TO SEE A LIVING WOMAN WHO REFUSED TO STAY DEAD!

WONDER WOMAN SENDS A MENTAL RADIOGRAM TO ETTA CANDY—

CALLING ETTA CANDY! BRING YOUR GIRLS TO THE INTERNATIONAL MILK PLANT QUICK! ALSO TELEPHONE MAJOR TREVOR!

BUT DE GYPPO REMEMBERS THE BARONESS'S WARNING THAT WONDER WOMAN HAS AN ARMY OF GIRLS IN HER LEAGUE—

AN ARMY OF PRETTY GIRLS MAY TRY TO RESCUE WONDER WOMAN! CAPTURE THEM—DON'T LET THEM VAMP YOUR MEN!

OKAY, CHIEF! NO DAMES CAN PUT ANYTHING OVER ON US!

ETTA AND HER GIRLS FIND THE MILK PLANT DESERTED.

NOBODY AROUND! THESE MEN ARE AFRAID OF US—THEY'VE RUN AWAY!

BET THEY'RE HIDING INSIDE—LET'S FIND THEM!

ENTERING AN EMPTY ROOM, THE GIRLS FIND THEMSELVES LOCKED IN!

THIS DOOR IS LOCKED!

SO IS THIS ONE! WE'RE TRAPPED!

WE'LL WAIT.... THE MEN WILL COME FOR US—THEN WE'LL GET THEM!

WONDER WOMAN FACES HER FATE!

CHAIN HER TO THE FRONT END OF THAT TANK CAR. DON'T START THE CAR DOWNHILL UNTIL THE BARONESS ARRIVES—SHE WANTS TO SEE WONDER WOMAN'S FINISH!

I HOPE THE BARONESS DOESN'T KEEP ME WAITING! THIS POSITION ISN'T VERY RESTFUL!

YOU'LL REST A LONG TIME, SISTER, AFTER THE CHIEF GETS THROUGH WIT' YA!

11

THERE SHE IS, BARONESS, AS YOU ORDERED!

WHAT A CHARMING PICTURE! TOO BAD THE NEWSPAPER MEN ARE NOT HERE TO PHOTOGRAPH THEIR WONDER WOMAN!

BEHOLD—A LIVING DEAD WOMAN! YOUR STUPID EXECUTIONERS KILLED ME! BUT WITH AN ELECTRICAL MACHINE I INVENTED, MY SLAVES RESTORED LIFE TO MY DEAD BODY!

YOU ARE CLEVER! BUT WHY BECOME A MILK RACKETEER? WHAT A COMEDOWN FOR THE CHIEF NAZI AGENT IN AMERICA!

FOOL! I HAVE SPENT SEVEN MILLION DOLLARS TO TAKE MILK FROM THE MOUTHS OF AMERICAN CHILDREN! YOUR RISING GENERATION WILL BE WEAKENED AND DWARFED! GERMANY, IN TWENTY YEARS, WILL CONQUER YOUR MILK-STARVED YOUTHS AND WILL RULE AMERICA!

WHEN THE BRAKES ARE RELEASED, THAT TANKCAR FULL OF MILK WILL ROLL DOWNHILL AND CRASH INTO A CASE OF HIGH EXPLOSIVES! WONDER WOMAN WILL BE BLOWN INTO A THOUSAND PIECES!

GOOD! I'LL START THE CAR!

STEVE, MEANWHILE, RESPONDING TO ETTA CANDY'S CALL, ENTERS THE MILK PLANT WITH HIS MEN.

SEARCH FOR WONDER WOMAN AND THE HOLLIDAY COLLEGE GIRLS!

STEVE RELEASES THE GIRLS.

ETTA CANDY! DID THEY TRAP YOU? WHERE IS WONDER WOMAN?

I DON'T KNOW! WOO WOO! WE'VE GOT TO FIND HER! HAVE A CHOCOLATE!

WONDER WOMAN'S LAST MOMENT IS AT HAND!

RELEASE THE BRAKES AND JUMP!

I'LL JUMP, BARONESS, DON'T WORRY!

THE 10,000-GALLON MILK CAR ROLLS SWIFTLY DOWNHILL, WITH WONDER WOMAN HELPLESS—OR IS SHE?

IT'S TIME TO STOP THIS NONSENSE!

12

RACING DOWN THE TRACK AHEAD OF THE FLYING TANK CAR, **WONDER WOMAN** PUSHES A TREE ACROSS IT'S PATH.

THIS WILL SAVE THOUSANDS OF GALLONS OF GOOD MILK FOR AMERICAN CHILDREN!

AT THE MILK PLANT, A BATTLE ROYAL IS IN PROGRESS!

SUDDENLY—A NEW FIGHTER ENTERS THE SCENE!

WONDER WOMAN! HOORAY! SOCK 'EM! FOLLOW WONDER WOMAN TO VICTORY! KEEP 'EM FLYING!

THE VENGEFUL BARONESS LEVELS HER AUTOMATIC AT STEVE'S **BACK**!

THIS WILL EVEN MY ACCOUNT WITH **WONDER WOMAN**—I SHALL KILL THE MAN SHE LOVES!

BUT AT THAT MOMENT **WONDER WOMAN'S** LASSO FALLS WITH DEADLY ACCURACY OVER THE BARONESS'S HEAD!

EE-EEK! THE DEVIL'S GOT ME!

MY BEAUTIFUL ANGEL - YOU HAVE SAVED MY LIFE AGAIN!

COMPELLED BY **WONDER WOMAN'S** MAGIC LASSO, BARONESS PAULA SIGNS A FULL CONFESSION OF THE MILK RACKET PLOT.

LEGALLY YOU CANNOT BE EXECUTED TWICE FOR MURDER-BUT YOU'LL GO TO PRISON!

NO ONE CAN HOLD ME PRISONER!

DIANA PRINCE RESENTS THE NATIONAL ACCLAIM GIVEN **WONDER WOMAN**!

I'M ALMOST JEALOUS OF MYSELF AS **WONDER WOMAN**—NOTHING I DO AS A NORMAL WOMAN, DIANA PRINCE, EVER IMPRESSES ANYBODY—I HAVE TO BECOME THE SENSATIONAL **WONDER WOMAN** BEFORE ANYBODY NOTICES ME!

WONDER WOMAN BREAKS MILK RACKET

THERE'S NOTHING IN THE WORLD SO DEAR AS CHILDREN- I LOVE EVERY ONE OF THEM AND THEY ALL NEED MILK, THE PERFECT FOOD! STRONG, HEALTHY CHILDREN TODAY MEANS A SAFE, HAPPY AMERICA TOMORROW!

WHAT STARTLING ADVENTURE WILL THE BEAUTIFUL AMAZON UNDERTAKE NEXT? FOLLOW **WONDER WOMAN'S** PERILS AND PROWESS EVERY MONTH IN **SENSATION COMICS**

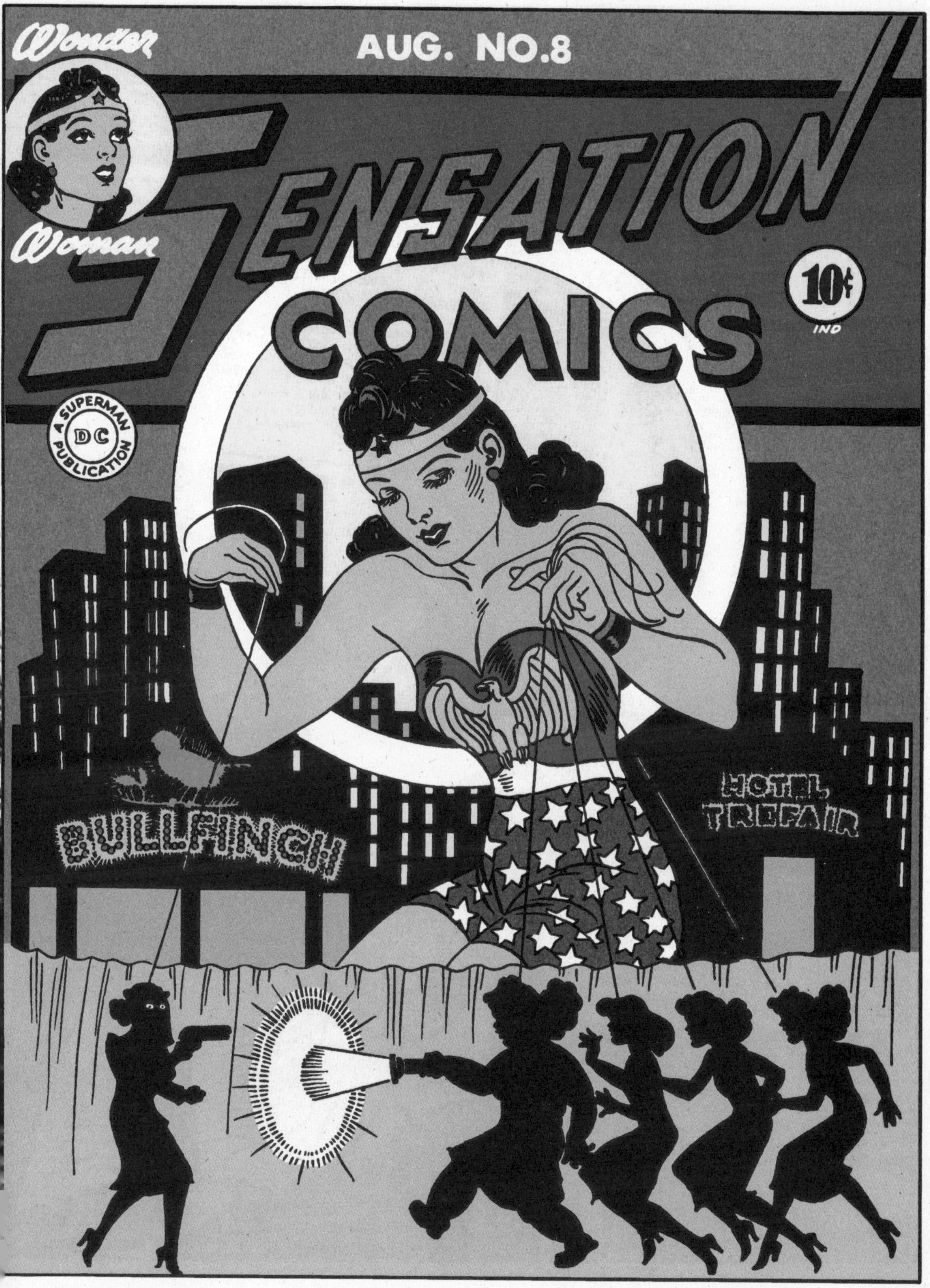
Wonder Woman
AUG. NO.8
SENSATION COMICS
10¢
IND
A SUPERMAN DC PUBLICATION
BULLFINCH
HOTEL TREFAIR

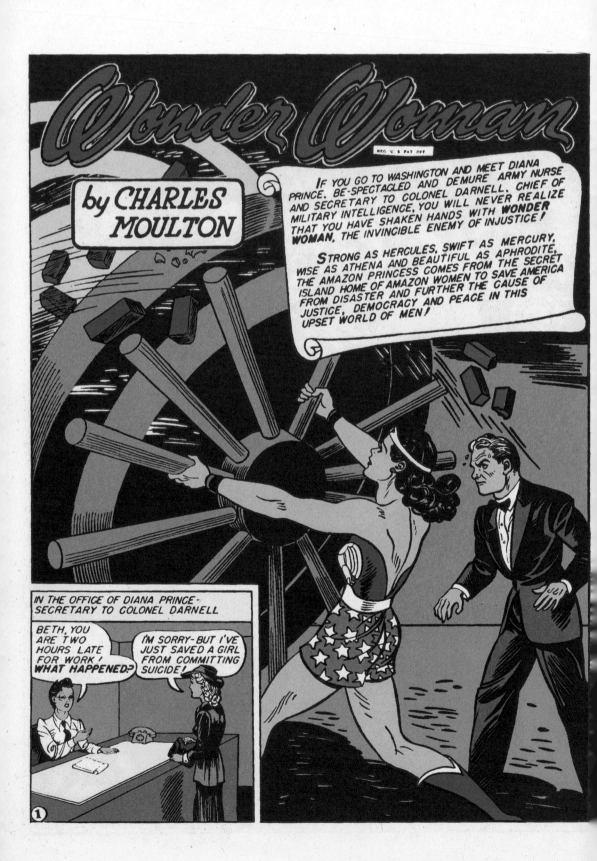

Wonder Woman

by CHARLES MOULTON

IF YOU GO TO WASHINGTON AND MEET DIANA PRINCE, BE-SPECTACLED AND DEMURE ARMY NURSE AND SECRETARY TO COLONEL DARNELL, CHIEF OF MILITARY INTELLIGENCE, YOU WILL NEVER REALIZE THAT YOU HAVE SHAKEN HANDS WITH **WONDER WOMAN**, THE INVINCIBLE ENEMY OF INJUSTICE!

STRONG AS HERCULES, SWIFT AS MERCURY, WISE AS ATHENA AND BEAUTIFUL AS APHRODITE, THE AMAZON PRINCESS COMES FROM THE SECRET ISLAND HOME OF AMAZON WOMEN TO SAVE AMERICA FROM DISASTER AND FURTHER THE CAUSE OF JUSTICE, DEMOCRACY AND PEACE IN THIS UPSET WORLD OF MEN!

IN THE OFFICE OF DIANA PRINCE—SECRETARY TO COLONEL DARNELL

BETH, YOU ARE TWO HOURS LATE FOR WORK! WHAT HAPPENED?

I'M SORRY—BUT I'VE JUST SAVED A GIRL FROM COMMITTING SUICIDE!

1

YOU DID **WHAT?** TELL ME ABOUT IT.

IT'S MY FRIEND HELEN- SHE'S JUST BACK FROM THE REFORM-ATORY! THIS IS WHAT SHE DID—

"HELEN AND HER FRIEND MOLLY WORKED FOR THE BULLFINCH DEPARTMENT STORES."

I'M ALL IN- IF THEY'D ONLY LET US SIT DOWN ONCE IN A WHILE.

THIS JOB IS TOO MUCH FOR YOU-- YOU'VE GOT TO SEE A DOCTOR!

"THE DOCTOR SAID MOLLY WAS RUN DOWN FROM OVERWORK AND INSUFFICIENT FOOD."

YOU'VE **GOT** TO EAT MORE, MISS, OR- ELSE---

I'VE KINDA LOST MY APPETITE, DOCTOR! WE BULLFINCH GIRLS ONLY MAKE ELEVEN DOLLARS A WEEK—

"THE DOCTOR SAID MOLLY COULDN'T LAST UNLESS SHE GOT MORE VITAMINS."

YOU MUST TAKE TWO OF THESE VITAMIN PILLS EVERY DAY.

I CAN'T DOC- THEY COST $3.98 A BOTTLE!

"HELEN PROMISED TO GET THE VITAMIN PILLS FOR HER FRIEND."

DON'T WORRY, MOLLY! I'LL GET YOU THOSE PILLS!

HALEY STOUT M.D.

BUT YOU CAN'T, YOU HAVEN'T GOT THE MONEY ANY MORE THAN I HAVE!

"SO THE NEXT DAY, HELEN STOLE THE PILLS FROM THE BULLFINCH DRUG COUNTER."

I HATE TO DO THIS- BUT I'LL PAY THE STORE BACK SOME TIME!

"BUT THE STORE DETECTIVE CAUGHT HELEN IN THE ACT."

ALL RIGHT, SISTER! I GOTCHA WITH THE GOODS!

OH **PLEASE** DON'T ARREST ME! MY FRIEND **MUST** HAVE THESE PILLS- SHE'S SICK---

"THE JUDGE **WOULD** HAVE SHOWN HELEN MERCY, BUT GOOGINS, THE STORE MANAGER—

THIS PRISONER HAD GOOD MOTIVES. IF I LET HER GO—

NO, YOUR HONOR! I **INSIST** YOU SEND THIS GIRL TO PRISON!

"HELEN, SENTENCED TO THE REFORMATORY, BEGGED ME TO LOOK AFTER MOLLY."

NEVER, MIND ME— IF YOU'LL ONLY GET MOLLY THOSE PILLS—

OF COURSE I WILL! I'LL TAKE CARE OF MOLLY, I PROMISE!

"I MADE MOLLY ROOM WITH ME. SHE GOT ENOUGH TO EAT, AND HER HEALTH IMPROVED."

GEE, BETH! YOU ARE SWELL TO ME!

YOU HAVE HELEN TO THANK FOR THAT, KID—I PROMISED HER TO LOOK AFTER YOU.

"HELEN'S DREARY PRISON DAYS WERE CHEERED BY MOLLY'S GRATEFUL LETTERS."

WELL, EVEN THOUGH MY OWN LIFE IS RUINED AT LEAST I SAVED MOLLY'S! THAT'S SOMETHING.

Dear Helen
The Doctor says
I am getting
better every
day. Beth has sure
been swell
to me...

"HELEN WAS RELEASED YESTERDAY. SHE STOPPED AT AT THE BULLFINCH STORE TO SEE MOLLY."

GEE, HELEN! I'M GLAD TO SEE YOU!

IT'S GRAND TO BE FREE AGAIN, YOU'RE LOOKING GREAT, MOLLY!

"BUT, GOOGINS, MANAGER OF THE STORE HAPPENED TO PASS BY—HE WAS FURIOUS."

WHAT DO YOU MEAN, YOUNG LADY, TALKING TO FRIENDS AND KEEPING CUSTOMERS WAITING?

OH! I'M S-SORRY—

"GOOGINS RECOGNIZED HELEN— AND FIRED MOLLY."

A HA! SO YOU ASSOCIATE WITH THIEVES AND JAILBIRDS! GET YOUR PAY AND CLEAR OUT!

OH, PLEASE, MR. GOOGINS,— DON'T FIRE ME!

YOU DIRTY SHYLOCK YOU—!!

"WHEN I REACHED HOME THAT NIGHT I FOUND MOLLY STRUGGLING TO PREVENT HELEN'S SHOOTING HERSELF."

HELEN, YOU MUSTN'T—-! GIVE ME THAT GUN!

DON'T STOP ME! I KEEP MAKING TROUBLE FOR YOU--LET ME DIE--SO YOU'LL BE FREE OF ME!

③

"WE HELD HELEN DOWN AND REASONED WITH HER."

LET ME KILL MYSELF! I'M A CRIMINAL, A JAILBIRD!

IT'S NOT YOUR FAULT, HELEN! BULLFINCH STORES RUINED BOTH OF US!

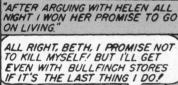

"AFTER ARGUING WITH HELEN ALL NIGHT I WON HER PROMISE TO GO ON LIVING."

ALL RIGHT, BETH, I PROMISE NOT TO KILL MYSELF! BUT I'LL GET EVEN WITH BULLFINCH STORES IF IT'S THE LAST THING I DO!

DIANA PRINCE, ALARMED, ASKS PERMISSION TO INVESTIGATE.

THESE CONDITIONS OUGHT TO BE REMEDIED, COLONEL DARNELL!

H'M--THOSE THINGS ARE OUT OF THE ARMY'S JURISDICTION- BUT I CAN GIVE YOU A LEAVE OF ABSENCE AND YOU CAN INVESTIGATE UNOFFICIALLY.

WHEN DIANA REACHES THE BULL-FINCH STORE, A COMMITTEE OF GIRLS IS PROTESTING TO MANAGER GOOGINS.

WE DEMAND A LIVING WAGE AND HEALTHY WORKING CONDITIONS!

YOU "DEMAND"! WHY OF ALL THE NERVE! YOU ARE DISCHARGED! ALL OF YOU! HUNDREDS OF GIRLS ARE WAITING FOR YOUR JOBS!

HE'S IN CONFERENCE. YOU CAN'T SEE HIM! ULP!!

"CAN'T" IS A WORD I DO NOT UNDERSTAND!

MR. GOOGINS MANAGER

ARE YOU BEING FAIR WITH THESE GIRLS, MR. GOOGINS?

IT'S NOT MY BUSINESS TO BE FAIR! I'M HIRED TO MAKE MONEY FOR THE BULLFINCH STORES!

FOR HUMANITY'S SAKE, WHY DON'T YOU GIVE THOSE GIRLS A LIVING WAGE?

NO USE APPEALING TO ME! I TAKE ORDERS FROM GLORIA BULLFINCH'S PERSONAL REPRESENTATIVE!

OUTSIDE, DIANA FINDS GIRL STRIKERS PICKETING THE STORE

HM-I THINK I'LL SEE GLORIA BULLFINCH TONIGHT.

OUR TOIL MAKES GLORIA GLAMOROUS

BULLFINCH STORES UNFAIR TO GIRLS

WE STARVE WHILE GLORIA BULLFINCH DINES AT THE 400 CLUB!

BUT STEVE, FOR THE FIRST TIME, ASKS DIANA TO GO OUT WITH HIM.

I SAY, DIANA, WILL YOU HAVE DINNER WITH ME TONIGHT?

OH, I'D LOVE TO!

OH, PHSHAW! AND ON THE VERY NIGHT I WANTED TO SEE GLORIA BULLFINCH--- HM I'VE AN IDEA!

DIANA, REMEMBERING THAT GLORIA FREQUENTS THE 400 CLUB, ASKS STEVE TO GO THERE.

THIS WAY, SIR.

YOU SURE PICKED A RITZY RESTAURANT, DIANA!

I HAVE A SPECIAL REASON FOR COMING HERE.

ISN'T THAT GLORIA BULLFINCH OVER THERE WITH THE HANDSOME FOREIGNER?

YES—THAT'S HER FIANCE, PRINCE GUIGI DEL SLIMO—THE WORLD'S NO. 1 FORTUNE HUNTER!

DIANA, LEAVING THE ASTONISHED STEVE, GOES TO GLORIA'S TABLE.

I AM DIANA PRINCE OF THE MILITARY INTELLIGENCE.

RE-AHLY HOW INT'- RESTING! WHAT AM I SUSPECTED OF? AN UN- AMERICAN TASTE IN HUSBANDS?

UNOFFICIALLY I HAVE BEEN INVESTIGATING CONDITIONS IN YOUR BULLFINCH STORES. THE GIRLS ARE TREATED ABOMINABLY!

WHAT NONSENSE!

IT IS THOSE SHOP GIRLS WHO TREAT MISS BULL- FINCH ABOMINABLY! THEY STEAL FROM HER A HALF- MILLION DOLLARS!

ALL MY BUSINESS IS HANDLED THRU MY PERSONAL AGENT. COME, GUIGI—LET US GO TO A MORE EXCLUSIVE CLUB WHERE COMMON PEOPLE CANNOT ANNOY ME!

QUITE! SEE MR. DOE AT THE HOTEL TREFAIR!

WHEN STEVE AND DIANA LEAVE THE CLUB AFTER A PLEASANT EVENING THEY ARE SUDDENLY SURROUNDED BY SINISTER FIGURES.

KEEP THOSE HANDS UP!

THIS IS THE DAME WE WANT! TIE HER UP AND LET'S GET GOING.

NOT SO FAST, MY FRIEND—THE LADY PREFERS ME FOR AN ESCORT!

OOF

BANG!!

⑤

AS THE GANGSTERS FLEE IN THEIR CAR, STEVE COMMANDEERS A TAXI.

I'VE GOT TO CATCH THOSE BIRDS—YOU DRIVE MY CAR HOME, DIANA!

COME BACK, STEVE! LET THEM GO!

STEVE FOLLOWS HIS QUARRY TO TREFAIR HOTEL AND SUDDENLY--- BLACK-OUT!

THIS'LL BE ALL FOR YOU, CHUM. YER TOO NOSEY!

HOTEL TREFAIR

DIANA, MEANWHILE HURRYING HOME, DONS THE GAY GARB OF WONDER WOMAN.

THERE'S ONLY ONE WAY TO HELP THE GIRLS IN BULL-FINCH STORES. I MUST TEACH SPOILED GLORIA A LESSON!

LATER THAT NIGHT, IN HER LUXURIOUS BOUDOIR, GLORIA BULL-FINCH ENTERTAINS AN UNEXPECTED VISITOR.

WHAT—WO—WONDER WOMAN-!?

SO THE GLAMOROUS GLORIA RECOGNIZES ME—HOW FLATTER-ING!

W-WON'T YOU SIT DOWN?

NO, THANKS- I AM TAKING YOU FOR A LITTLE TRIP. PUT YOUR HANDS BEHIND YOU, PLEASE!

GLORIA STRUGGLES BUT THE MAGIC LASSO IMMEDIATELY SUBDUES HER

LET ME G--- WHY, WHAT'S HAPPENED TO ME?

NOTHING-YOU JUST RELAX- WE'RE GOING FOR A LITTLE TRIP-

ETTA CANDY AND HER GIRLS ARE WAITING AT HOLLIDAY COLLEGE.

WOO-WOO-!! ITS GLORIA BULLFINCH!

WHEE! A NEW MEMBER FOR BEETA LAMBDA!

WAIT, GIRLS! THIS IS NO INITIA-TION-ITS A SERIOUS EXPER-IMENT IN REFORMING HUMAN CHARACTER.

YOU ARE BOUND WITH THE MAGIC LASSO-YOU MUST OBEY ME! YIELD YOUR WILL TO MINE! YOU ARE HYPNOTIZED - SUBMIT!

I—I MUST OBEY! I WILL SUBMIT!

YOU WILL FORGET THAT YOU ARE GLORIA BULLFINCH! WHEN YOU AWAKE YOU WILL BE RUTH SMITH, A POOR GIRL LOOKING FOR WORK.

YES—YES,---- I AM --- RUTH SMITH!

GO TO THE BULLFINCH STORE IN WASHINGTON. TAKE RUTH SMITH—THERE ARE JOBS OPEN FOR ALL OF YOU: FIFTY GIRLS HAVE JUST BEEN DISCHARGED FOR INSUBORDINATION. WORK THERE AND KEEP YOUR EYES OPEN UNTIL YOU HEAR FROM ME!

ETTA ENJOYS HER WORK AT THE CANDY COUNTER—

CANDY MAKES YOU STRONG AND BEAUTIFUL! LOOK AT ME! COME ON, FOLKS, BUY A BIG BOX OF THIS DELICIOUS CANDY!

HA! HA! I'LL TAKE TWO POUNDS!

GIVE ME FIVE!

BUT POOR RUTH STRAINS EVERY NERVE AND MUSCLE TO HOLD HER JOB!

DON'T SIT DOWN. SHOW SOME PEP—SMILE AT THE CUSTOMERS!

YES, SIR! OH, MY FEET ARE KILLING ME. WILL THIS DAY NEVER END?

MEANWHILE, BETH GIVES DIANA SOME STARTLING INFORMATION.

OH, MISS PRINCE! HELEN JONES ASKED MOLLY TO HELP HER ROB THE BULLFINCH STORE TO-NIGHT! OF COURSE MOLLY REFUSED, BUT SHOULD WE TELL THE POLICE?

NO! I'LL FIND A WAY TO STOP HELEN MYSELF!

DIANA CALLS ETTA CANDY—

LISTEN! THE STORE MAY BE ROBBED TONIGHT—I WANT YOU GIRLS TO PREVENT IT! HIDE IN THE STORE AFTER WORK INSTEAD OF GOING HOME, AND WATCH FOR THE ROBBER!

WOO-WOO WONDER WOMAN! COUNT ON US, KID—

AS HOURS PASS AND STEVE FAILS TO APPEAR AT THE OFFICE, DIANA BECOMES INCREASINGLY ANXIOUS.

THAT GANG MUST HAVE KIDNAPPED STEVE! I HAVE A HUNCH THAT GLORIA'S AGENT MR. DOE IS MIXED UP IN THIS! I'LL SEE HIM—

AT THE TREFAIR HOTEL **WONDER WOMAN** RACES UP TEN FLIGHTS OF STAIRS TO AVOID RECOGNITION.

I'VE SEEN SNAKES AN' PINK ELEPHANTS—BUT I'VE NEVER BEFORE SEEN HUMAN LIGHTNIN'!

E-EEK! A GALLOPIN' GHOST!

THIS IS DOE'S ROOM—I'LL BREAK THE LOCK GENTLY SO NO ONE WILL HEAR ME!

THE ROOM'S EMPTY—DOE HAS GONE! BUT **WHAT** HAVE THEY DONE WITH STEVE?

JUST FOR FUN, LET'S SEE WHO'S IN THE NEXT ROOM!

STEPPING THROUGH THE DOOR, **WONDER WOMAN** IS CONFRONTED BY A MASKED GUN GIRL!

STICK 'EM UP! WHY—IT'S **WONDER WOMAN**!

GUNS ARE DANGEROUS PLAY-THINGS FOR LITTLE GIRLS! WHY THE MASQUERADE?

OH I—I'M JUST PRACTICING—

PRACTICING TO BE A GUN GIRL, EH? WHO ARE YOU?

NEVER MIND TH'—— **LOOK OUT!**

AS **WONDER WOMAN** DODGES AT HELEN'S WARNING THE DEADLY BLOW FALLS ON A SENSITIVE SPOT, THE BASE OF THE BRAIN, STUNNING EVEN THE MIGHTY AMAZON MAIDEN.

GOOD WORK, BABY—WE GOT HER!

UMPH!

WHY NOT BOP HER OFF NOW? IT'D BE EASIER THAN TYIN' HER UP!

THE BOSS SAYS NO—WANTS TO QUESTION HER.

8

SHE MAKES A NIFTY BUNDLE, EH?

ROPE HER TIGHTER—WE GOTTA MAKE HER FIT THE TRUNK!

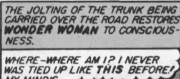

THE JOLTING OF THE TRUNK BEING CARRIED OVER THE ROAD RESTORES **WONDER WOMAN** TO CONSCIOUSNESS.

WHERE—WHERE AM I? I NEVER WAS TIED UP LIKE **THIS** BEFORE! MY MIND'S FOGGY—I CAN'T THINK!

MEANWHILE, IN THE BULLFINCH DEPARTMENT STORE—

NOBODY'LL LOOK FOR US IN THESE ELECTRIC REFRIGERATORS! WE'LL TURN OFF THE CURRENT AND FIX THE DOORS SO THEY WON'T LATCH. WHEN I SAY "WOO WOO," YOU ALL COME OUT.

BUT POOR "RUTH SMITH" COLLAPSES—THE LIFE OF A BULLFINCH SALES GIRL HAS BEEN TOO MUCH FOR HER.

B-RR

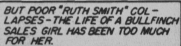

WHEN ALL IS QUIET IN THE GREAT DIMLY LIGHTED STORE, ETTA GIVES HER SIGNAL AND THE GIRLS STEAL FROM THEIR HIDING PLACES.

WOO WOO!

I FEEL LIKE A COLD CHICKEN!

SHH! QUIET!

ETTA LEADS HER DETECTIVE ARMY ON A TOUR OF THE STORE.

WOO-WOO! LOOKS LIKE MURDER!

IT'S THE NIGHT WATCHMAN! THE STORE THIEF MUST HAVE SHOT HIM!

SUDDENLY THE BEAM OF A FLASHLIGHT PENETRATES THE DARKNESS OF THE STORE—

HEY, LOOK! THERE'S OUR MAN GIRLS, WE'VE GOT TO CATCH HIM!

A RUSH—A SHRIEK, THE LIGHT GOES OUT! AND IN THE DARK, A SHOT IS FIRED!

EEE-EEEEK!

BANG!

EE-EEK!

WHEN THE LIGHTS COME ON, THE THIEF APPEARS TO BE CAPTURED—

YOU'RE NOT SO TOUGH, BABY! WHAT'S YOUR NAME?

HELEN JONES, I USED TO WORK HERE. I HATE THIS STORE AND EVERYONE IN IT!

SEE THOSE DRESSES? I STOLE THEM! I'LL GET REVENGE ON THE BULLFINCH STORE IF IT KILLS ME!

IT MAY HAVE KILLED YOU ALREADY, HONEY-CHILE! THERE'S A DEATH PENALTY FOR MURDER!

THE SHOT HAS ATTRACTED THE POLICE WHO ENTER THE STORE AND ARREST EVERYBODY!

A NICE BUNCH O'DAMES! SHOT THE WATCHMAN AND PACKED A TRUCK FULL OF STOLEN GOODS!

WHAT TRUCK? YOU'RE CRAZY!

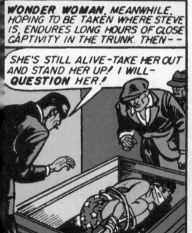

WONDER WOMAN, MEANWHILE, HOPING TO BE TAKEN WHERE STEVE IS, ENDURES LONG HOURS OF CLOSE CAPTIVITY IN THE TRUNK. THEN—

SHE'S STILL ALIVE—TAKE HER OUT AND STAND HER UP! I WILL—QUESTION HER!

THIS IS NOT THE GIRL I TOLD YOU TO GET, YOU FOOLS!

BUT BOSS! THIS ONE CAME INTO ROOM 1002 LIKE YOU SAID SHE WOULD—

DON'T BLAME YOUR MERRY MEN, MR. DOE! THEY DID A SPLENDID JOB OF TYING ME UP!

SO! YOU CALL ME DOE! WHO ARE YOU? ZUT! YOU'RE WONDER WOMAN!

WON'T I DO AS WELL AS DIANA PRINCE? I'LL TELL YOU WHAT-EVER YOU WANT TO KNOW—IF YOU'LL TAKE ME TO STEVE TREVOR!

TREVOR! HA! YOU KNOW TOO MUCH! I MUST KILL YOU! GOOGINS, OPEN THE VAULT!

WELL, WELL — DEAR OLD GOOGINS! SO THIS IS THE BULLFINCH DEPARTMENT STORE! WHERE IS MAJOR TREVOR?

DON'T BE IMPATIENT! YOU'LL JOIN HIM IN A MOMENT!

BULLFI STOR

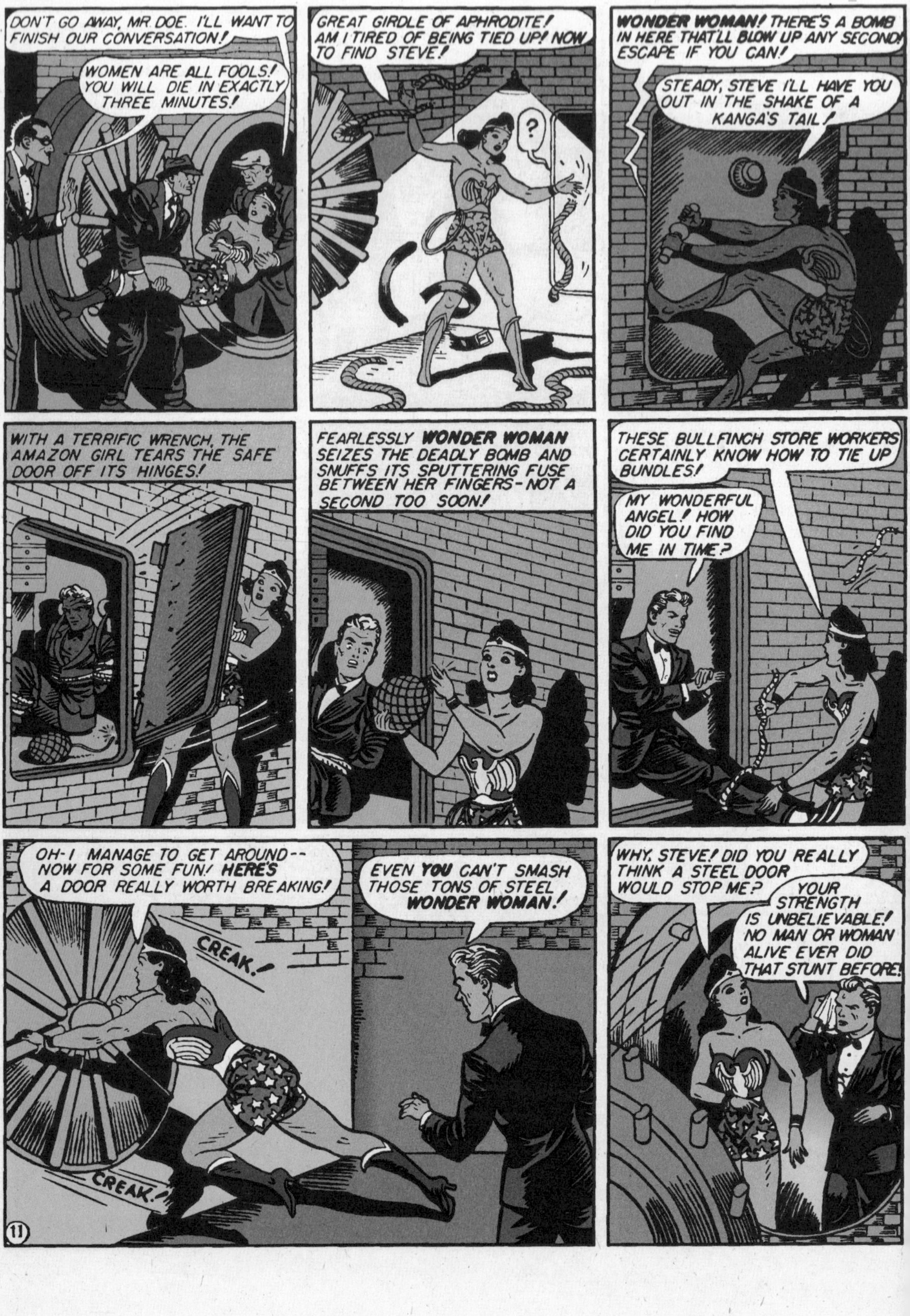
DON'T GO AWAY, MR. DOE. I'LL WANT TO FINISH OUR CONVERSATION!
WOMEN ARE ALL FOOLS! YOU WILL DIE IN EXACTLY THREE MINUTES!
GREAT GIRDLE OF APHRODITE! AM I TIRED OF BEING TIED UP! NOW TO FIND STEVE!
?
WONDER WOMAN! THERE'S A BOMB IN HERE THAT'LL BLOW UP ANY SECOND! ESCAPE IF YOU CAN!
STEADY, STEVE I'LL HAVE YOU OUT IN THE SHAKE OF A KANGA'S TAIL!
WITH A TERRIFIC WRENCH, THE AMAZON GIRL TEARS THE SAFE DOOR OFF ITS HINGES!
FEARLESSLY WONDER WOMAN SEIZES THE DEADLY BOMB AND SNUFFS ITS SPUTTERING FUSE BETWEEN HER FINGERS-NOT A SECOND TOO SOON!
THESE BULLFINCH STORE WORKERS CERTAINLY KNOW HOW TO TIE UP BUNDLES!
MY WONDERFUL ANGEL! HOW DID YOU FIND ME IN TIME?
OH-I MANAGE TO GET AROUND-- NOW FOR SOME FUN! HERE'S A DOOR REALLY WORTH BREAKING!
CREAK!
CREAK!
11
EVEN YOU CAN'T SMASH THOSE TONS OF STEEL WONDER WOMAN!
WHY, STEVE! DID YOU REALLY THINK A STEEL DOOR WOULD STOP ME?
YOUR STRENGTH IS UNBELIEVABLE! NO MAN OR WOMAN ALIVE EVER DID THAT STUNT BEFORE!

OUR FRIENDS SEEM TO HAVE LEFT IN A HURRY!

THEY EXPECTED THE EXPLOSION ANY MINUTE! IT WOULD BE BLAMED ON BURGLARS. BUT DOE AND GOOGINS TOOK THE MONEY FROM THE SAFE THEMSELVES!

BULLFINCH STORES

COME ON, STEVE— AFTER THEM! I HAVE A YEARNING TO UNMASK MR. DOE!

THAT'LL KEEP 'EM FLYING!

WHILE ESCAPING THROUGH THE STORE, THE REAL LOOTERS ARE STOPPED BY SERGEANT CLANCY.

NOW WHO WOULD YE BE, AND WHAT ARE YE DOIN' HERE?

I AM MR GOOGINS, THE MANAGER OF THIS STORE! THIS IS MR. DOE, MISS BULLFINCH'S PERSONAL AGENT. WE'RE HERE TO INVESTIGATE THEFTS!

WE'VE GOT THEM THIEVES, MR. GOOGINS!

WE CAUGHT 'EM LOADIN' A TRUCK WITH STOLEN GOODS AN' THAT FAT DAME SHOT THE WATCHMAN!

SPLENDID! SHOW THE GIRLS NO MERCY, SERGEANT. EVERY ONE OF THEM MUST GO TO PRISON!

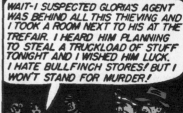

WAIT—I SUSPECTED GLORIA'S AGENT WAS BEHIND ALL THIS THIEVING AND I TOOK A ROOM NEXT TO HIS AT THE TREFAIR. I HEARD HIM PLANNING TO STEAL A TRUCKLOAD OF STUFF TONIGHT AND I WISHED HIM LUCK. I HATE BULLFINCH STORES! BUT I WON'T STAND FOR MURDER!

YOU LITTLE LIAR! I'LL TEACH YOU TO BLACKMAIL A GENTLEMAN—

SMACK!

TEACH ME, TOO, MR. DOE! LET'S SEE HOW HARD A "GENTLEMAN" CAN HIT A WEAK WOMAN!

VERY WELL— YOU ASKED FOR IT!

12

OW-WOW! MY HAND!

NOW IT'S MY TURN, STAND UP AND TAKE IT!

WHAM

LET ME INTRODUCE HIS PHONY HIGHNESS, GUIGI DEL SLIMO, PRINCE OF PILFERING AND FILCHING FIANCE OF GLAMOROUS GLORIA BULLFINCH!

RUTH SMITH, AWAKENED BY THE NOISE, FINDS HER MEMORY RESTORED AT **WONDER WOMAN'S** GESTURE.

WHY— I AM GLORIA BULLFINCH! BUT I AM **NOT** ENGAGED TO PRINCE DEL SLIMO—HE IS A FAKE, A TRAITOR AND A THIEF.

MY BELOVED! CAN YOU FORGET THE DIAMOND DIADEM OF THE DEL SLIMOS— OUCH!

I HOPE I CAN! I ONLY WISH I COULD PUNCH LIKE **WONDER WOMAN!**

A FEW DAYS LATER, GLORIA BULLFINCH TAKES OVER THE MANAGEMENT OF HER OWN STORES WITH HELEN JONES AS HER ASSISTANT.

GIRLS, STARTING NOW YOUR SALARIES ARE DOUBLED, YOUR HOURS AND WORKING CONDITIONS WILL BE IMPROVED! **WONDER WOMAN** MADE ME WORK LIKE YOU AND NOW I UNDERSTAND!

THREE CHEERS FOR GLORIA!

STORES

THE NEWSPAPERS PRAISE DIANA PRINCE FOR BETTERING THE GIRLS' LIVING CONDITIONS

BY JOVE, DIANA! YOU'RE A PUBLIC HEROINE!

I OWE IT ALL TO **WONDER WOMAN** AND SHE ONLY CAME AROUND TO SAVE **YOU!**

DIANA PRINCE WINS HER FIGHT FOR THE WORKING GIRLS

13

Wonder Woman
-SAYS-
DO YOUR DUTY FOR UNCLE SAM BY BUYING **U.S SAVINGS STAMPS AND BONDS!**

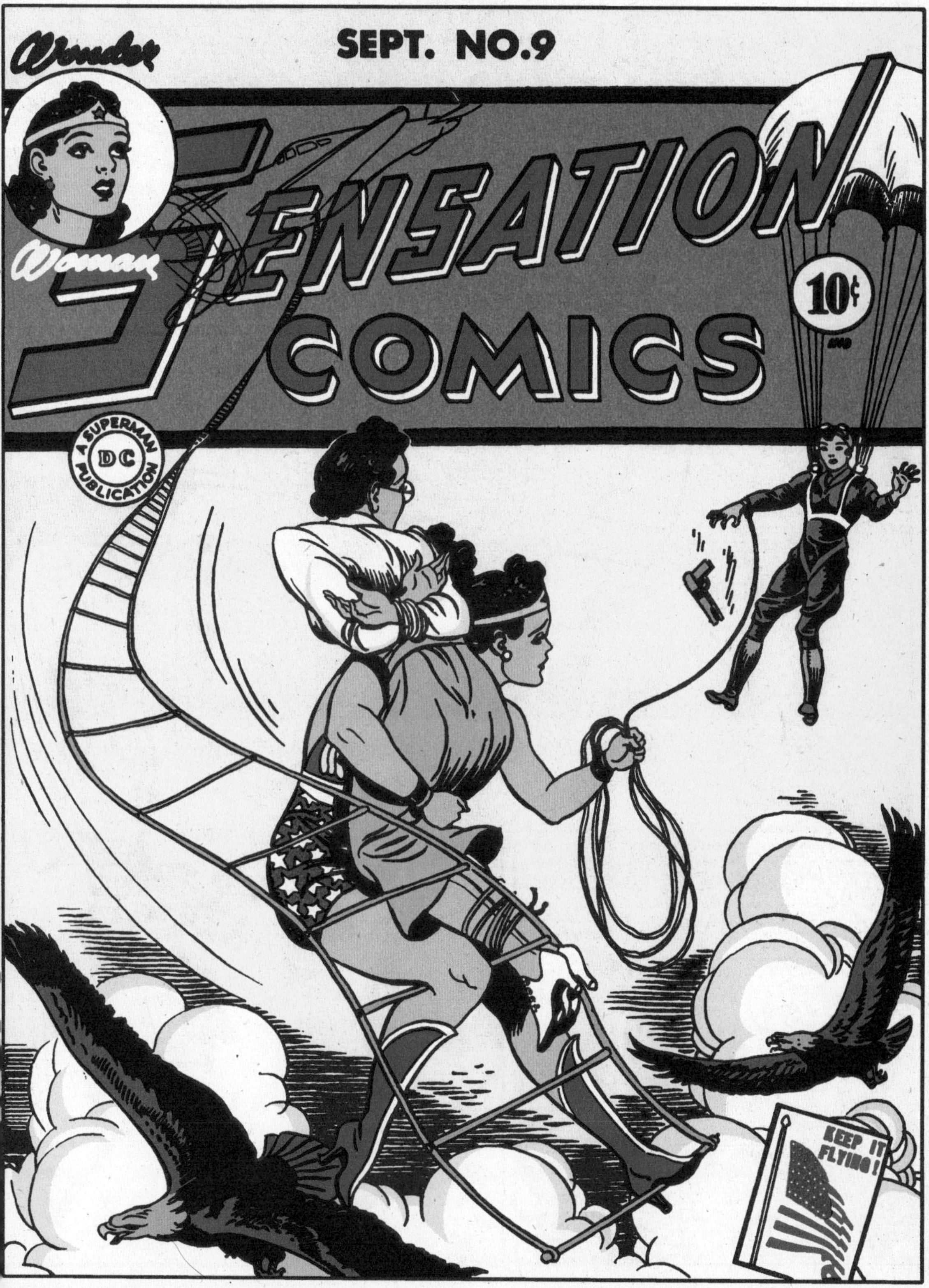
SEPT. NO.9
Wonder Woman
SENSATION COMICS
10¢
A SUPERMAN DC PUBLICATION
KEEP IT FLYING!

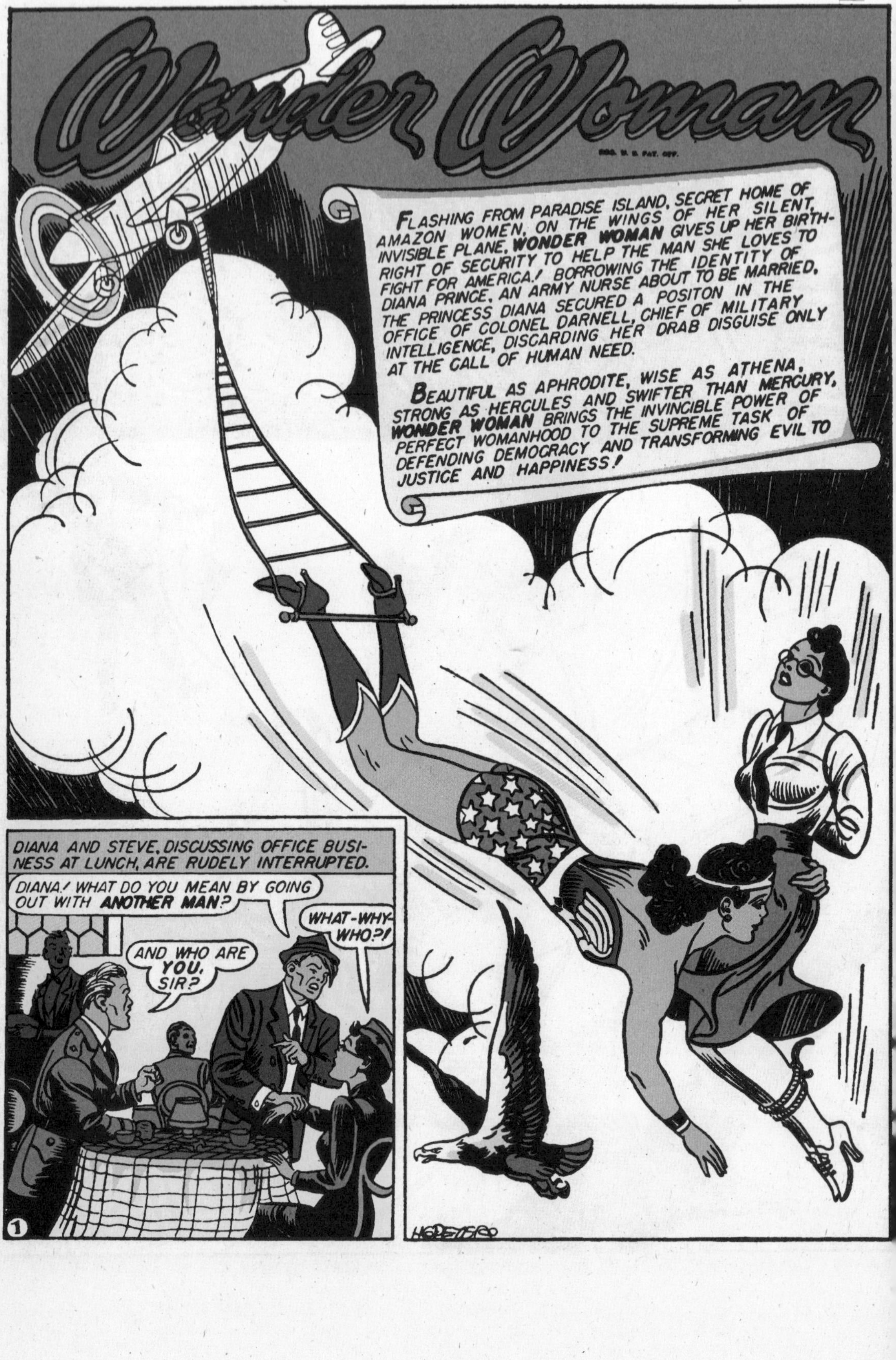
Wonder Woman
FLASHING FROM PARADISE ISLAND, SECRET HOME OF AMAZON WOMEN, ON THE WINGS OF HER SILENT, INVISIBLE PLANE, WONDER WOMAN GIVES UP HER BIRTH-RIGHT OF SECURITY TO HELP THE MAN SHE LOVES TO FIGHT FOR AMERICA! BORROWING THE IDENTITY OF DIANA PRINCE, AN ARMY NURSE ABOUT TO BE MARRIED, THE PRINCESS DIANA SECURED A POSITON IN THE OFFICE OF COLONEL DARNELL, CHIEF OF MILITARY INTELLIGENCE, DISCARDING HER DRAB DISGUISE ONLY AT THE CALL OF HUMAN NEED.
BEAUTIFUL AS APHRODITE, WISE AS ATHENA, STRONG AS HERCULES AND SWIFTER THAN MERCURY, WONDER WOMAN BRINGS THE INVINCIBLE POWER OF PERFECT WOMANHOOD TO THE SUPREME TASK OF DEFENDING DEMOCRACY AND TRANSFORMING EVIL TO JUSTICE AND HAPPINESS!
DIANA AND STEVE, DISCUSSING OFFICE BUSINESS AT LUNCH, ARE RUDELY INTERRUPTED.
DIANA! WHAT DO YOU MEAN BY GOING OUT WITH ANOTHER MAN?
WHAT-WHY-WHO?!
AND WHO ARE YOU, SIR?
1

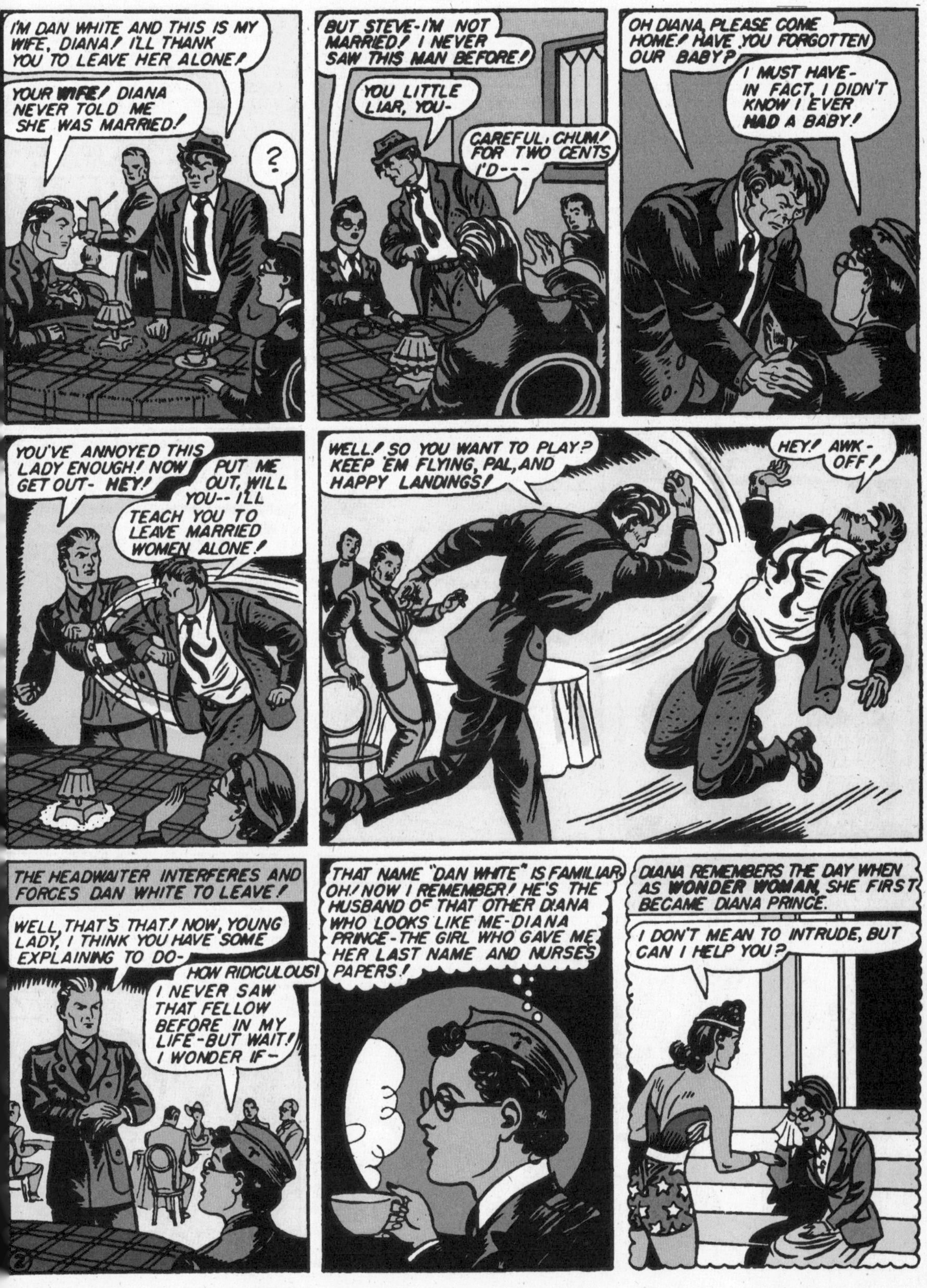
I'M DAN WHITE AND THIS IS MY WIFE, DIANA! I'LL THANK YOU TO LEAVE HER ALONE!
YOUR WIFE! DIANA NEVER TOLD ME SHE WAS MARRIED!
?
BUT STEVE-I'M NOT MARRIED! I NEVER SAW THIS MAN BEFORE!
YOU LITTLE LIAR, YOU-
CAREFUL, CHUM! FOR TWO CENTS I'D---
OH DIANA, PLEASE COME HOME! HAVE YOU FORGOTTEN OUR BABY?
I MUST HAVE- IN FACT, I DIDN'T KNOW I EVER HAD A BABY!
YOU'VE ANNOYED THIS LADY ENOUGH! NOW GET OUT- HEY!
PUT ME OUT, WILL YOU-- I'LL TEACH YOU TO LEAVE MARRIED WOMEN ALONE!
WELL! SO YOU WANT TO PLAY? KEEP 'EM FLYING, PAL, AND HAPPY LANDINGS!
HEY! AWK- OFF!
THE HEADWAITER INTERFERES AND FORCES DAN WHITE TO LEAVE!
WELL, THAT'S THAT! NOW, YOUNG LADY, I THINK YOU HAVE SOME EXPLAINING TO DO-
HOW RIDICULOUS! I NEVER SAW THAT FELLOW BEFORE IN MY LIFE-BUT WAIT! I WONDER IF-
THAT NAME "DAN WHITE" IS FAMILIAR. OH! NOW I REMEMBER! HE'S THE HUSBAND OF THAT OTHER DIANA WHO LOOKS LIKE ME-DIANA PRINCE-THE GIRL WHO GAVE ME HER LAST NAME AND NURSES PAPERS!
DIANA REMEMBERS THE DAY WHEN AS WONDER WOMAN, SHE FIRST BECAME DIANA PRINCE.
I DON'T MEAN TO INTRUDE, BUT CAN I HELP YOU?

THE GIRL HAD TOLD **WONDER WOMAN** THAT SHE WAS AN ARMY NURSE JUST APPOINTED TO THIS HOSPITAL----

AND TODAY MY FIANCE JUST GOT A JOB IN SOUTH AMERICA, BUT HE CAN'T SEND FOR ME BECAUSE HIS SALARY IS TOO SMALL AT THE MOMENT.

THAT'S TERRIBLE, AND JUST THINK-ALL WOULD WORK OUT RIGHT IF YOU ONLY HAD A LITTLE MONEY.

I JUST NOTICED-WITH THESE GLASSES OFF YOU LOOK LIKE ME! I HAVE AN IDEA! IF I GAVE YOU MONEY, WOULD YOU SELL ME YOUR CREDENTIALS?

YOU- YOU MEAN YOU WANT TO TAKE MY PLACE HERE AT THE HOSPITAL? BUT I CAN'T- I MEAN-

LOOK- BY TAKING YOUR PLACE I CAN SEE THE MAN I LOVE AND YOU CAN MARRY THE MAN YOU LOVE! NO HARM DONE, FOR I'M A TRAINED NURSE, TOO- JUST A LITTLE MONEY AND A SUBSTITUTION-

AND WE'D BOTH BE HAPPY! I'LL DO IT! OH- THIS IS WONDERFUL!

OH, BY THE WAY- MY NAME IS DIANA. WHAT'S YOURS?

WHY THAT'S AN AMAZING COINCIDENCE- I'M DIANA TOO! DIANA PRINCE! AND YOU'D BETTER REMEMBER THAT LAST NAME — BECAUSE IT'LL BE YOURS FROM NOW ON.

LATER, NURSE DIANA RECEIVED A LETTER FROM THE OTHER DIANA IN SOUTH AMERICA.

*Dear Diana "Prince"
I married Dan White today and I am so happy! Dan is assistant engineer working for the government of Brazil on anti-aircraft shells. Thank you for making my marriage possible.
Diana
(Mrs. Dan White)*

SUDDENLY REMEMBERING WHITE'S IDENTITY, DIANA REALIZES THAT HE MISTOOK HER FOR HIS WIFE, WHO IS HER DOUBLE.

I'VE GOT TO CATCH THAT MAN- I WANT TO SEE HIS WIFE!

AH-HA! SO YOU DO KNOW HIM! TOO LATE- HE'S GONE!

DAN WHITE, HURRYING HOME, FINDS HIS WIFE THERE BEFORE HIM.

'BOUT TIME YOU GOT BACK, DAN! I'VE BEEN WAITING AN HOUR FOR YOU!

YOU'VE BEEN WAITING! HOW'D YOU GET HOME AHEAD OF ME-FLY?

BLA-BLA-DA-DA-GOOGLE.

WHAT DO YOU MEAN, DAN? I HAVEN'T BEEN OUT OF THIS HOUSE TODAY.

WHAT ARE YOU LYING FOR? I LEFT YOU WITH THAT ARMY GUY IN THE RESTAURANT NOT TEN MINUTES AGO AND YOU KNOW IT!

LOOK AT THAT STEW, DAN WHITE! D'YOU THINK I COULD HAVE MADE THAT IN TEN MINUTES? YOU MISTOOK SOME OTHER GIRL FOR ME!

WELL MAYBE I DID, AT THAT!

BUT GEE, DIANA! THAT GIRL WAS YOUR DOUBLE! SHE WORE A NURSE'S UNIFORM!

IT MUST BE THAT OTHER DIANA—THE GIRL WHO TOOK MY JOB AS A NURSE. GREAT SOUPSPOON! THAT GIVES ME AN INSPIRATION!

DAN'S WIFE RENEWS AN OLD ARGUMENT.

DAN DEAR, I'VE JUST THOUGHT OF SOMEBODY WHO'LL GIVE ME A NURSE'S JOB. PLEASE LET ME GO TO WORK, DAN!

NO! MY WIFE DOESN'T HAVE TO WORK.

BUT DAN, WE'RE DOWN TO OUR LAST DOLLAR AND THE BABY MUST HAVE FOOD.

DON'T WORRY! GENERAL HARD IS SEEING ME TODAY ABOUT MY INVENTION.

MY ANTI-AIRCRAFT DISINTEGRATOR SHELL WILL PROTECT AMERICA FROM COAST TO COAST! IT WILL---

SKIP IT, DAN! I'VE HEARD ALL THAT A HUNDRED TIMES. YOUR SHELL WON'T FEED US, SO I'VE GOT TO.

COME BACK HERE! TAKE OFF THAT UNIFORM! I WON'T LET YOU—

YOU CAN'T STOP ME! LUCKY I KEPT MY ARMY NURSE'S UNIFORMS— I'M GOING TO WORK!

DIANA PRINCE, ENTERING HER OWN OFFICE, SEES HERSELF SITTING AT HER DESK!

BY THE GREAT HAMMER OF HERCULES! AM I ME OR, AM I YOU?

I AM THE REAL DIANA PRINCE! REMEMBER? I LENT YOU MY NAME—NOW I WANT IT BACK!

BUT..BUT..AFTER ALL.. BOTH OF US CAN USE THE SAME NAME—

BUT I WANT MY NURSE'S PAPERS, TOO. THIS JOB IS MINE BY RIGHTS, AND I NEED IT!

183

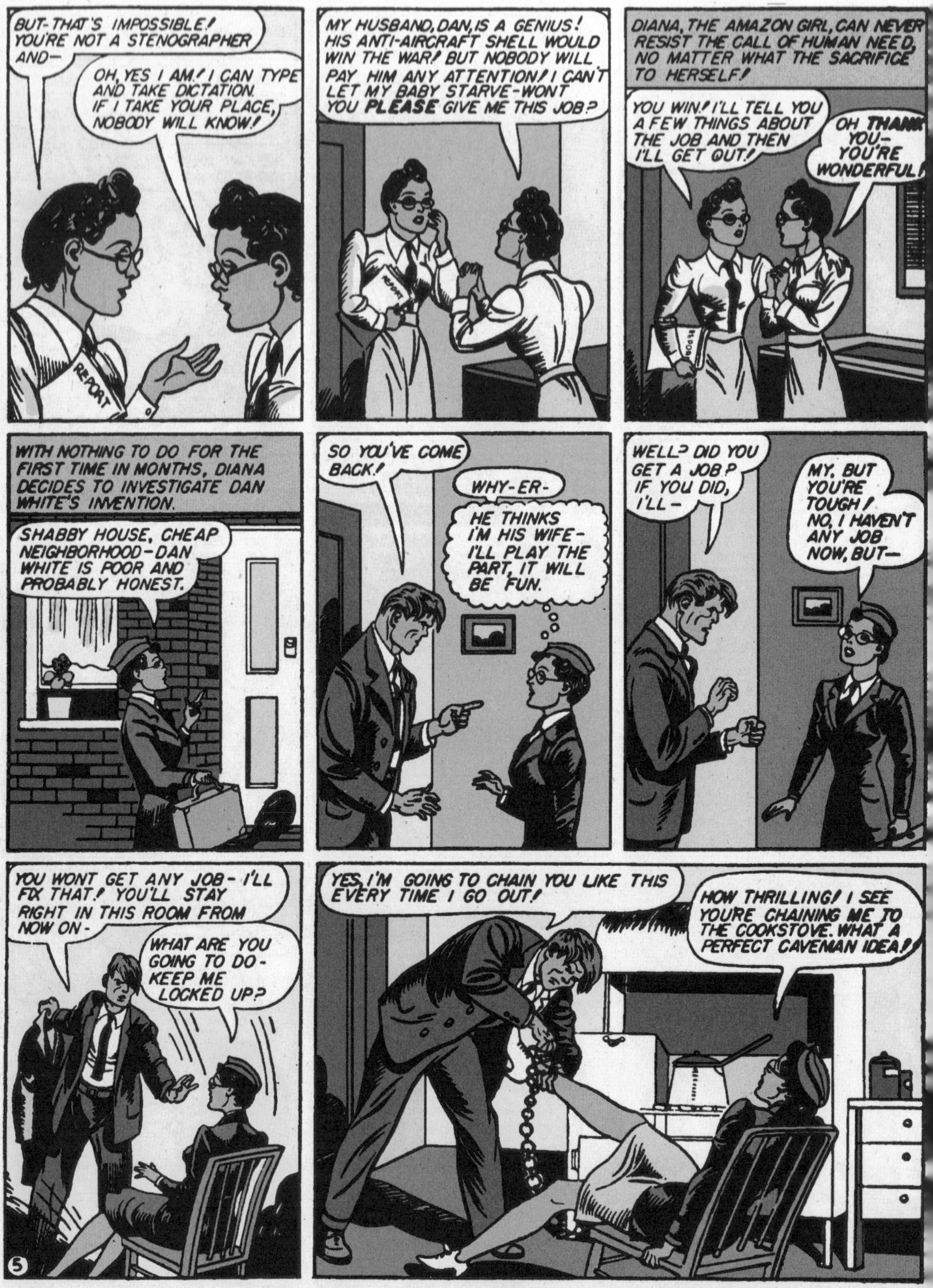
BUT-THAT'S IMPOSSIBLE! YOU'RE NOT A STENOGRAPHER AND—
OH, YES I AM! I CAN TYPE AND TAKE DICTATION. IF I TAKE YOUR PLACE, NOBODY WILL KNOW!
REPORT
MY HUSBAND, DAN, IS A GENIUS! HIS ANTI-AIRCRAFT SHELL WOULD WIN THE WAR! BUT NOBODY WILL PAY HIM ANY ATTENTION! I CAN'T LET MY BABY STARVE-WONT YOU PLEASE GIVE ME THIS JOB?
REPORT
DIANA, THE AMAZON GIRL, CAN NEVER RESIST THE CALL OF HUMAN NEED, NO MATTER WHAT THE SACRIFICE TO HERSELF!
YOU WIN! I'LL TELL YOU A FEW THINGS ABOUT THE JOB AND THEN I'LL GET OUT!
OH THANK YOU— YOU'RE WONDERFUL!
WITH NOTHING TO DO FOR THE FIRST TIME IN MONTHS, DIANA DECIDES TO INVESTIGATE DAN WHITE'S INVENTION.
SHABBY HOUSE, CHEAP NEIGHBORHOOD—DAN WHITE IS POOR AND PROBABLY HONEST.
SO YOU'VE COME BACK!
WHY-ER-
HE THINKS I'M HIS WIFE- I'LL PLAY THE PART, IT WILL BE FUN.
WELL? DID YOU GET A JOB? IF YOU DID, I'LL—
MY, BUT YOU'RE TOUGH! NO, I HAVEN'T ANY JOB NOW, BUT—
YOU WONT GET ANY JOB- I'LL FIX THAT! YOU'LL STAY RIGHT IN THIS ROOM FROM NOW ON-
WHAT ARE YOU GOING TO DO- KEEP ME LOCKED UP?
5
YES, I'M GOING TO CHAIN YOU LIKE THIS EVERY TIME I GO OUT!
HOW THRILLING! I SEE YOU'RE CHAINING ME TO THE COOKSTOVE. WHAT A PERFECT CAVEMAN IDEA!

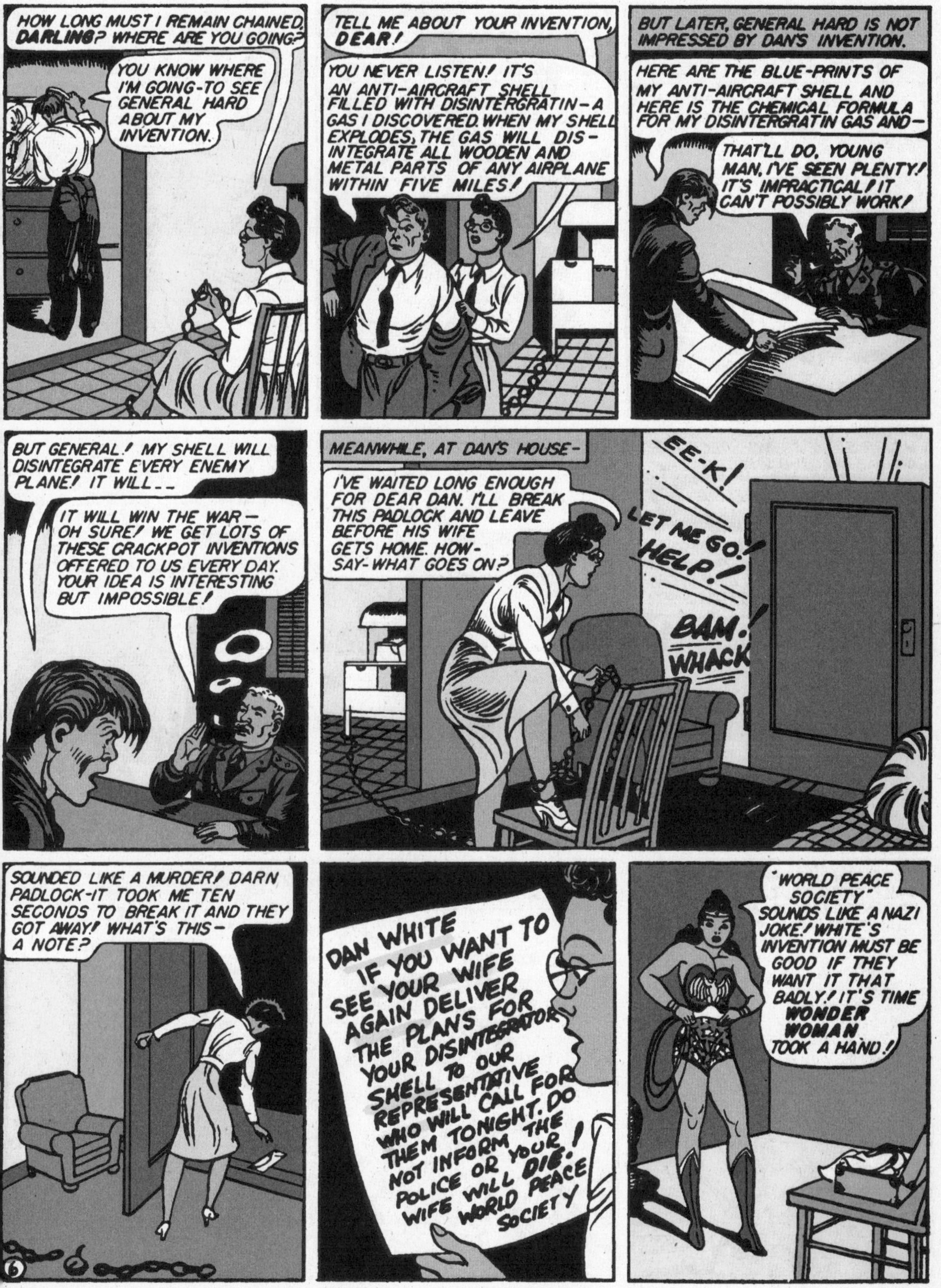
HOW LONG MUST I REMAIN CHAINED, DARLING? WHERE ARE YOU GOING?
YOU KNOW WHERE I'M GOING-TO SEE GENERAL HARD ABOUT MY INVENTION.
TELL ME ABOUT YOUR INVENTION, DEAR!
YOU NEVER LISTEN! IT'S AN ANTI-AIRCRAFT SHELL FILLED WITH DISINTERGRATIN-A GAS I DISCOVERED. WHEN MY SHELL EXPLODES, THE GAS WILL DISINTEGRATE ALL WOODEN AND METAL PARTS OF ANY AIRPLANE WITHIN FIVE MILES!
BUT LATER, GENERAL HARD IS NOT IMPRESSED BY DAN'S INVENTION.
HERE ARE THE BLUE-PRINTS OF MY ANTI-AIRCRAFT SHELL AND HERE IS THE CHEMICAL FORMULA FOR MY DISINTERGRATIN GAS AND-
THAT'LL DO, YOUNG MAN, I'VE SEEN PLENTY! IT'S IMPRACTICAL! IT CAN'T POSSIBLY WORK!
BUT GENERAL! MY SHELL WILL DISINTEGRATE EVERY ENEMY PLANE! IT WILL--
IT WILL WIN THE WAR- OH SURE! WE GET LOTS OF THESE CRACKPOT INVENTIONS OFFERED TO US EVERY DAY. YOUR IDEA IS INTERESTING BUT IMPOSSIBLE!
MEANWHILE, AT DAN'S HOUSE-
I'VE WAITED LONG ENOUGH FOR DEAR DAN. I'LL BREAK THIS PADLOCK AND LEAVE BEFORE HIS WIFE GETS HOME. HOW- SAY- WHAT GOES ON?
EE-K!
LET ME GO!
HELP!
BAM!
WHACK
SOUNDED LIKE A MURDER! DARN PADLOCK-IT TOOK ME TEN SECONDS TO BREAK IT AND THEY GOT AWAY! WHAT'S THIS- A NOTE?
6
DAN WHITE IF YOU WANT TO SEE YOUR WIFE AGAIN DELIVER THE PLANS FOR YOUR DISINTEGRATOR SHELL TO OUR REPRESENTATIVE WHO WILL CALL FOR THEM TONIGHT. DO NOT INFORM THE POLICE OR YOUR WIFE WILL DIE! WORLD PEACE SOCIETY
"WORLD PEACE SOCIETY" SOUNDS LIKE A NAZI JOKE! WHITE'S INVENTION MUST BE GOOD IF THEY WANT IT THAT BADLY! IT'S TIME WONDER WOMAN TOOK A HAND!

RACING THROUGH THE STREETS FASTER THAN THE EYE CAN FOLLOW, **WONDER WOMAN** MEETS DAN WHITE LEAVING THE WAR BUILDING.

DAN WHITE! I WANT TO SEE YOU!

WHY, IT'S **WONDER WOMAN!** YOU WANT TO SEE **ME**? MUST BE SOME MISTAKE!

BLUE PRINTS

YOUR WIFE IS KIDNAPPED! THE KIDNAPPERS DEMAND THE SECRET OF YOUR DISINTEGRATOR SHELL FOR RANSOM!

I'LL LET 'EM HAVE IT TO SAVE DIANA! GENERAL HARD THINKS MY SHELL IS A CRACKPOT INVENTION ANYWAY!

EVEN A GENERAL MAY BE WRONG! I'VE GOT AN IDEA—BUT WE'LL HAVE TO HURRY!

PUT ME DOWN! WHAT ARE YOU, A FEMALE GORILLA?

MAJOR STEVE TREVOR RECEIVES AN UNEXPECTED VISITOR.

BY ALL THAT'S MARVELOUS— **WONDER WOMAN!**

HELLO, STEVE! I'M BRINGING YOU A PACKAGE OF TROUBLE! MEET DAN WHITE, INVENTOR OF THE DISINTEGRATOR SHELL!

I'VE MET THIS SCREWBALL BEFORE—HAD TO THROW HIM OUT OF A RESTAURANT. BUT IF **YOU** BACK HIS INVENTION, **WONDER WOMAN**, IT MUST BE GOOD!

I WANT YOU TO TEST DAN'S SHELL, STEVE!

OKAY—I'LL ARRANGE A TEST. IF THIS DISINTEGRATOR SHELL WORKS, IT WILL ELIMINATE THE MENACE OF ENEMY AIRPLANES TO AMERICAN CITIES!

BUT WHAT ABOUT MY WIFE? I'VE GOT TO SAVE DIANA!

DON'T WORRY ABOUT YOUR WIFE, DAN—I HAVE A PLAN! I WANT YOU TO GIVE ME SOME FAKE BLUE-PRINTS AND A FALSE FORMULA—

7

THAT EVENING **WONDER WOMAN** MEETS THE KIDNAPPER'S AGENT AT DAN'S HOUSE.

I'M AN AGENT OF THE "WORLD PEACE SOCIETY." I CAME TO SEE DAN WHITE— WHO.. WHY.. YOU'RE **WONDER WOMAN!**

YES. I'M HERE TO DELIVER MRS. WHITE'S RANSOM.

GIVE ME THE PAPERS. IF THEY'RE WHAT WE WANT, MRS. WHITE WILL BE RELEASED.

NOT SO FAST! BEFORE I GIVE YOU THESE, I MUST SEE DIANA WHITE—ALIVE—WITH MY OWN EYES!

AGENT X AGREES TO TAKE **WONDER WOMAN** TO SEE THE KIDNAPPED GIRL.

DR. CUE—WHAT AN ODD NAME!

HIS NAME IS AH—ER—ENGLISH. THE DOCTOR SPECIALIZES IN STRANGE DISEASES AND CHEMICALS—LIKE DAN WHITE'S DISINTEGRATING GAS.

I.M. CUE M.D.

B-ZZ B-ZZ B-ZZ

WHILE SEATED IN THE DOCTOR'S WAITING ROOM, **WONDER WOMAN** RECEIVES UNEXPECTED MEDICAL ATTENTION!

I WASN'T EXPECTING DR. CUE TO OPERATE ON ME SO SOON!

JEHOSAPHAT! THE DAME'S SKULL IS MADE OF CONCRETE!

BAM! CRACK!

TELL THE DOCTOR I JUST CAN'T WAIT TO SEE HIM!

DR. CUE PRIVATE OFFICE

GLUG-A-GLOP-OWWW!

DIANA ENTERS THE OFFICE TO BE CONFRONTED BY A TELEVISION SCREEN.

I AM DR. CUE. I LET YOU SEE ME BY TELEVISION ONLY, **WONDER WOMAN**, BECAUSE I RESPECT YOUR SUPERHUMAN STRENGTH.

WHERE ARE YOU AND WHERE IS DIANA WHITE, THE GIRL YOU KIDNAPPED?

MRS. WHITE IS HERE IN MY PRIVATE HOSPITAL. I WILL LET HER SPEAK WITH YOU.

THIS DOCTOR IS A FIEND! HE IS DEVELOPING DISEASE GERMS TO ATTACK AMERICA! HE TRIES OUT THE GERMS ON HIS "PATIENTS." TELL DAN NOT TO GIVE CUE HIS INVENTION!

MRS. WHITE HAS SAID ENOUGH! I SHALL INOCULATE HER WITH MY BEST BUBONIC PLAGUE BACILLI, UNLESS **WONDER WOMAN** SURRENDERS THE PAPERS IMMEDIATELY!

8

WONDER WOMAN GIVES AGENT X A CLEVER IMITATION OF THE REAL PAPERS

I'LL GIVE YOU FIFTEEN MINUTES TO BRING ME DIANA WHITE AS AGREED. IF SHE ISN'T HERE —

I WILL HURRY! WAIT HERE, WONDER WOMAN.

WONDER WOMAN'S SUPER-KEEN SENSE OF SMELL DETECTS A FAINT ODOR OF ANAESTHETIC GAS IN THE ROOM!

THEY'RE TRYING TO GAS ME! I'LL HAVE TO HOLD MY BREATH UNTIL THEY THINK I'M KNOCKED OUT.

THE MINUTES SEEM LIKE HOURS! EVEN WONDER WOMAN'S POWERFUL LUNGS ARE ALMOST BURSTING.

THANK APHRODITE THEY'RE COMING FOR ME AT LAST!

THE GAS GOT HER, ALL RIGHT!

YEAH, BUT HURRY! IF SHE COMES TO, SHE'LL KNOCK US INTO THE MIDDLE OF NEXT WEEK!

I HOPE THEY TAKE ME TO DR. CUE'S HOSPITAL

IN THE SECRET LABORATORY OF THE SINISTER DR. CUE, OMINOUS PREPARATIONS ARE MADE TO DISPOSE OF WONDER WOMAN!

THIS WIRE WILL MELT, WON'T IT?

NOT UNTIL IT'S TOO LATE FOR HER TO BUST LOOSE!

NOT EVEN WONDER WOMAN CAN GET OUTA THIS BRONZE "ROASTING BOX" WHEN IT'S LOCKED!

MAYBE NOT, BUT I'LL FEEL EASIER WHEN SHE'S IN THE ELECTRIC FURNACE!

THE DOC'S PATIENTS ALL END HERE. BUT THE OTHERS WAS DEAD WHEN WE PUT 'EM IN!

SHE'LL BE DEAD SOON ENOUGH! I'LL TURN ON THE HEAT.

9

BUT NO SOONER IS THE OVEN DOOR LOCKED -----

EXCUSE MY CARELESSNESS, BOYS, BUT YOU SHOULDN'T STAND IN A LADY'S WAY!

KONK!

BLAM!

I HIT 'EM TOO HARD—THEY'RE OUT COLDER THAN A COUPLE OF MACKERELS! NOW HOW IN THE WORLD AM I GOING TO FIND DR. CUE'S HOSPITAL? I'LL CALL ETTA CANDY!

ETTA AND HER HOLLIDAY COLLEGE GIRLS ARE TESTING CANDIDATES FOR BEETA LAMDA.

ASSUME THE POSITION!

SING "BUBBLES"

BEETA LAMDA

I'M FOREVER BLOWING BUBBLES—

WAIT! WOO! WOO! WONDER WOMAN IS CALLING US ON HER MENTAL RADIO!

BRR-ING

————GIRLS WILL COME TO DR. CUE'S HOUSE. ETTA WILL PRETEND TO FAINT. WE'LL FOLLOW HER—

WOO! WOO! COME ON, GIRLS - GET OUR CHICKEN CRATE!

THERE WERE TWENTY GIRLS ON A SUMMER'S NIGHT WE HAD A COUPLE OF MEN IN SIGHT ONE OF THEM WAS A MIDDIE, TIGHT— SING CHEERILY GALS, LET'S GO!

KEEP 'EM BUYIN'

WOO WOO

AT CUE'S HOUSE ETTA IS EXAMINED BY AN ASSISTANT DOCTOR.

WHERE DO YOU SAY DER PAIN ISS?

RIGHT HERE, DOC—NO—ER, I MEAN — THERE!

WHEW! AH-H! WHAT A LOAD!

YOU HAF WERRY PECOOLIA SYMPTOMS! I SEND YOU TO DR. CUE'S PRIVATE HOSPITAL FOR OBSERVATION.

ETTA IS PLACED ON AN ELEVATOR WHICH DESCENDS FAR DOWN INTO THE DEPTHS OF THE EARTH!

WHERE ARE WE GOING, DOC? DOES THIS ELEVATOR RUN EXPRESS TO CHINA?

NEFFER MIND! YOU VILL SEE.

IN THE UNDERGROUND HOSPITAL, ETTA, LIKE THE OTHER PATIENTS, IS MADE SECURE!

HEY, WHAT ARE YOU DOING TO ME?

WE MUST KEEP YOU IN BED! YOU ARE TOO SICK TO GET UP UND YOU ARE GOING TO BE SICKER!

WONDER WOMAN, MEANWHILE, RIPS OPEN THE DOOR OF THE ELEVATOR SHAFT ABOVE AND LEADS HER GIRLS DOWN THE CABLES.

COME ON, GIRLS! FOLLOW ME!

REACHING THE ELEVATOR SHE TEARS OFF ITS METAL TOP AND DESCENDS THROUGH THE CAR TO THE HIDDEN HOSPITAL.

WONDER WOMAN REACHES ETTA CANDY JUST IN TIME!

NO HURRY ABOUT TREATING THE PATIENT, DOCTOR! I WANT TO CONSULT YOU FIRST.

SOCKO

WOO! WOO!

WOO! WOO! THAT BIG HEINIE WAS GOING TO SHOOT ME FULL OF GERMS OR SOMETHING—BUT LISTEN, WONDER WOMAN, THEY TOOK DIANA AWAY—I HEARD THE ORDERLIES TALKING!

TELL ME—WHERE IS DIANA WHITE?

WONDER WOMAN, WITH HER PERSUASIVE MAGIC LASSO, MAKES THE NAZI DOCTOR TALK!

NO! BUT SOMETHING SEEMS TO MAKE ME OBEY YOU! CUE FLIES DER WOMAN IN HIS AIRPLANE TO WHERE DISINTEGRATOR SHELL ISS TESTED. IF DER SHELL VORKS, IT KILLS DER INVENTOR'S FRAU—A GOOT JOKE, YAH?

LEAVING ETTA IN CHARGE OF THE HOSPITAL, WONDER WOMAN RACES FASTER THAN THE WIND TO HER INVISIBLE PLANE.

I OUGHT TO MAKE IT IN TIME—BUT HOW CAN I RESCUE DIANA?

GENERAL HARD, MEANWHILE, AT STEVE'S REQUEST, IS PREPARING TO TEST DAN'S DISINTEGRATOR SHELL.

THIS IS THE RIGHT TIME FOR THE TEST—JUST BEFORE DAWN.

BUT I'M NOT SATISFIED WITH OUR TARGET.

THAT TARGET'S ALL RIGHT! ACCORDING TO YOU, MR. WHITE, THE GAS FROM YOUR SHELL WILL DISINTEGRATE IT COMPLETELY!

ONLY THE WOOD AND METAL PARTS, SIR! IT WON'T DISINTEGRATE THE BALLOON—SINCE IT IS NOT MADE OF WOOD OR STEEL.

ALL READY, SIR! IT'D BE HARD TO MISS THAT TARGET!

FIRE!

BANG!

YOUR AIM WAS TOO GOOD! YOU SHOULDN'T HAVE HIT THE BALLOON: WE CAN'T TELL NOW WHETHER THE PLANE' WING WAS DISINTEGRATED OR NOT!

HAVE YOU GOT ANOTHER SHELL, DAN?

YES — ONE MORE!

WELL, SEND UP ANOTHER TARGET. BUT I BELIEVE WE'RE WASTING OUR TIME!

FAR ABOVE A PLANE SPEEDS TOWARD THE SCENE, PILOTED BY AGENT X.

THE AXIS POWERS MUST KNOW FOR CERTAIN WHETHER THIS SHELL WORKS. I SHALL CIRCLE A MILE ABOVE THE SHELL-BURST. IF YOUR HUS-BAND'S INVENTION IS EFFECTIVE, OUR PLANE WILL BE DISINTE-GRATED!

GREAT CAESAR'S GHOST! THAT PLANE DISSOLVED INTO SMOKE WHEN THE DISINTEGRATOR GAS HIT IT!

AMAZING! TWO PEOPLE FALLING — AND ONLY ONE HAS A PARACHUTE.

I HAVE ONE SATISFACTION — YOU'LL FALL TO YOUR DEATH ALONG WITH ME.

AH NO! OBSERVE — I WEAR A PARACHUTE, YOU HAVE NONE. YOU MUST NOT LIVE TO BETRAY DR. CUE!

12

ON THE GROUND BELOW, STEVE TREVOR SIGHTS THE PLANE A SPLIT SECOND TOO LATE!

THERE'S A PLANE UP THERE! HOLD YOUR FIRE!

SORRY, SIR! I'VE ALREADY LET HER GO!

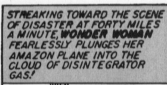
STREAKING TOWARD THE SCENE OF DISASTER AT FORTY MILES A MINUTE, *WONDER WOMAN* FEARLESSLY PLUNGES HER AMAZON PLANE INTO THE CLOUD OF DISINTEGRATOR GAS!

THIS PLANE ISN'T MADE OF WOOD OR METAL—WILL IT DISINTEGRATE? WE'LL SOON FIND OUT!

FLYING BENEATH THE FALLING GIRL *WONDER WOMAN* SETS HER ROBOT PILOT AND—

IF THIS LADDER WERE ONLY A LITTLE LONGER—

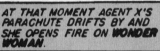
AT THAT MOMENT AGENT X'S PARACHUTE DRIFTS BY AND SHE OPENS FIRE ON *WONDER WOMAN*.

TOO MUCH IS ENOUGH! I'LL PUT A STOP TO THIS NONSENSE!

WONDER WOMAN, REMOVING X'S MASK AND WIG, DISCOVERS DR. CUE!

SO YOU ARE "DR. CUE," ACTUALLY COLONEL TOGO KU CHIEF OF JAPANESE SPIES IN AMERICA!

EVEN SO! I LOSE NO FACE IN BEING DEFEATED BY *WONDER WOMAN*

⑬

OH, DAN! HOW WONDERFUL THAT YOU'RE TO BE IN CHARGE OF MAKING DISINTEGRATOR SHELLS! NOW THE OTHER DIANA CAN HAVE HER JOB BACK!

I'LL TELL HER.

LATER —

I AM DIANA WHITE AND YOU ARE DIANA PRINCE FROM NOW ON. WE DON'T LOOK SO MUCH ALIKE EITHER WITH MY NEW HAIR-DO!

I'M GLAD TO GET MY POSITION BACK. BUT I ENVY YOU YOURS, AS WIFE AND MOTHER.

FOLLOW *WONDER WOMAN'S* FASCINATING PERILS AND ADVENTURES EVERY MONTH *IN SENSATION COMICS —*